Technology and Creativity

"Many pundits have talked up the disruptive influence of digital technology on traditional industries, but this lovely volume turns the argument around and addresses how digitalization has enabled, empowered, and reshaped creative industries, oftentimes in surprising ways. Ranging from food to painting to film, the provocative essays in the volume are a treat for the mind."

—Walter W. Powell, *Stanford University, USA*

"Over sixty years ago Joseph Schumpeter coined the term 'creative destruction' to describe the somewhat contradictory process of industrial renewal through revolution. As Strandgaard, Khaire and Slavich demonstrate in this marvelous collection of essays, even the creative industries are not immune to the power of creative destruction. The digital revolution has transformed the creative industries from within and this book offers an essential road map to the path ahead."

—Roy Suddaby, *Peter B. Gustavson School of Business, University of Victoria, USA*

Jesper Strandgaard Pedersen ·
Barbara Slavich · Mukti Khaire
Editors

Technology and Creativity

Production, Mediation and Evaluation in the Digital Age

palgrave
macmillan

Editors
Jesper Strandgaard Pedersen
Department for Organization
Copenhagen Business School
Frederiksberg, Denmark

Barbara Slavich
IÉSEG School of Management
Paris, France

Mukti Khaire
Cornell University
Ithaca, NY, USA

ISBN 978-3-030-17565-8 ISBN 978-3-030-17566-5 (eBook)
https://doi.org/10.1007/978-3-030-17566-5

This Palgrave Macmillan imprint is published by the registered company Springer Nature Switzerland AG
The registered company address is: Gewerbestrasse 11, 6330 Cham, Switzerland

Preface

This edited volume brings together papers that have been presented and discussed during the Standing Workgroup on Creative Industries that has been running under the auspices of the European Group of Organization Studies (EGOS) for a number of years. The 2017 edition of the Standing Work Group took place at Copenhagen Business School (CBS) and was titled, "New Frontiers for the Creative Industries: Digitization, Mediation and Valuation." The majority of the chapters in this edited volume was presented in this setting. One of the inspirational sources for this theme was the call by Lampel, Shamsie, and Lant in their book, *The Business of Culture*, for more research on,

> ….'the role of technology in shaping the future of cultural industries; the increasing importance of experts, critics and other institutions that shape tastes in the cultural industries…' (Lampel, Shamsie, & Lant, 2006: 290)

As organizers of the 2017 edition of the Standing Workgroup on Creative Industries, we are very grateful to the EGOS and CBS for making it possible for us to engage in this exciting research and collect knowledge on such an important topic. We would also like to thank the entire group of participants in the Standing Work Group for their inspiring intellectual engagement in the various sessions throughout the conference. We are also grateful to the two anonymous reviewers as well as Palgrave Macmillan for enabling this volume. Finally, we would like to thank Mie Strandgaard Pedersen for her invaluable work in preparing the manuscript for publication.

The venture of writing this edited volume mirrors many of the topics covered in the volume.

From the early digital signing of contracts with the publisher to how digitalization influences almost all other parts of the work process leading to the publication of this volume. For example, our ability to communicate with the publisher and the contributors, to coordinate and transfer texts across different time zones, as well as the ability to write, comment on, and revise texts to mention but some of the obvious ways digitalization influences this type of academic and creative work. Digitalization, however, also means that text disappears, versions get confused, and emails are caught in spam filters. Questions like, how should the book be titled? What kind of audience(s) should it address? How will the reviewers and our readers receive the volume? These are all relevant issues concerned with positioning and evaluation of the volume, and raised during the work process. They are all pertinent questions discussed in several chapters in the edited volume, but also questions we as editors have been confronted with and have had to deal with along the two-year-long journey from the Standing Workgroup at the EGOS colloquium in Copenhagen till the publication of the book.

Frederiksberg, Denmark — Jesper Strandgaard Pedersen
Paris, France — Barbara Slavich
Ithaca, USA — Mukti Khaire

Reference

Lampel, J., Shamsie, J., & Lant, T. K. (2006). Towards a deeper understanding of cultural industries. In J. Lampel, J. Shamsie, & T. K. Lant (Eds.), *The business of culture: Strategic perspectives on entertainment and media*. London: Lawrence Erlbaum Associates, Publishers.

Contents

Notes on Contributors

Gino Cattani is Associate Professor of Management and Organization at the Stern School of Business, New York University. He received his Ph.D. in Business Administration from the Wharton School of Management, University of Pennsylvania. His research focuses on creativity, innovation, and market/industry formation and evolution. In his current research, he has investigated the socio-structural foundations of individual creativity by looking at the role of audiences recognizing and endorsing creative work and individuals' position along the core/periphery continuum of the field's social network.

Thomas Collas received a Ph.D. in sociology from Sciences Po (Paris, France). He is now Chargé de recherches F.R.S.- FNRS in sociology at UC Louvain (Belgium). His research interests lie in economic sociology, the sociology of occupations, political sociology, and methods of social science.

Denise Falchetti is a Postdoctoral Associate at Boston University, Questrom School of Business. During her Ph.D., she visited NYU Stern School of Business for three years. She got her Ph.D. in Management at the University of Bologna in 2018. Her research activity is on social evaluation processes focusing on three main topics: creativity, entrepreneurship, and innovation. For her dissertation project, she employs experiments to look at how personal traits, social factors, and ideas' framing affect the processes of novelty evaluation.

Simone Ferriani is Full Professor of Management at the University of Bologna and Honorary Visiting Professor at Cass Business School. He is also a lifetime member of Clare Hall College at Cambridge University. He received his Ph.D. in Business Administration from the University of Bologna. Recent publications have focused on the emergence and evaluation of novelty, social network determinants of individual creativity, and technology-based entrepreneurship.

Santi Furnari is Professor of Strategy at Cass Business School, City, University of London. He completed his Ph.D. at Bocconi University and was visiting scholar at the University of Chicago. His research interests include the emergence of new fields and practices, the micro-foundations of institutional logics, and the use of fuzzy-set/Qualitative Comparative Analysis (fs/QCA) in organizational and management theory. His research has been published in journals such as the *Academy of Management Review*, *Human Relations*, *Industrial and Corporate Change*, *Journal of Management*, *Organization Studies*, and *Strategic Organization* (among others). His paper titled "Interstitial Spaces" has received the AMR Best Paper Award for the best paper published in the *Academy of Management Review* in 2014. He serves on the Editorial Boards of the *Academy of Management Review, Organization Studies* and *Journal of Management Studies*.

Mia Rosa Koss Hartmann is a psychologist and a postdoctoral researcher, jointly at MIT Sloan School of Management and Copenhagen Business School. Her work is primarily ethnographic and deals with creativity and innovation processes in contexts as diverse as police work and visual art production, and reaches into social psychology and organization theory. In addition to her academic work, she collaborates with Stalke Art Gallery as curator and has contributed to books on modern art.

Mukti Khaire is the Girish and Jaidev Reddy Professor at Cornell Tech and in the Johnson School at Cornell University. Her work primarily focuses on the creation of new markets and the reinterpretation of value constructs and consequent cultural change, particularly in the context of cultural industries. She has extensively studied the Indian art and fashion markets. Her book, *Culture and Commerce: The Value of Entrepreneurship in Creative Industries*, was published in 2017.

Raissa Pershina is a Doctoral Research Fellow at the University of Oslo, Norway, research section "Digitization and Entrepreneurship" (DIGENT). Raissa holds two master degrees, one in "Innovation and Entrepreneurship" (University of Oslo) and one in "3D Graphics and Design" (Saint Petersburg State Technical University). Before joining the Ph.D. program, she gained professional experience in the digital games, 3D animation, and music industries. Her research interests include digitization and digital innovation management, cross-domain collaboration, institutional logics, and creative entrepreneurship. She currently studies the various organizational and institutional processes involved in the creation of innovative digital products, also in the context of the creative and cultural industries.

Ursula Plesner is an Associate Professor at the Department of Organization, Copenhagen Business School. Most of her work examines the relationship between digital technologies and organization—for instance, how work is transformed into digitized public sector organizations or how professions develop in heavily digitized environments. She uses her research-based insights in executive teaching focusing on how to organize and manage work around digital technologies. Ursula is striving to develop a nuanced position that neither overlooks nor overestimates the role of new technologies in organizations—a position that is developed in her forthcoming book *Digital Organizing—Revisiting Themes in Organization Studies* (co-authored with Emil Husted). This is done on the basis of extensive qualitative studies of work and management practices in various types of digitized organizations. Her work has appeared in, for instance, *Organization and Strategic Organization.* Her work on journalism and digitization has been published in *Journalism—Theory, Practice and Criticism* and *Journal of Organizational Change Management.*

Mauro Romanelli is Assistant Professor of Organization Studies and Human Resource Management at University of Naples Parthenope,

Department of Business and Economics. Teaching activities: organization design and theory, organizational behavior and human resource management, ethics, human resources and organizational behavior, change, and reform within public administration. He is member of academic and professional associations such as Egos, Euram, Irspm, Assioa, BS-Lab, ItAis, and Icto. He attended Italian and International Conferences (Euram, Egos, Woa, Ifkad, Iceird, Strategica, Irspm, Itais, Icto, BS-Lab, MobilityIoT) as track chair, presenter, reviewer, and member of the Scientific Committee. He was visiting scholar at SNSPA, Faculty of Management in Bucharest, Romania. Research interests and themes: communications at international conferences, papers and articles in journals, book chapters and books concerning the organizational change and human resource management within public administration and organizations, employment relationships, regulation and organization, ethics and organization within public administration, the role of information and communication technologies within public organizations and administration, parliaments, museums, big data, intellectual capital, cultural heritage and healthcare organizations: management, organization, and governance aspects; hybrid organizations, social and rural entrepreneurship, smart and sustainable cities and digital ecosystems, e-governance, e-government, e-healthcare, smart communities and knowledge sharing, ICTs for sustainable peace and value co-creation.

Stoyan V. Sgourev is Professor of Management at ESSEC Business School, France, where he teaches courses on art management and art history. He received his Ph.D. in Sociology from Stanford University and was a Postdoctoral Fellow at MIT Sloan. His research interests include social networks and market construction in historical perspective, and innovation and evaluation practices in the creative industries. His research has been featured in the *American Journal of Sociology, American Sociological Review, Organization Science and Academy of Management Journal*, among others. He has published on a wide array of topics in the creative industries, including evaluation of excellence in art, innovation practices in opera, ballet and art, the connection between the art market and finance, and approval of stylistic inconsistency. His latest work examines creativity at the interstices of social networks, artistic mobility, and processes of social diffusion.

Barbara Slavich is Associate Professor of Organization and Management and Academic Director of the Master in Fashion Management at IÉSEG School of Management (LEM-CNRS 9221), Paris. She has been visiting scholar and a member of the research center "The Initiative for the Study and Practice of Organized Creativity and Culture" at Columbia University, New York, USA. Her research focuses on creativity management and on organizational mechanisms and processes in creative industries. She has extensively studied high-end restaurants and the fashion industry.

Adriano Solidoro is Senior Lecturer at Università di Milano-Bicocca in Organisational Theory and Design and Associate Editor at *Industrial and Commercial Training* at Emerald Publishing.

He is Director at ISOB (Observatory Innovation and Organisational Development for Public Libraries), Università di Milano-Bicocca, Department of Human Sciences for Training.

He maintains an active research agenda that examines issues emerging in the fields of digital transformation, soft skills, change management, creativity, and innovation. He has published books and peer-reviewed journal articles and other academic publications. He participates in multiple training professional associations via consultancy, committees, editorial leadership, conference presentations, and board memberships. He has professional experience in management consultancy, coaching, training and development, and EU-funded research programs.

Birthe Soppe is Professor of Business Administration with a focus on Organization at the University of Innsbruck, Austria. She is also Associate Professor at the University of Oslo, Norway. She holds a Ph.D. in Business Administration from the University of Regensburg, Germany, and a Postdoctoral from Stanford University, USA. Birthe's research activities revolve around novel organizational phenomena. She bridges insights from institutional and organization theory as well as economic sociology to enhance the understanding of the fundamental social, institutional, and organizational underpinnings that shape new market fields and novel forms of organizing, such as crowdfunding. She also works on organizational collaborations (coopetition) as well as efforts to gain legitimacy for innovations and novel economic activities. Empirically, her research often addresses periods of transitions, such as the sustainability and digital transition. Her work has been published among others in *Organization Studies*, *Research in the Sociology of Organizations*, and *Journal of Small Business Management*, *Social Psychology*, and *Energy Policy*.

Jesper Strandgaard Pedersen is Professor at Copenhagen Business School, where he also serves as Director of '*Imagine* .. Creative Industries Research Centre' and as Chairman of SCANCOR. His overall research interest focuses on organizational and institutional change and stability. Pursuing this research interest, he is addressing issues of institutional action and agency, industry emergence and field structuring, and organizational identity construction and legitimacy. Studies include cultural transformation processes in high-tech firms, mergers, and acquisitions in knowledge-intensive firms, diffusion and institutionalization of managerial concepts and practices in creative and knowledge-intensive firms, and studies on strategies for organizing and managing creative enterprises in the film and media field. Recent research focuses on the role of cultural intermediaries and forms of evaluative practices in the culinary and film-making fields and is published in international journals and in the co-edited volumes: *The Negotiation of Values in the Creative Industries: Fairs, Festivals and Competitive Events* (2011) Cambridge University Press, and *Misfits, Mavericks and Mainstreams—Drivers of Innovation in Creative Industries* (2016), Special issue of Organization Studies.

Gianluigi Viscusi, Ph.D. is Research Fellow at the Chair of Corporate Strategy and Innovation (CSI) of the EPFL, Switzerland. His areas of expertise include information systems strategy and planning, business modeling, e-government, information quality and value, social study of information systems. Nowadays, his research focus is on three research streams concerning digital economy and society: crowd-driven innovation; science and innovation valuation through digital platforms; digital governance. His research has been published in a range of books, conference proceedings, and journals such as *Government Information*

Quarterly and *The DATA BASE for Advances in Information System (ACM SIGMIS)*. In 2010, he has co-authored with Carlo Batini and Massimo Mecella the book *Information Systems for eGovernment: A Quality-of-Service Perspective* (Springer) and, in 2018, he co-edited with Christopher Tucci and Allan Afuah the book *Creating and Capturing Value Through Crowdsourcing* (Oxford University Press).

List of Figures

List of Tables

1

Technology and Creativity: Production, Mediation and Evaluation in the Digital Age

Jesper Strandgaard Pedersen, Barbara Slavich and Mukti Khaire

Introduction

Technology and creativity seem to be two core constructs that have dominated recent debates for understanding the driving forces in twenty-first-century economies, and in particular capitalist economies, debated under such terms as 'Experience Economy' (Pine & Gilmore, 1999) or 'Name Economy' (Moeran, 2003) or the more general term 'New Economy' to mention but a few of the terms coined. On the

J. Strandgaard Pedersen (✉)
Department for Organization, Copenhagen Business School, Københavns, Denmark
e-mail: Js.ioa@cbs.dk

B. Slavich
IÉSEG School of Management, Paris, France

M. Khaire
Cornell University, Ithaca, NY, USA
e-mail: mvk34@cornell.edu

J. Strandgaard Pedersen et al. (eds.), *Technology and Creativity*,
https://doi.org/10.1007/978-3-030-17566-5_1

connection between technology and creativity, Lampel, Shamsie and Lant (2006) outline their view on the role of technology in the evolution of the cultural industries by stating that,

> Cultural industries owe their existence to a series of technical innovations such as electrical sound recording, motion picture photography, television broadcasting and the Internet. These technologies opened new frontiers that grew into great industries. The expansion phase, however, was championed not by the technologically knowledgeable, but by the creative and business talent. (Lampel et al. 2006: 12)

Thus, emphasizing the significance of the technology as a driver, but not as an end in itself, Lampel et al. (2006) also emphasize the importance of content and that the technology at the end of the day is in the minds and hands of creative individuals and business organizations. The editors sympathize and concur with this view, but also propose that it is important, nonetheless, to understand the implications and influence on creative and cultural industries of technological advances, especially recent digital technologies, which have had far-ranging and rapidly evolving impact. This volume attempts to shed light on these changes, while still placing them in the broader historical, institutional, cultural and economic context in which these industries operate.

Recent economic transformation, technological advances and globalization seem to continue to alter how organizations and individuals define and organize work and how societies consume what organizations and individuals produce. The development of the Internet, in particular, has played an increasingly important role in such economic and sociocultural change. An array of Information and Communication Technology (ICT) tools has allowed for increased digitalization of information media and social interactions, and consumers are turning to digitally mediated communication in their social and professional connectivity, decision-making as well as to digital channels for consumption (Munar et al. 2013).

These recent technological advances have increasingly influenced organizations and individuals in creative industries, by leading to a 'disintermediation' and resulted in a loss of power of traditional actors, such as critics and producers (Hirsch & Gruber, 2015), as well as in an increased power of consumers. Indeed, the development has taken place by bringing (traditionally conceived) passive consumers of creative products to being active agents in the creative process. This takes place through different processes and developments. For example, by opening up new opportunities for collaborations and by offering new ways of consuming cultural products (Munar & Gyimóthy, 2013). Examples of these changes include for instance the high-end restaurant industry[1] where diners post online comments on their experiences on platforms such as TripAdvisor, influencing restaurants' reputation and reducing the traditional impact of critics' reviews (Müller, 2018). In music and performing arts, online platforms such as YouTube give artists the opportunity to publish their music and contents online entering into a direct contact with the audiences.

The current digitalization has also pushed a deinstitutionalization of media conglomerates, which leads to new opportunities for creators to reach wider audiences (Hirsch & Gruber, 2015). Furthermore, new business models, made possible by digital technologies, allow creators to generate and appropriate more value from their own work. Social media platforms grow by creating value from users' contributions. This is made possible due to the digitization of, for example, text, sound and images. Users contribute with knowledge and creativity in a fast-expanding global upload–download phenomenon, and user-generated content (UGC) has become massively popular, shaping and changing the public perception of products and organizations. Thus, ICT and social media change the traditional production function to co-create value across historical producer–consumer boundaries and redefine the role of intermediaries, gatekeepers and experts, which has greater implications in the creative industries than in others, due to their very nature, described below.

Creative Industries: Creativity at the Center

The broad term 'creative industries' refers to a number of sectors that derive value through the creativity involved in the products developed and the processes used (Jones, Lorenzen, & Sapsed, 2015). These industries, for example, such as architecture, advertising, fashion, design, film, the fine arts and haute cuisine, encompass individuals and organizations that produce, develop and distribute products or experiences that convey symbolic and aesthetic value (Caves, 2000; Lampel et al., 2006). Several studies have tried to understand what industries should be seen as creative, and there has been a lot of debate around the use of the term 'creative' versus 'cultural industry,' with several scholars agreeing on the view of cultural industries as a subset of creative industries (Jones et al., 2015). In his influential work, 'Creative industries: Contracts between art and commerce,' the economist Richard Caves (2000) suggested a number of properties defining what characterizes creative industries—'Nobody knows,' 'Art for art's sake,' 'Motley crew,' 'Infinite variety,' 'A list/B list,' 'Time flies' and 'Ars longa' (Caves, 2000: 2–10)—in an attempt to define and capture the creative industries. Based on these properties, Caves came up with the following list of creative industries,

> They include book and magazine publishing, the visual arts (painting, sculpture), the performing arts (theatre, opera, concerts, dance), sounds recordings, cinema and TV films, even fashion and toys and games. (Caves, 2000: 1)

In spite of this ground-breaking and influential work, Caves' list from 2000 also illustrates very well the problem of such a list. Rather than asking, 'what *is* the creative industries?' another approach (and probably a more interesting question to ask) is to contextualize to a particular time and place—'who is *considering* what goods and activities to be creative expressions and therefore belonging to the creative industries?' Therefore no final or universal list of the creative industries makes sense or could meaningfully be listed, as it is a social construction and a dynamic one at that. Creative industries develop due to industry change and become more (or less) artistic and experience-driven over time (e.g., the culinary field) and new industries emerge driven by new technologies (e.g., video games and virtual reality). Finally, what is considered to belong to the category of creative industries is highly dependent on context and seems to differ, for example, from country to country (e.g., some countries have a strong tradition for considering cooking an almost artistic venture and associated with pleasure, whereas other countries consider it primarily a question about nutrition and associate it with guilt).

In the creative industries, creativity is a central input of the production process and creative organizations survive by their 'creative output.' Creativity has been defined in many ways, but one of the most accepted definitions of the term is the production of a novel, useful and appropriate response, product, or solution to an open-ended task (Amabile, 1996). Differently from innovation, creativity is mainly the result of an individual and a team effort (Lampel et al. 2000). A vast literature exists on what makes people more or less creative (see Runco 2004 for a review). Generally, this literature treats individual creativity as separate and largely unrelated to creativity in and of groups. In addition, one limitation of nearly all creativity research—on individuals as well as groups—is the prevailing assumption that creativity is an objective fact that can be singled out. The problem with this assumption, we find, is that it disguises the fact that in (non) research settings 'creativity' is a social judgment, not an objective property of the creation, which can be assessed independently of its social context. Indeed, we have no other way of knowing the intrinsic properties of an object other than through our subjective perceptions. Thus, in the extreme, it can be claimed that an idea or object is not creative until it is perceived as such. According to this observation, what is fundamental to understanding creativity and its potential impact is its acceptance (and hence potential adoption) within a wider community of people, as noted by Howard Becker in his foundational book from 1982, 'Art Worlds,' with his distinction between 'integrated professionals and mavericks' (Becker, 1982). In the same vein, Csikszentmihalyi (1999) has argued that definitions of creativity should acknowledge the importance of perceivers, and the wider group context within which their evaluations take place. Building on this work, Khaire (2017) takes it further and identifies the set of actors within the field of cultural production to be constituted by creators, producers, market intermediaries and consumers. The ability to come up with new ideas is surely relevant to the competitiveness of companies across different industries, and the creative industries are organized in a search to increase and take advantage of the value of creativity.

It is argued that compared to products and services produced in a range of other (traditional) industries, the cultural-creative industries (CCIs) and their products are characterized by being intangible, symbolic, experiential and highly subjective goods and services (Caves, 2000; Hirsch, 1972; Lampel et al., 2000). This makes them extremely difficult to evaluate—no legitimate institutionalized criteria, bodies or codified standards in the industry offers a formalized or standardized framework for evaluation. Nevertheless, creative products are constantly being evaluated by various actors, means and arrangements. Individual critics offer their opinion on food or artistic exhibitions in newspapers, and committees and juries decide on architecture, film or music, and users are encouraged to rate their culinary or travel experience to mention just some examples of evaluative practices in the creative industries. An evaluation is necessary when decisions are to be made on who should win an award or receive government subsidies allocated to project applications in the creative industries, for example, film subsidies to film project proposals. But how do you evaluate the potential of a film manuscript or book proposal as these pitches and ideas undergo developments and transformations during their realization process? The chapters in this volume take up the question of assessment and evaluation of creativity together with other questions related to technology and creativity.

The Volume

This edited volume is concerned with examining and understanding the role of technology and primarily the digital challenge for enterprises operating within creative industries and its impact on production, meaning-making, valuation and the consumption of creative products and experiences. It focuses on several types of digital changes and challenges for a range of creative organizations, together with studies of its impact on the mediation of experiences and consumption of creative products, as well as how creative work is influenced following from these developments. The volume approaches the task of understanding the implications for creative industries of digitalization in a comprehensive and multidimensional manner by inviting a range of scholars to contribute work that provides historical, conceptual and empirical insights. Fundamentally, the digital medium has facilitated and rendered easier all three stages in the value chain of creative industries—creation, commentary, commerce and consumption (Khaire, 2017)—and in so doing, has changed the way the industries function. These changes have had both positive and negative implications for all stakeholders involved, and the chapters in this volume aim to shed light on what was gained, what was lost, and what, if anything, has stayed the same.

Naturally, before exploring the implications of digitalization, it behooves scholars to problematize the very context that has been disrupted by the technology. In Chapter 2, Cattani et al., therefore, start there, asking, what is creativity and theorize how creative work is accepted and recognized. This is fundamental to understanding the further chapters because the process by which creative work(s) are viewed, understood, evaluated and endorsed is rapidly changing due to the digital medium, which in turn changes markets for cultural-creative goods. In Chapter 3, Sgourev takes an historical approach based on the rightly rational premise that the Internet and digital technologies are not the first technological advances to have an impact on markets in general, and on CCIs in particular. The technology he focuses on is particularly pertinent to the CCIs—the advent of oils as a medium for painting. This approach helps us specifically place in context the most recent development of digitalization, and its implications for creators and their process of creation, and, in turn, for the economic/market exchange of these goods.

The following three chapters, by Furnari, by Hartmann and by Collas, respectively, mirror the previous chapters by Cattani et al. and by Sgourev, exploring similar questions in a contemporary setting. Chapter 4 by Furnari conducts a theoretical analysis of where the boundaries of CCIs should be drawn, given the near complete penetration of the digital medium in all parts of the value chain of what used to be considered the limits of the CCIs. Indeed, with firms like Apple (with the iTunes product) now being distributors of music, for example, the author asks if it is any longer possible to sharply define the CCIs in the way they used to be—'comprising firms that produce goods of greater symbolic than material value' (Hirsch, 1972)—and what that means for this volume and for explorations of digitalization in markets for cultural and creative works. Chapter 5 by Hartmann takes this line of thought further when she enters the world of digital art to understand its definition and how it is created, exhibited, evaluated and exchanged. Hartmann identifies transformative as well as antagonist synergies between visual art and the Internet and discusses how these two forces must be carefully attended to. In Chapter 6, taking the reader to chocolate confectionery manufacturing field, Collas follows up on the field view by viewing a particular rating system as a technology and its influence on the market. He demonstrates how the chocolate confectionery manufacturing market in France reacts to and is influenced by the rating system and quality standards of a specialized guide (*Club des croquers de chocolat*), which is a highly influential guide and tastemaker.

The next four chapters in the book then examine the changes wrought by the digital medium in other steps of the value chain in the art market. Chapter 7 by Pershina and Soppe looks at a particular constituent and crucial phenomenon—funding—and how a new entity, Kickstarter.com, enables artists to both raise money and garner attention for their work. This unprecedented interpenetration of economic and cognitive resources so crucial to the creation of art is possible in a seamless way on the digital medium, which in turn, affects how and who interacts with art. This chapter raises the intriguing question of whether art and artists are helped or hindered by this interpenetration, and whether the kind of art created through this kind of funding serves to entertain or enlighten society. Chapter 8 by Romanelli then correspondingly deeply examines how museums, classic arbiters of quality and therefore of streams of funding and audience attention, have been affected by digitalization. He argues that the very role and purpose of museums in the value chain and even society has changed owing to digitalization and explains the implications of that for art markets. Chapter 9 by Plesner offers an analysis of professional struggles around digitalization in a public service broadcaster, showing how new technologies and tasks become elements in cultural journalism in new ways. The chapter analyzes changes in the professions and practices in the work of cultural journalists and how the digital medium is changing ways in which cultural journalists' work is understood. It poses the relevant and interesting question how actors renegotiate or 'reassemble' cultural journalism in the digital age and proposes that changes in roles, tasks and values are slowly changing journalism as an occupation. Finally, Chapter 10 by Solidoro and Viscusi sheds light on the last stage in the value chain—the audience/consumers. They take on the interesting task of studying how digitalization affected the film industry, an industry that, except for the music industry, was seemingly easy to adapt to digitalization. The authors examine how digitalization has impacted the film industry and the classical business model for film exhibition and, in doing so the authors focus on one particular invention, 'Movieday.it,' that aims at combining digitalization with the cinema theater experience.

To round off the volume, the editors have written an afterword. It is not a conclusion but rather a reflection on the various chapters and their findings. We find that this line of research on the role of technology and creativity is still in its adolescence and that more work still needs to be done. After many years of almost unison glorification and hype with regard to technology, and particular ICT and digitalization, we find that we need and would like to call for research that not just embraces technology but also takes a critical stance toward ICT and digitalization.

Note

1. For studies of the culinary field, high-end restaurants and evaluative practices, see, for example, Christensen and Strandgaard Pedersen (2013), Ferguson (1998, 2004), Lane (2014), Rao, Monin and Durand (2005), Slavich and Castelucci (2016), and Svejenova, Mazza and Planellas (2007), Trubek (2000).

References

Amabile, T. (1996). *Creativity in context: Update to the social psychology of creativity*. Boulder, CO: Westview Press.

Becker, H. S. (1982). *Art Worlds*. Berkeley and Los Angeles, CA: University of California Press.

Caves, R. (2000). *Creative industries: Contracts between art and commerce*. Cambridge, MA: Harvard University Press.

Christensen, B. T., & Strandgaard Pedersen, J. (2013). Restaurant rankings in the culinary field. In B. Moeran & B. T. Christensen (Eds.), *Exploring creativity: Evaluative practices in innovation, design and the arts* (pp. 235–259). Cambridge: Cambridge University Press.

Csikszentmihalyi, M. (1999). *Creativity*. New York: HarperCollins.

Ferguson, P. (1998). A cultural field in the making: Gastronomy in 19th-century France. *American Journal of Sociology, 104,* 597–641.

Ferguson, P. (2004). *Accounting for Taste: The triumph of French cuisine*. Chicago: University of Chicago Press.

Hirsch, P. M. (1972). Processing fads and fashions: An organization-set analysis of cultural industry systems. *American Journal of Sociology, 77,* 639–659.

Hirsch, P. M., & Gruber, D. A. (2015). Digitizing fads and fashions. In C. Jones, M. Lorenzen, & J. Sapsed (Eds.), *The Oxford handbook of creative industries* (pp. 420–436). Oxford, UK: Oxford University Press.

Jones, C., Lorenzen, M., & Sapsed, J. (2015). *The Oxford handbook of creative industries*. Oxford, UK: Oxford University Press.

Khaire, M. (2017). *Culture and commerce: The value of entrepreneurship in creative industries*. Stanford, CA: Stanford University Press.

Lampel, J., Lant, T. K., & Shamsie, J. (2000). Balancing act: Learning from organizing practices in cultural industries. *Organization Science, 11,* 263–269.

Lampel, J., Shamsie, J., & Lant, T. K. (2006). Towards a deeper understanding of cultural industries. In J. Lampel, J. Shamsie, & T. K. Lant (Eds.), *The business of culture: Strategic perspectives on entertainment and media*. London: Lawrence Erlbaum Associates, Publishers.

Lane, C. (2014). *The cultivation of taste: Chefs and the organization of fine dining*. Oxford: Oxford University Press.

Moeran, B. (2003). Celebrities and the name economy. In *Anthropological perspectives on economic development and integration* (Vol. 22, pp. 299–321). Amsterdam: Elsevier.

Moeran, B., & Christensen, B. T. (Eds.). (2013). *Exploring creativity: Evaluative practices in innovation, design, and the arts*. Cambridge: Cambridge University Press.

Müller, F. H. (2018). *When valuators are valuated: An analysis of the perception and description of valuation devices in fine-dining* (Doctoral dissertation). Retrieved from Doctoral School of Organization and Management Studies, Copenhagen Business School.

Munar, A. M., & Gyimóthy, S. (2013). Critical digital tourism studies. In A. M. Munar, S. Gyimóthy, & L. Cai (Eds.), *Tourism social media: Transformations in identity community and culture* (Vol. 18, pp. 245–262). Emerald: Bingley.

Munar, A. M., Gyimóthy, S., & Cai, L. (Eds.). (2013). *Tourism social media: Transformations in identity, community and culture*. Emerald: Bingley.

Pine, J. B., & Gilmore, J. H. (1999). *The experience economy*. Boston, MA: Harvard Business School Press.

Rao, H., Monin, P., & Durand, R. (2005). Border Crossing: Bricolage and the erosion of categorical boundaries in French gastronomy. *American Sociological Review, 70*(6), 968–991.

Runco, M. A. (2004). Creativity. *Annual Review of Psychology, 55*, 657–687.

Slavich, B., & Castellucci, F. (2016). Wishing upon a star: How apprentice-master similarity, status and career stage affect critics' evaluations of former apprentices in the haute cuisine industry. *Organization Studies, 37*(6), 823–843.

Svejenova, S., Mazza, C., & Planellas, M. (2007). Cooking up change in haute cuisine: Ferran Adrià as an institutional entrepreneur. *Journal of Organizational Behavior, 28*(5), 539–561.

Trubek, A. B. (2000). *Haute cuisine: How the French invented the culinary profession*. Philadelphia, PA: University of Pennsylvania Press.

2

Innovators' Acts of Framing and Audiences' Structural Characteristics in Novelty Recognition

Gino Cattani, Denise Falchetti and Simone Ferriani

Introduction

When are novel ideas more likely to obtain recognition? Research on creativity and innovation has long been catalyzed by the belief that major creative achievements are sparked by imaginative and uniquely gifted individuals who succeed in bringing novel ideas to life. Several scholarly

The original version of this chapter was revised: An acknowledgement content has been added to this chapter. The correction to this chapter is available at https://doi.org/10.1007/978-3-030-17566-5_12

G. Cattani (✉)
Stern School of Business, New York University, New York, USA
e-mail: gcattani@stern.nyu.edu

D. Falchetti
Questrom School of Business, Boston University, Boston, MA, USA

S. Ferriani
University of Bologna, Bologna, Italy

Cass Business School, London, UK

J. Strandgaard Pedersen et al. (eds.), *Technology and Creativity*,
https://doi.org/10.1007/978-3-030-17566-5_2

contributions have supported this view, spurring a vibrant body of work that has contributed to enhancing our understanding of which individual dispositions, talents and agentic characteristics underlie the emergence of novelty. Although the individual—i.e., the person who serves as the source of variation in the field—is critical, it is the field that ultimately sanctions whether or not an idea deserves recognition (e.g., Amabile, 1982, 1996; Csikszentmihályi, 1990, 1996; Gardner, 1993; Mumford & Gustafson, 1988). One important implication of this observation is that the success of novelty in gaining recognition is located in neither the creator nor the outcome of the creator's efforts, but rather the interaction between the creator and the field's audiences that selectively retain or reject novelty (Kasof, 1995). Thus, an essential determinant of whether novel ideas (and those who pitch them) are recognized as worthy of attention and support is whether audiences (e.g., peers, critics, investors or users) perceive those ideas as valuable on the basis of cues that matter to them. As noted by Kasof (1995: 366), "it may be useful to think of creativity as a form of persuasive communication, in which the creator is the source, the original product is the message, and the judge [audience] is the recipient."

Of particular interest here is the role of social audiences in charge of channeling the symbolic and/or material resources that innovators need to further their ideas. An audience-based perspective, in fact, helps to expose some puzzling facets of novelty recognition. Consider, as an example, the groundbreaking work on mobile genetic elements by Barbara McClintock who was rejected by top biology journals for many years before being recognized and honored with a Noble Prize. Johann Sebastian Bach's extraordinary innovation in harmony and counterpoints was eclipsed for more than one hundred years and rediscovered by Felix Mendelssohn during the nineteenth century. John Harrison struggled for almost 40 years before his marine chronometer was recognized as the most effective solution to measure the longitude at sea (Cattani, Ferriani, & Lanza, 2017). Similarly, George Orwell's novel *Animal Farm* was rejected by several editors before becoming an American classic (Mueller, Melwani, Loewenstein, & Deal, 2018).

The previous cases suggest that novelty recognition is challenging and fraught with uncertainty in any field of cultural production (i.e., art and science). However, novelty recognition is also "the crucial starting point in the long process of putting new ideas generated into good use" (Zhou, Wang, Song, & Wu, 2017: 180) as relevant social audiences must come to appreciate those ideas before they take hold and achieve success (Adarves-Yorno, Postmes, & Haslam, 2007; Cattani & Ferriani, 2008; Cattani, Ferriani, & Allison, 2014; Perry-Smith & Mannucci, 2017; Wijnberg, 1995; Wijnberg & Gemser, 2000). As stressed by Mueller et al. (2018: 95), the question of "why decision-makers can sometimes view groundbreaking ideas as "trivial" and not creative or worth pursuing remains an unresolved puzzle and one that carries potentially far-reaching consequences" (Mueller et al., 2018: 95). Thus, we ask: When do novel ideas elicit favorable evaluations from relevant audiences and then progress in their journey toward recognition?

Our goal is to advance understanding of novelty recognition by bringing together insights into the enabling role of rhetoric in framing novelty-claims with recent findings on audience-based evaluative mechanisms. In particular, we argue that innovators can deploy *acts of framing*—through the skillful use of storytelling and rhetorical tactics—to try to influence audiences' evaluation and, in so doing, the recognition of their novel ideas. The effectiveness of those acts of framing, however, depends on the level of audience evaluative heterogeneity—that is, the extent to which audience members are diverse in their evaluation criteria, and on whether an evaluating audience is *internal* or *external* to an innovator's professional community. Marrying a rhetorical with an audience-mediated perspective is important because novelty recognition is as much the result of an innovator's agentic (micro-level) efforts (here *acts of framing*), as it is the result of audience (meso-level) features that do not fall under an innovator's direct control but can render fields more or less permeable to the reception of novel ideas. Integrating these two perspectives affords a window into a more nuanced understanding of how novel ideas become recognized and eventually accepted in the field, thus contributing several insights into research on innovation and entrepreneurship and, more generally, social evaluation.

The chapter is organized as follows. We start by examining the *framing* approach and theorize on how innovators can frame their novel ideas in order to enhance their chances of winning audience recognition for them. In the next two paragraphs, we expose two main audience-level structural characteristics and elucidate how they can affect field permeability to novel ideas. Finally, we discuss some important implications of focusing on the interplay between innovators' acts of framing and the identified audience features and delineate possible venues for future research.

Novelty and the Act of Framing

Innovators' struggle for recognition is a central theme in the literature on creativity, entrepreneurship and innovation (e.g., Cattani, Colucci & Ferriani, 2016; Cattani et al., 2017; Mueller, Melwani & Goncalo, 2012; Zhou et al., 2017). One way by which innovators can overcome the liability of newness of their ideas is through the use of rhetorical tools (e.g., Aldrich & Fiol, 1994; Czarniawska, 1998; Gabriel, 2004). A growing body of research in management and entrepreneurship now adopts a framing approach to study creativity and innovation, where framing refers to "the use of rhetorical devices in communication to mobilize support and minimize resistance to a change" (Cornelissen & Werner, 2014: 185). Several studies in entrepreneurship, for instance, emphasize the importance of *acts of framing* (e.g., storytelling and narratives) in reducing audiences' perceived risk of novel entrepreneurial ideas, but also motivating them to commit capital to a new venturing idea (Garud, Gehman, & Giuliani, 2014; Manning & Bejarano, 2016; Martens, Jennings, & Jennings, 2007; Pollack, Rutherford, & Nagy, 2012; van Werven, Bouwmeester, & Cornelissen, 2015). The frames innovators use as well as the terms and categories they borrow from dominant discourse are critical to gain access to audiences' symbolic and/or material resources (Lounsbury & Glynn, 2001; Navis & Glynn, 2011).

Recent research further suggests that innovators should elaborate frames that match the novelty level of their ideas. For instance, van Werven et al. (2015) argue that a specific type of rhetoric can be effective in convincing an audience when the idea is incremental but not when an idea is radical and vice versa. Indeed, the degree of novelty of an idea ultimately determines the informational content that innovators should incorporate in their acts of framing: *What* exactly they should communicate during an entrepreneurial pitch, and *how* it should be communicated. It is then critical for innovators to rely on different types of *cues* in framing their ideas and also use cues that match the degree of novelty of those ideas.

An apt illustration of the importance of choosing the appropriate framing is Thomas Edison's invention of the electric light system. Edison designed the incandescent light around many of the concrete features of the already-familiar gas system by drawing on "the public's preexisting understandings of the technology, its value, and its uses" (Hargadon & Douglas, 2001: 480), and this proved critical to obtain audiences' recognition. Embedding radical ideas in familiar forms that evoke existing categories has important implications for the success of an innovation (Rindova & Petkova, 2007). Framing radical ideas around cues that evoke familiarity requires innovators to identify those features that members of the evaluating audience are likely to know and understand. For instance, radical ideas can build on materials or techniques with which social audiences are familiar or be characterized by familiar designs or uses. Also, innovators may tailor their more radically novel claims to fit or match the preexisting prototypic expectations held by those who evaluate them (Elsbach & Kramer, 2003). Hence, innovators who have more accurate knowledge about audience-specific familiar prototypes will be in a better position to know which features or attributes to emphasize (or downplay) in their framing strategies. In short, after identifying familiar cues, innovators can strategically frame their presentation (or pitch) around such cues to enhance the probability of obtaining audiences' recognition.

In the case of incremental ideas, on the contrary, the use of familiar cues might hinder their recognition. Because their value is more easily understood, incremental ideas are less appealing to relevant audiences (Rindova & Petkova, 2007). Framing them around familiar cues can actually downplay their perceived novelty. Innovators can enhance the probability of recognition by relying instead on cues with which relevant audiences are less familiar: Unfamiliar cues are more likely to evoke novelty and make incremental ideas more appealing. For instance, innovators can strategically frame their ideas around features (e.g., materials, design, applications, etc.) that audience members do not know as yet. Accordingly, acts of framing should aim to carefully balance the degree of novelty and the use of (un)familiar cues.

The justification for the previous arguments rests on the idea that the novel and the familiar must combine in ways that neither bury the novelty nor shed the familiar. As suggested by Hargadon and Douglas (2001: 493) "Innovations that distinguish themselves too much from the existing institutions are susceptible to blind spots in the public's comprehension and acceptance, particularly those innovations viewed as radical or discontinuous. But innovations that hew too closely to particular understandings and patterns of use may incite resistance or assimilation into the current technological environment" (Hargadon & Douglas, 2001: 493). Accordingly, we propose:

Proposition 1 *Radical (incremental) ideas are more likely to be recognized when innovators frame them by using familiar (unfamiliar) cues.*

Thus far, we have considered actions (i.e., *acts of framing*) that fall under the innovators' direct control delineating ways in which innovators can proactively enhance audiences' receptiveness of their novel ideas. In order to understand how the process of novelty recognition actually unfolds, one must also account for the structural characteristics of the evaluating audiences—in particular, whether they are *internal* or *external* to cultural producers' (innovators') professional community and their degree of *heterogeneity*—to which we now turn.

Novelty and Internal/External Audiences

As previously noted, although novel ideas originate from an innovator's agentic efforts, it is up to the audiences that populate the field to decide whether or not to recognize them. By controlling the material or symbolic resources innovators need to advance their ideas, audiences are in a critical position to shape which new ideas are taken up and how. They form the field and set the criteria by which competing ideas are evaluated, rejected or recognized as desirable, proper or appropriate (Suchman, 1995)—and hence legitimate—often regardless of their comparative technical superiority. Audiences not only set the criteria by which competing ideas are evaluated, but also act as gatekeepers by evaluating to what extent novel ideas conform or depart from those criteria. As Crane put it: "If an innovator wishes to win recognition for his innovations [...] he must conform to the cognitive norms concerning the appropriate problems or themes for innovation [...] He must also follow technical norms concerning the appropriate methods and techniques for use in producing innovations" (1976: 720).

Following Crane's (1976) reward systems model, we distinguish between *internal* and *external* audiences. This distinction is important to shed light on the type of criteria that audience members are likely to apply as they evaluate novel ideas. When audiences are internal to the field, their constituency is made up of members of the same field as the innovators they evaluate, although they take on different roles (Debackere, Clarysse, Wijneberg, & Rappa, 1994). In this case, audience members are usually recruited from a restricted group of insiders that are élite representatives of the field's dominant canons. This is, for instance, the case in most scientific fields where gatekeepers are recruited from prominent scientists. As Wijnberg noted, science can be understood as "a competitive process in which scientists attempt to successfully market scientific products. Published papers are the best equivalents of products [...] Consumers are also producers, fellow-scientists: the editors and referees of journals, other writers who quote you and use your models and theories" (1995: 226). Acting as field gatekeepers, insiders set the canons against which future work (including their own) is evaluated. As such, they have the authority to determine the legitimate definition of a given type of work and, by extension, the authority to define which works configure the field's canon (Bourdieu, 1993). Therefore, they tend to define excellence as "what is most like me" (Lamont, 2009) and provide a disproportionate amount of material and/or symbolic resources to "members of the field who are more strongly associated with its dominant canons" (Cattani et al., 2014: 262).

Different considerations can be made for external audiences such as critics, analysts, policymakers and regulators that are not directly involved in setting the field's dominant canons—thought they can theorize on and contribute to the institutionalization of those canons. In general, external audiences represent what White (1992: 69) called "onlookers"—i.e., actors who observe, comment on and even influence what innovators do and how they do it. As such, they usually enjoy what Simmel (1971) called the objectivity of the stranger—he who is not bound by stable social ties to other group members. Critics are the typical example of external audience. Of course, critics are members of the same field as cultural producers, but they can be considered an external audience as they are not embedded in the same professional community. In principle, this situation should promote an unprejudiced perception, understanding and assessment of producers' work, thus "allowing critics to make evaluations with more objectivity" (Cattani et al., 2014: 264). They also have a greater incentive than peers to discover new talents with the potential to rise to fame (Bourdieu, 1984). Indeed, it may be "dangerous for critics not to embrace a new style, as they risk losing reputation if that style becomes popular" (Cattani et al., 2014: 264).

Although in reality the situation is less polarized, focusing on the extremes of the continuum between internal and external audiences helps explain some key theoretical and empirical differences between the two cases. As argued earlier, internal audiences have the power to shape the field's subsequent evolution, but also the incentive to resist work that does not conform to field's dominant canons. In the field of photography, for instance, Robert Frank's groundbreaking book, *The Americans*, was disliked by peer photographers when it first appeared in 1958 since it departed from the then conventional view. Indeed, "[…] the angriest responses to *The Americans* came from photographers and photography specialists… Who recognized how profound a challenge Frank's work was to the standards of photographic style—photographic *rhetoric*—that were in large part shared even by photographers of very different philosophical postures" (quoted in H. Becker, 1982: 112).

By contrast, external audiences usually hold different norms and standards of evaluation and, therefore, should be less vested in the field's dominant standards. Accordingly, external audiences might help different perspectives to coexist, thus offering crucial entry points for radical ideas. For instance, evidence from the context of French cuisine indicates how code-violating changes introduced by creative chefs enhanced external third parties' evaluations (i.e., the number of stars awarded by *Guide Michelin*) rather than triggering penalties (Durand, Rao, & Monin, 2007).[1] For these reasons, we propose:

Proposition 2 *Innovators' radical (incremental) ideas are more (less) likely to receive recognition from external than internal audiences. Unlike internal audiences that tend to favor ideas that conform to the field's dominant canons, external audiences are more open toward ideas that depart from such canons.*

Novelty and Audience Evaluative Heterogeneity

The previous distinction between internal and external audiences does not address explicitly whether audiences are homogeneous in their evaluative criteria—and hence their members tend to agree on which novel ideas deserve recognition—or multiple diverse criteria coexist within the same audience, each embodying distinct set of norms and standards of evaluation (Cattani, Ferriani, Negro, & Perretti, 2008). Moreover, any audience—whether internal or external—is never fully homogenous but usually consists of groups or segments that can embrace rather different standards and norms by which novelty is evaluated. Audience evaluative heterogeneity, in other words, stems from the coexistence of multiple types of audiences—e.g., peers, critics, investors or users—but also from diversity within each audience type. Substantial variation, for example, may exist among audiences of critics in their openness to novelty, with prestigious critics paying significantly greater attention to the work of established cultural producers (Janssen, 1997). Given the lack of compelling empirical grounds for accepting or rejecting novel ideas, a critic may be more or less inclined to risk her reputation by expressing a judgment that differs from those of her colleagues. Because they have more to lose, established critics may be less inclined to support and recognize radical ideas (Cattani et al., 2017). In the field of literary criticism, for instance, Janssen (1997) found that more occasional, and therefore less established, reviewers tended to make more deviant choices.[2]

Conceptualizing evaluative plurality as the result of both inter- and intra-audience heterogeneity is important because it helps explain why this structural characteristic does not necessarily overlap with the previous distinction between internal and external audiences. Diana Crane's seminal 1976 work on reward systems in cultural institutions (such as art, science and religion) was among the first to examine how the existence of heterogeneous evaluative criteria may affect innovation. Crane suggested that it is easier for members of an internally homogenous audience to agree on which criteria should be used to evaluate individuals' work and also to identify deviant behaviors promptly. Such audiences are willing to tolerate lower amounts of variation (in terms of new ideas, perspectives or styles) and are more likely to enforce restricted cognitive styles supported with reified symbols and dogmatic rules—leading to continuity in the types of ideas being produced and lower tolerance for dissenting ideas. In contrast, when audiences are heterogeneous in their evaluative criteria, the coexistence of various types of evaluation is possible—which, in turn, allows for more cosmopolitan and liberal cognitive styles, thus raising the chance that innovators will find a homologous[3] space, that is, friendly to their subversive ideas. Overall, this plurality of perspectives makes for a more receptive social space where both conforming and dissenting ideas can be voiced and listened to by interested audiences. As Aldrich and Martinez recently pointed out, discrepancies "in expectations across multiple audiences […] can create opportunities for entrepreneurs to select niches in which they can satisfy one set of expectations while being shielded, at least temporarily, from alternative expectations" (2015: 449). Despite lack of widespread consensus on what novel ideas should be supported, the presence of multiple evaluative criteria facilitates recognition. A novel idea might indeed stand outside the field of comparison of—and hence fail to elicit affirmative commitment from—one evaluator, but still win the "intellectual attention space" (Collins, 1998) of another one whose criteria differ from those adopted by the focal evaluator.

In sum, the contemporary presence of heterogeneous evaluative criteria provides greater opportunities for experimentation and tolerance for ideas that vary in their degree of novelty. Conversely, homogeneity fosters the formation of consensus on a common set of norms and standards that specify what novel ideas are worth recognizing, thus restricting the required latitude in novelty assessments. Since this generalized consensus is more easily achieved when the ideas under evaluation do not deviate or deviate only marginally from the field's dominant canons, audience homogeneity in evaluative criteria is likely to encourage innovators to advance ideas that conform with rather than break away from those canons. Taken together, the previous arguments lead to the following proposition:

Proposition 3 *The likelihood that radical (incremental) ideas will be recognized is higher when audiences' evaluative criteria are heterogeneous (homogeneous). Members of heterogeneous (homogeneous) audiences are less (more) likely to share the same set of norms and standards, thereby exhibiting more (less) openness towards ideas that deviate from (conform to) the field's dominant canons.*

Discussion

Novelty emerges from actions that combine elements of otherwise disconnected categories. Many studies demonstrate that some novel combinations hold the potential for great impact and change, yet they also consistently find that more radical combinations typically encounter resistance—if not outright opposition—rather than support (Cattani et al., 2017; De Vaan, Stark, & Vedres, 2015; March, 2010, Chap. 4). Understanding the journey of a novel idea, therefore, requires one to distinguish between the production and the recognition of novelty. Distinguishing between these two phases places the study of novelty as a social process on stronger theoretical foundations. Contrary to popular wisdom, in fact, the recognition of an idea as novel is less contingent upon an individual's actual achievements than it is upon the social consensus that forms around her unique contribution within a particular field. A systematic study of the journey of a novel idea, therefore, must take into account the processes through which social audiences come to recognize novel contributions. Although many studies have focused primarily on the generation of novel ideas, only recently have scholars started to examine systematically the process by which novelty becomes recognized (Anderson, Potočnik, & Zhou, 2014; Cattani et al., 2014, 2017; Perry-Smith & Mannucci, 2017). Drawing on psychological research that distinguishes between incremental and radical novelty

(Kirton, 1994; Madjar, Greenberg, & Chen, 2011), we proposed a framework that combines agentic and non-agentic mechanisms that account for novelty recognition.

In our conceptualization, the reception of novel ideas stems from an innovators' ability to communicate their ideas as well as the characteristics of the social space that decides whether or not to recognize those ideas (Csikszentmihályi, 1996; Elsbach & Kramer, 2003; Kasof, 1995). Innovators deploy rhetorical strategies—e.g., narratives or storytelling—in an effort to influence the sense-making processes of relevant audiences, whose members have the authority or power to decide whether or not novel ideas are socially valuable. In particular, we argued that innovators can enhance the likelihood of obtaining recognition for their *radical* ideas by framing them around familiar cues, whereas the use of unfamiliar cues is more helpful for the recognition of incremental ideas.

We further argued that audiences vary in their openness toward novelty. We identified two important audience-level features that are relevant in this regard: audience evaluative heterogeneity and whether an audience is internal or external to novelty producers' professional community. Internal audiences, whose members belong to the same community as the producers they evaluate, typically have an interest in defending the field's dominant canons. As a result, they tend to resist ideas that have the potential of disrupting such canons and challenging the very basis of their legitimacy and prominence in the field. External audiences, on the contrary, are more amenable to those ideas because their members are less interested in perpetuating the field's prevailing canons. That explains why we expect innovators to be more likely to see their radical ideas be recognized by external than internal audiences. Audiences' degree of evaluative heterogeneity has additional implications for the type of novel ideas the field tends to validate. Consensus on which novel ideas deserve recognition is indeed more easily reached when audiences are homogeneous in their evaluative criteria. In this case, ideas that conform to those criteria are more likely to be recognized. On the contrary, when audiences are heterogeneous, the coexistence of multiple evaluative criteria opens up opportunities for dissenting ideas to emerge and, therefore, enhances the chances that even radical ideas will find a supportive audience willing to recognize them.

Implications for Theory

Our conceptualization extends current research on novelty recognition by building upon and integrating three distinct but complementary research streams: research on narratives in innovation and entrepreneurship (Garud et al., 2014; Kahl & Grodal, 2016; Navis & Glynn, 2011; Vaara, Sonenshein, & Boje, 2016); research on field-level features shaping its permeability to novel ideas (Cattani et al., 2014; Padgett & Powell, 2012; Sgourev, 2013); and research on novelty evaluation (Anderson et al., 2014; Cattani et al., 2017; Perry-Smith & Mannucci, 2017; Zhou et al., 2017). By focusing on the *evaluative* rather than the *generative* phase of the journey of a novel idea (Burt, 2004; Lingo & O'Mahony, 2010; Perry-Smith, 2006; Uzzi & Spiro, 2005), we theorized on the role of agentic and non-agentic mechanisms that are responsible for idea recognition: acts of framing at the individual level and structural characteristics at the audience level.

By focusing on *acts of framing*, we elucidated how individual can communicate a novel idea by strategically framing it so as to enhance its recognition. While scholars debate on the different type of rhetoric that can aid innovators to garner support from critical audiences (Garud et al., 2014; van Werven et al., 2015), our theory suggests that the choice of *what* innovators should communicate and *how* they should communicate it critically depends on the degree of novelty of their ideas. Framings that are focused on *familiar* cues enhance audiences' receptiveness of radical ideas; on the contrary, framings that are focused on *unfamiliar* cues are more appropriate for incremental ideas. This insight represents an extension of extant research on entrepreneurial narratives (for a recent review, see Vaara et al., 2016) that has recently suggested that the power of a rhetorical strategy is contingent upon the novelty of the ideas (van Werven et al., 2015). Exploring entrepreneurial narratives in crowdfunding campaigns, for instance, Manning and Bejarano (2016) identified two main styles to frame novel ideas—the *results-in-progress* frame and the *ongoing journey* frame. Among the features of an idea that influence the effectiveness of the frame, they found technological sophistication to play a relevant role in the act of framing an idea. Their findings reveal that "projects based on sophisticated technology, such as 3D printers and software, are typically presented as results-in-progress, whereas projects relying on more basic technology, such as food or clothing, are predominantly presented as ongoing journeys" (Manning & Bejarano, 2016: 20). As they suggest, sophisticated technologies (i.e., radical ideas) will benefit from a *results-in-progress* frame because this frame allows audience members to appreciate the value of their utility, but simple technologies (i.e., incremental ideas), whose utility can be easily appreciated, will benefit from an *ongoing journey* frame that highlights "the new contexts in which they will be used" (Manning & Bejarano, 2016: 20). Our framework complements this line of work by proposing that social audiences evaluate radical ideas more positively when these ideas are grounded in *familiar* cues, yet incremental ideas are more appealing when *unfamiliar* cues are used to frame them.

The article also extends prior research examining field-level features that might render them more or less permeable to the recognition of novelty (Padgett & Powell, 2012). By focusing on audience-level structural characteristics, we could explain why an audience-mediated perspective sheds new light on the conditions that facilitate the recognition of novel ideas as well as the individuals to whom those ideas are credited (Csikszentmihályi, 1990, 1996). But while extant studies typically consider the role of one single monolithic audience, only recently have scholars begun to recognize the role of multiple audiences whose members may hold different evaluation criteria and, therefore, exhibit different dispositions toward novelty (e.g., Cattani et al., 2014; Goldberg, Hannan, & Kovács, 2016; Pontikes, 2012). As noted by Parker and Corte (2017: 269): "in fields with a plurality of gatekeeping units, there are multiple potential venues for receiving creative legitimation, and some kinds of gatekeepers may be more likely to reward avant-garde contributions [...] in fields where gatekeeping is centralized [...] creative deviance is most often met with intense emotional resistance and criticism." We conceptualized heterogeneity in two ways. First, we distinguished between internal and external audiences. We think this is especially important in the context of social evaluation studies, because in spite of the burgeoning body of work looking at categorization processes as determinants of innovation (Khaire & Wadhwani, 2010), the discussion of how we ought to "bridge between studies of internal and external classification" (Vergne & Wry, 2014: 78) seems to be missing (Seong & Godart, 2018). We contributed to such debate by elaborating on the evaluative differences that shape attributions of novelty across internal and external audiences. Second, and perhaps more importantly, in our framework heterogeneity is not limited to audience plurality (e.g., peers, critics, investors or users) but encompasses evaluative differences among members of the same audience type (e.g., high- vs. low-brow critics), implying that novel ideas may be evaluated relative to a variety of perspectives rather than a single dominant one.

Responding to recent calls for more research on the evaluation phase of novelty (e.g., Anderson et al., 2014; Zhou et al., 2017), some scholars have argued that innovators can activate different social networks to enhance their odds of success throughout different stages of a novel idea journey (Perry-Smith & Mannucci, 2017). We have attempted to respond to this call by looking instead at how innovators can strategically deploy acts of framing to shape audience evaluations, as well as examining audience-level features that affect the recognition of novelty. Consistently with recent research on social movements and institutional theory suggesting that the effect of framing varies with the centralized or fragmented structure of the field (Furnari, 2018), we elucidated the reasons why innovators should strategize their acts of framing based on the structural characteristics of the social audiences evaluating their novel ideas as well as the degree novelty of these ideas. Since these audiences contribute to defining the criteria by which novel ideas are evaluated, exposing which characteristics affect their disposition toward certain ideas as opposed to others is crucial for any study concerned with the conditions that facilitate or inhibit novelty recognition. To this end, idea framing is an important factor in shaping audience disposition. If in fact audience heterogeneity increases the chance that radical ideas will find a receptive social space—that is, an audience willing to recognize and support them—it is still critical to frame them using familiar cues. As we argued before, familiar cues will enhance an audience's understanding of radical ideas and, by implication, their likelihood of being recognized. Focusing on the dynamic interplay between acts of framing and audience-level characteristics, we believe, constitutes a promising area for future research on novelty recognition in cultural fields.

Implications for Practice

Our theoretical framework has several important implications for innovators. At a general level, the notion that novelty is determined as much by the innovators' acts of framing as by the receptiveness of the field should make innovators more sensitive to the rhetorical strategies available to them and organizations more sensitive to the evaluative systems responsible for recognizing individuals' novel ideas. The present study suggests that innovators can increase their probability of receiving support for their novel ideas by making strategic use of acts of framing. For instance, innovators are more likely to obtain recognition for their radical ideas if they frame them by using *familiar cues*; in contrast, incremental ideas have a better chance of being recognized if innovators employ *unfamiliar cues* to frame them. This idea is consistent with Kahl and Grodal's (2016) work on discursive strategies showing how IBM's communication strategy of making the computers' radical technology seem familiar helped the company to outperform Remington Rand in the introduction of the computer among insurance firms.

The importance of being able to recognize novel ideas with high creative potential is obvious. One significant practical implication of our model is that it might help organizational decision makers run more discriminating assessments of novelty by informing their organizational design choices. Our arguments suggest that managers should design evaluative systems that are coherent with the type of novelty under evaluation. For instance, if the objective is to further pursue radical ideas, managers should staff internal selection committees (those evaluating new investment proposals) including also non-peer members who might be more open to deviant ideas. Relying on peer selection committees, in fact, might be more suitable for ideas that do not entail any major departure from the status quo (Cattani et al., 2014). In this regard, it is important to note that these design features appear to run counter to such prevailing practices such as the selection of leading experts into scientific panels, accomplished professionals into artistic juries or top managers into companies' investment committees. By following these practices, which privilege the design of internally oriented audiences, decision makers may routinely favor incremental novelty, while passing on truly disruptive ideas that do not fit well with the evaluative orientation of peer-based audiences. The question of how to define the optimal composition of a selection committee (e.g., the NFS or NIH panelists involved in grant allocation decisions or the jury members of the Cannes or Venice Film Festival) is, therefore, central to any future research that aims to study the recognition of novelty.

Novelty Framing and Social Audiences in the Era of Digitalization

Our framework has also the potential of shedding light on the phenomenon of digitalization in cultural industries. The digital transformation we are observing nowadays has further increased the importance of innovators' act of framing and social audiences' characteristics. Indeed, innovators can decide whether or not to put their novel ideas online, which community to reach using different platforms or social networks, and how to frame the stories they want to tell about their novel ideas. Also, digitalization increases the innovators' chances of finding a supportive audience as they can now bypass traditional gatekeepers and directly reach out to multiple audiences (e.g., different user groups) that do not share the same evaluative criteria and, therefore, may be more open to their novel ideas. Finally, the digital transformation has triggered new dynamics among different audiences: While in the non-digital age innovators could reach their target users only through the mediating role of traditional gatekeepers (whose endorsement was critical), users can now decide on their own which novel ideas to recognize.

An interesting example illustrating this new dynamic is the case of the famous fashion blogger, Chiara Ferragni, who is listed among the top-ten ultra-influencers by the Financial Times (Harrod, 2018). The Harvard case *The Blonde Salad* (Keinan, Maslauskaite, Crener, & Dessain, 2015) documents Chiara Ferragni's phenomenal immediate success: Since the very beginning, the fashion blogger's posts attracted many viewers, allowing her to gain popularity as well as the attention of various designers. Dior Italy was one of the first to ask the fashion blogger to create a partnership. Contrary to the traditional sequence, it is the critical audience (i.e., Dior Italy) that now reaches out to the innovator (i.e., Chiara Ferragni). More importantly, as the case study emphasizes, the key of *The Blonde Salad*'s success was the fashion blogger's selectivity in choosing which designers to collaborate with: "[…] the stories Ferragni would tell about these brands had to reflect her own lifestyle" (Keinan et al., 2015: 5). Specifically, "Chiara would tell a story about wearing a certain garment, having a trip, driving a car – just having a particular experience that she was living with the company – and would include a couple of companies' website links in the text. This would really engage her followers who were then way more likely to convert – to click on the link leading to the brand's website and to buy" (Keinan et al., 2015: 5). Besides emphasizing the importance of innovators' act of framing when they tell their stories in the digital age, this case also confirms the role that multiple heterogeneous audiences play and how the fashion blogger has captured their attention over time: "With the strategic shift from being a blog to becoming an online lifestyle magazine, the audience of The Blonde Salad changed significantly … In 2011, the main followers of my blog were young girls who were inspired by what I was doing. In 2014, fashion insiders, who previously looked down on bloggers, came to read the blog" (Keinan et al., 2015: 11). In sum, our conceptualization affords a more nuanced understanding of how digitalization is shaping cultural industries.

Conclusion

The emergence of novelty has long been center stage in scholarly research in strategic management, organization theory and sociology. Yet several questions pertaining to the recognition of novelty still demand further investigation. In this article, we argued that novelty recognition stems from the individual ability to communicate novel acts and the enabling social space that decides whether or not to recognize and eventually endorse such acts. We emphasized how innovators can use storytelling strategies (i.e., framings acts) to present their novel ideas and discuss the implications that those framing acts hold for their recognition depending on the degree of novelty of those ideas. We further argued that the recognition of novel ideas varies with specific audience-level characteristics. In this article, we focused in particular on whether audiences are *internal* or *external* to the innovators' professional community, as well as their degree of evaluative heterogeneity. Although these characteristics shed important light on the reasons why certain ideas are eventually recognized while others are not, future research might explore additional characteristics (e.g., audience members' cognitive orientations or an audience's internal dynamic during the evaluative process) that might further influence the observed evaluative outcomes.

Acknowledgements The authors gratefully acknowledge financial assistance from European Research Council ("Blindspot" [Grant: 695256]), the MIUR-PRIN ("Creativity, Audiences and Social Evaluation" [Grant: 2015LJXRXJ] and the University of Bologna (Alma Idea Funding Scheme).

Notes

1. "A code-preserving change is any variation that conforms to the rules of conduct representative of the social form within which the organization is nested. By contrast, a code-violating change is any variation that violates the rules of conduct representative of the social form" (Durand et al., 2007: 457).
2. This resonates with Bourdieu's view of cultural fields as networks of relationships among actors struggling for legitimacy: "The structure of the field of cultural production is based on two fundamental and quite different oppositions: first, the opposition between the sub-field of restricted production and the sub-field of large-scale production, i.e. between two economies, two time-scales, two audiences, which endlessly produces and reproduces the negative existence of the sub-field of restricted production and its basic opposition to the bourgeois economic order; and secondly, the opposition, within the sub-field of restricted production, between the consecrated avant-garde and the avant-garde, the established figures and the newcomers, i.e., between artistic generations, often only a few years apart, between the 'young' and the 'old',

the 'neo' and the 'paleo', the 'new' and the 'outmoded', etc.; in short, between cultural orthodoxy and heresy" (Bourdieu, 1993: 53).

3. According to Bourdieu (1980), a structural homology signals the presence of a social space whose members share the same or very similar dispositions as those of the focal actor and thus whose view of the social world, beliefs and tastes are attuned to the focal actor's ones.

References

Adarves-Yorno, I., Postmes, T., & Haslam, S. A. (2007). Creative innovation or crazy irrelevance? The contribution of group norms and social identity to creative behavior. *Journal of Experimental Social Psychology, 43*(3), 410–416.

Aldrich, H. E., & Fiol, C. M. (1994). Fools rush in? The institutional context of industry creation. *Academy of Management Review, 19*(4), 645–670.

Aldrich, H. E., & Martinez, M. A. (2015). Why aren't entrepreneurs more creative? Conditions affecting creativity and innovation in entrepreneurial activity. In *The Oxford handbook of creativity, innovation, and entrepreneurship: Multilevel linkages* (pp. 445–456). Oxford: Oxford University Press.

Amabile, T. M. (1982). Social psychology of creativity: A consensual assessment technique. *Journal of Personality and Social Psychology, 43*(5), 997.

Amabile, T. M. (1996). *Creativity in context.* Boulder, CO: Westview Press.

Anderson, N., Potočnik, K., & Zhou, J. (2014). Innovation and creativity in organizations: A state-of-the-science review, prospective commentary, and guiding framework. *Journal of Management, 40*(5), 1297–1333.

Becker, H. S. (1982). *Art Worlds.* Berkeley: University of California Press.

Bourdieu, P. (1980). The production of belief: Contribution to an economy of symbolic goods. *Media, Culture and Society, 2*(3), 261–293.

Bourdieu, P. (1984). *Distinction: A social critique of the judgment of taste.* Cambridge, MA: Harvard University Press.

Bourdieu, P. (1993). *The field of cultural production.* New York: Columbia University Press.

Burt, R. S. (2004). Structural holes and good ideas. *American Journal of Sociology, 110*(2), 349–399.

Cattani, G., Colucci, M., & Ferriani, S. (2016). Chanel's creative trajectory in the field of fashion: The optimal network structuration strategy. In *Multidisciplinary contributions to the science of creative thinking* (pp. 117–132). Singapore: Springer.

Cattani, G., & Ferriani, S. (2008). A core/periphery perspective on individual creative performance: Social networks and cinematic achievements in the Hollywood film industry. *Organization Science, 19*(6), 824–844.

Cattani, G., Ferriani, S., & Allison, D. (2014). Insiders, outsiders, and the struggle for consecration in cultural fields: A core-periphery perspective. *American Sociological Review, 79*(2), 258–281.

Cattani, G., Ferriani, S., & Lanza, A. (2017). Deconstructing the outsider puzzle: The legitimation journey of novelty. *Organization Science, 28*(6), 965–992.

Cattani, G., Ferriani, S., Negro, G., & Perretti, F. (2008). The structure of consensus: Network ties, legitimation, and exit rates of US feature film producer organizations. *Administrative Science Quarterly, 53*(1), 145–182.

Collins, R. (1998). *The sociology of philosophies: A global theory of intellectual change*. Cambridge, MA: Harvard University Press.

Cornelissen, J. P., & Werner, M. D. (2014). Putting framing in perspective: A review of framing and frame analysis across the management and organizational literature. *The Academy of Management Annals, 8*(1), 181–235.

Crane, D. (1976). Reward systems in art, science, and religion. *American Behavioral Scientist, 19*(6), 719–734.

Csikszentmihályi, M. (1990). *Flow the psychology of optimal experience*. New York: Harper & Row.

Csikszentmihályi, M. (1996). *Creativity, flow and the psychology of discovery and invention*. New York: HarperCollins.

Czarniawska, B. (1998). *A narrative approach in organization studies*. Thousand Oaks, CA: Sage.

Debackere, K., Clarysse, B., Wijneberg, N. M., & Rappa, M. A. (1994). Science and industry: A theory of networks and paradigms. *Technology Analysis & Strategic Management, 6*(1), 21–38.

De Vaan, M., Stark, D., & Vedres, B. (2015). Game changer: The topology of creativity. *American Journal of Sociology, 120*(4), 1144–1194.

Durand, R., Rao, H., & Monin, P. (2007). Code and conduct in French cuisine: Impact of code changes on external evaluations. *Strategic Management Journal, 28*(5), 455–472.

Elsbach, K. D., & Kramer, R. M. (2003). Assessing creativity in hollywood pitch meetings: Evidence for a dual-process model of creativity judgments. *Academy of Management Journal, 46*(3), 283–301.

Furnari, S. (2018). When does an issue trigger change in a field? A comparative approach to issue frames, field structures and types of field change. *Human Relations, 71*(3), 321–348.

Gabriel, Y. (2004). Narratives, stories and texts. In D. Grant, C. Hardy, C. Oswick, & L. Putnam (Eds.), *The Sage handbook of organizational discourse* (pp. 61–77). London: Sage.

Gardner, H. E. (1993). *Frames of minds: The theory of multiple intelligences.* New York: Basic Books.

Garud, R., Gehman, J., & Giuliani, A. P. (2014). Contextualizing entrepreneurial innovation: A narrative perspective. *Research Policy, 43*(7), 1177–1188.

Goldberg, A., Hannan, M. T., & Kovács, B. (2016). What does it mean to span cultural boundaries? Variety and atypicality in cultural consumption. *American Sociological Review, 81*(2), 215–241.

Hargadon, A. B., & Douglas, Y. (2001). When innovations meet institutions: Edison and the design of the electric light. *Administrative Science Quarterly, 46*(3), 476–501.

Harrod, H. (2018, November 16). The rise and rise of the ultra-influencer. *Financial Times*. https://www.ft.com/content/fad9e714-e8c0-11e8-8a85-04b8afea6ea3.

Janssen, S. (1997). Reviewing as social practice: Institutional constraints on critics' attention for contemporary fiction. *Poetics, 24*(5), 275–297.

Kahl, S. J., & Grodal, S. (2016). Discursive strategies and radical technological change: Multilevel discourse analysis of the early computer (1947–1958). *Strategic Management Journal, 37*(1), 149–166.

Kasof, J. (1995). Explaining creativity: The attributional perspective. *Creativity Research Journal, 8*(4), 311–366.

Keinan, A., Maslauskaite, K., Crener, S., & Dessain, V. (2015). The blonde salad. *Harvard Business School Case* 515-074. Boston, MA: HBS Press.

Khaire, M., & Wadhwani, D. (2010). Changing landscapes: The construction of meaning and value in a new market category—Modern Indian art. *Academy of Management Journal, 53*(6), 1281–1304.

Kirton, M. J. (1994). *Adaptors and innovators: Styles of creativity and problem solving*. New York, NY: Routledge.

Lamont, M. (2009). *How professors think*. Cambridge, MA: Harvard University Press.

Lingo, E. L., & O'Mahony, S. (2010). Nexus work: Brokerage on creative projects. *Administrative Science Quarterly, 55*(1), 47–81.

Lounsbury, M., & Glynn, M. A. (2001). Cultural entrepreneurship: Stories, legitimacy, and the acquisition of resources. *Strategic Management Journal, 22*(6–7), 545–564.

Madjar, N., Greenberg, E., & Chen, Z. (2011). Factors for radical creativity, incremental creativity, and routine, noncreative performance. *Journal of Applied Psychology, 96*(4), 730.

Manning, S., & Bejarano, T. A. (2016). Convincing the crowd: Entrepreneurial storytelling in crowdfunding campaigns. *Strategic Organization, 15*(2), 194–219.

March, J. G. (2010). *The Ambiguities of Experience*. Ithaca, NY: Cornell University Press.

Martens, M. L., Jennings, J. E., & Jennings, D. (2007). Do the stories they tell get them the money they need? The role of entrepreneurial narratives in resource acquisition. *Academy of Management Journal, 50*(5), 1107–1132.

Mueller, J. S., Melwani, S., & Goncalo, J. A. (2012). The bias against creativity: Why people desire but reject creative ideas. *Psychological Science, 23*(1), 13–17.

Mueller, J., Melwani, S., Loewenstein, J., & Deal, J. J. (2018). Reframing the decision-makers' dilemma: Towards a social context model of creative idea recognition. *Academy of Management Journal, 61*(1), 94–110.

Mumford, M. D., & Gustafson, S. B. (1988). Creativity syndrome: Integration, application, and innovation. *Psychological Bulletin, 103*(1), 27.

Navis, C., & Glynn, M. A. (2011). Legitimate distinctiveness and the entrepreneurial identity: Influence on investor judgments of new venture plausibility. *Academy of Management Review, 36*(3), 479–499.

Padgett, J. F., & Powell, W. W. (2012). *The emergence of organizations and markets*. Princeton, NJ: Princeton University Press.

Parker, J. N., & Corte, U. (2017). Placing collaborative circles in strategic action fields: Explaining differences between highly creative groups. *Sociological Theory, 35*(4), 261–287.

Perry-Smith, J. E. (2006). Social yet creative: The role of social relationships in facilitating individual creativity. *Academy of Management Journal, 49*(1), 85–101.

Perry-Smith, J. E., & Mannucci, V. (2017). From creativity to innovation: The social network drivers of the four phases of the idea journey. *Academy of Management Review, 42*(1), 53–79.

Pollack, J. M., Rutherford, M. W., & Nagy, B. G. (2012). Preparedness and cognitive legitimacy as antecedents of new venture funding in televised business pitches. *Entrepreneurship Theory and Practice, 36*(5), 915–939.

Pontikes, E. G. (2012). Two sides of the same coin: How ambiguous classification affects multiple audiences' evaluations. *Administrative Science Quarterly, 57*(1), 81–118.

Rindova, V. P., & Petkova, A. P. (2007). When is a new thing a good thing? Technological change, product form design, and perceptions of value for product innovations. *Organization Science, 18*(2), 217–232.
Seong, S., & Godart, F. (2018). Semantic strategies for influencing the influencers: Trading a stock of names for higher creativity evaluations. *Academy of Management Journal, 61*(3), 966–993.
Sgourev, S. V. (2013). How Paris gave rise to Cubism (and Picasso): Ambiguity and fragmentation in radical innovation. *Organization Science, 24*(6), 1601–1617.
Simmel, G. (1971). *On Individuality and Social Forms*. Chicago: University of Chicago Press.
Suchman, M. C. (1995). Managing legitimacy: Strategic and institutional approaches. *Academy of Management Review, 20*(3), 571–610.
Uzzi, B., & Spiro, J. (2005). Collaboration and creativity: The small world problem. *American Journal of Sociology, 111*(2), 447–504.
Vaara, E., Sonenshein, S., & Boje, D. (2016). Narratives as sources of stability and change in organizations: Approaches and directions for future research. *The Academy of Management Annals, 10*(1), 495–560.
van Werven, R., Bouwmeester, O., & Cornelissen, J. P. (2015). The power of arguments: How entrepreneurs convince stakeholders of the legitimate distinctiveness of their ventures. *Journal of Business Venturing, 30*(4), 616–631.
Vergne, J. P., & Wry, T. (2014). Categorizing categorization research: Review, integration, and future directions. *Journal of Management Studies, 51,* 56–94.
White, H. C. (1992). *Identity and control: A structural theory of social action.* Princeton, NJ: Princeton University Press.
Wijnberg, N. M. (1995). Selection processes and appropriability in art, science and technology. *Journal of Cultural Economics, 19,* 221–235.
Wijnberg, N. M., & Gemser, G. (2000). Adding value to innovation: Impressionism and the transformation of the selection system in visual arts. *Organization Science, 11*(3), 323–329.
Zhou, J., Wang, X. M., Song, L. J., & Wu, J. (2017). Is it new? Personal and contextual influences on perceptions of novelty and creativity. *Journal of Applied Psychology, 102*(2), 180.

3

The Alchemy of Painting: How the Technology of Oil Paint Transmuted Art

Stoyan V. Sgourev

That technology is such an integral part of our lives has also made it appear invisible—it is typically taken for granted as a key ingredient in the processing of information or the completion of job-related tasks. This may explain its relative absence in organizational research (Orlikowski & Scott, 2008), as attention is concentrated on the more visible aspects of organizing, thereby reinforcing the perception that technology is but a product of cultural or economic forces.

Technology constitutes a "bundle of material and symbol properties" (Orlikowski, 2000: 408)—a physical object and a social product at the same time (Barley, 1986). It is frequently observed that studies of technology and organizing tend to follow the social (Leonardi & Barley, 2008; Orlikowski & Scott, 2008): the interactions, perceptions, and behaviors around a technology (e.g., Barley, 1986; Orlikowski, 2000). Even when a research context is chosen in relation to a particular

S. V. Sgourev (✉)
ESSEC Business School, Cergy, France
e-mail: sgourev@essec.edu

J. Strandgaard Pedersen et al. (eds.), *Technology and Creativity*,
https://doi.org/10.1007/978-3-030-17566-5_3

technology, attention is typically focused on patterns of use and practices of organizing, not on the technology itself. The desire to avoid technological determinism has resulted in disproportionate interest in the social dynamics of technology, relative to its material properties.

To rectify this tendency, Leonardi and Barley (2008) provide several guidelines. One is to recognize the importance of material artefacts, features, and practices to human activities and relations (Gieryn, 2002; Jones, Meyer, Jancsary, & Hollerer, 2017). Others include broadening the range of studied technologies and analyzing both development and use. But probably most important is their suggestion to avoid cross-sectional demonstrations that technologies can have different outcomes in different contexts, examining instead different outcomes of the same technology over time.

These guidelines define the overarching objective of this chapter—documenting long-term effects of the material aspects of a technology in a creative industry. As scholars observe, adopting a longitudinal perspective is essential in disentangling the dynamic interplay between the technological and social domains (e.g., Leonardi & Barley, 2008). The co-evolution between technologies, people, and organizations is well established in scholarship (e.g., Barley, 1986; Orlikowski, 1992, 2000). The dual nature of technology—as a product and a process—underlies a complex interaction through which organizing is accomplished (Orlikowski & Scott, 2008). To understand and capture this complexity demands attention to both the social aspects (i.e., perception or interpretation) and the constraints and affordances of the technology—what it allows users to do or prevents them from doing (Zammuto, Griffith, Majchrzak, Dougherty, & Faraj, 2007). To avoid cultural and technological determinism requires that scholars describe not only how users make sense of a technology and apply it in constructing relations or identities, but also the ways in which the material features of technologies give rise to or condition the evolution of social practices (Clarke & Fujimura, 1992; Knorr-Cetina, 1997).

In an integrative approach of this kind, technology is analyzed as a constellation of features, processes, and practices (e.g., Perrow, 1967). Technology does not determine practices of organizing, but it creates and constrains possibilities for the application of material features, encouraging users to do old things in new ways or to try completely new things. To capture the interplay of agency and determinism in a co-evolutionary process (e.g., Padgett & Powell, 2012) requires scholars to initially identify and describe the complexity of a technology and then follow the relations between technology and social structure (Roberts & Grabowski, 1996). Similarly, Leonardi and Barley (2008) argue that to study the co-evolution of the material and social, it may make more sense to follow the technology.

This is the approach adopted in a historical analysis of one of the fundamental innovations in the history of art—oil paint. What makes oil paint appropriate in methodological terms is that it is irreducible to a cultural artifact, constituting a quintessentially material development. This seemingly unassuming invention had profound impact on the development of artistic genres and individual styles. The introduction of oil paint reorganized the process of picture making and redefined the social status of the artist. The substantive contribution of the analysis is in articulating how the technology of oil paint reinforced contradictions within the culture and facilitated the bifurcation of the representational and expressive functions of art. Rather than a mere cultural product, oil paint was an active agent of change in a complex interplay between technological and cultural forces that unfolded over centuries.

Technology in the Creative Industries

Characterized by the constant pursuit of new ideas (Caves, 2000), the creative industries have attracted surprisingly little scholarly interest in their technological aspects. The history of innovation encompasses ideas, relations, and methods (Mokyr, 2016), but methods have been largely absent from sociological and organizational accounts.[1] In studies of innovation, attention is typically focused on the process of evaluation and not on the underlying technology (e.g., Cattani, Ferriani, & Lanza, 2017), presented as a product of cultural and relational practices. Rare are the studies adopting the viewpoint of the producer and inquiring about production techniques, choice of materials, or craftsmanship. For example, if recognized in the sociology of art that techniques are one of the intermediaries between the artwork and the social context, there is disproportionately more attention devoted to the role of other intermediaries, such as patrons, collectors, dealers, critics, guilds, or studios (Hennion, 2015).

This relative neglect is reflected in the tendency to present the artwork as little more than the end product of social influences, denying its capacity to be an active agent in the production process or an autonomous source of aesthetic pleasure. Yet, as DeNora (2000) observes for music, its formal properties result from a process of interaction, whereby the social is inscribed into music, but music affects reciprocally social life (Acord & DeNora, 2008). Similarly, Baxandall (1985) recognizes the social and economic aspects of art, encoded in the social organization of art production, but argues that artistic agency is irreducible to them. Redefining the production of art as the interaction of labor and materials, Baxandall (1980) attributes a key role in the social construction of agency to material practices, which allowed Renaissance painters to evade religious conventions by connecting directly with the everyday experiences of craftsmen or merchants as buyers of art. The intuitive comprehension of craft, materials, and tools created a common ground between producers in different domains, leading to fundamental shifts in the perception of aesthetic and economic value.[2]

As these accounts suggest, technologies and practices are important to study because of their implications for creativity, evaluation, and professional identity. The concept of "affordance" can be instrumental in understanding these implications and the nature of the interaction between people and technologies (Leonardi, 2013). Affordances are broadly defined as possibilities for action (Gibson, 1982) or the use to which an object or technology makes itself available to others. They are relational in nature, connecting the attributes of users and those of technologies (Hutchby, 2001). As an analytic tool, affordances allow to document the capacity of technologies to create a possibility space[3] (Moeran, 2013). While shaped by the cultural environment, affordances exercise autonomous effects by framing the possibilities for action in relation to a technology (Hutchby, 2001: 444). Referring to properties that are used by individuals for their own specific purposes, affordances contain a range of possible activities that are circumscribed by conventions. This concept is well suited to analyzing the various ways in which creative processes are both inhibited and enabled in a social context (Moeran, 2013).

In this framework, materials afford technologies and technologies afford styles (Moeran, 2013). The divide between style and technology describes a wide array of human activities (Ambrose, 2001) and is fundamental to evaluation and the construction of identities in the creative industries (Cappetta et al., 2006; Eisenman, 2013). For example, photographers articulate their artistic objectives not only through their aesthetic choices, such as a specific color or theme in their portfolio (Aspers, 2001), but also through technological choices, such as digital and analog photography (Munir & Phillips, 2005). The relationship between these dimensions is complex and historically contingent. For example, in the last decades of the twentieth century the technological complexity of traditional cuisine was played down at the expense of aesthetic complexity (Rao et al., 2003), similar to what occurred in art in the early twentieth century (Sgourev, 2013). In what follows, I document the less familiar scenario in scholarship of a suddenly increasing degree of technological complexity, as observed in art in the late fifteenth and early sixteenth centuries. The development of the technology of oil paint not only ameliorated the quality of painting, affording more realistic visual representation, but also created new possibilities for stylistic differentiation and aesthetic idiosyncrasy in the application of the paintbrush. This was the outset of a momentous shift in the history of art whereby the technicality of picture making started to weigh in heavily in determining the aesthetic appeal and resonance of the work of art (e.g., Baxandall, 1988).

The analysis of the oil paint technology covers two key developments—the emergence of the technique in fifteenth-century-Flanders and its refinement in early sixteenth-century-Venice. Spanning a century, the narrative presents an account of the inception and diffusion of the technology over time. By tracing the technology, the analysis tries to tease out the intricate interplay between technological and cultural factors, highlighting different outcomes of the same technology over time (Leonardi & Barley, 2008). The two contexts are geographically distant but connected in time—the oil paint technology migrated from Flanders to Venice, interacting with the local culture.

The analysis is based on a systematic survey of research on oil paint in art history. Given the limited volume of research dedicated to this topic, I was able to cover existing scholarship in English and French. Key observations were cross-validated across accounts, suggesting ways to develop the theoretical model (Siggelkow, 2007). After an overview of the affordances of oil paint, I document how the introduction of the technology reflected back on the culture and the mode of art production.

Oil Paint: Affordances

It is somewhat surprising that such a major development in the history of art, such as the introduction of oil paint in fifteenth-century Europe and its diffusion and elaboration in the sixteenth century, has received so little attention in art history. This is probably due to the relative obscurity to which technical issues have been relegated in scholarship dominated by theoretical matters, where attention is directed more to the reception of works than their conception. However, the introduction of oil paint represents undoubtedly a landmark moment in the history of art, as it helped usher in an unprecedented wave of technical and stylistic innovations in the sixteenth century.

Oil painting was not an invention of sudden discovery, but gradually developed over a period of hundred years by artists who strived to adapt to changing times and styles (Meyer, 1969). The oil-based paints were originally developed in the early twelfth century but found wide use only in Flanders in the early fifteenth century (Langlais, 1959).[4] As Flemish art became increasingly popular, the oil-based techniques diffused gradually throughout Europe. They were first adopted in the Southern, Spanish-dominated regions of the Italian peninsula, before reaching Venice around 1475. Oil became the most important medium by the early sixteenth century and was to remain so until the end of the nineteenth century.

The primary medium before the introduction of oil was egg tempera. While it served well the requirements of fourteenth-century-easel painting, it had a distinct characteristic that limited its versatility. The paint dried very fast, compelling the artist to complete work on a section at high speed and in a very precise manner, before the pigments dried. Furthermore, the resultant colors were rather muted, with limited opportunities for rendering shading effects. When light hit the surface of the canvass, it did not penetrate to lower layers of color, impairing the creation of a visual illusion. The dry, linear quality of tempera was out of step with the demands of a changing cultural landscape, marked by aspirations for veracity and the broadening of genres beyond religious content. From the early fifteenth century, painters increasingly turned to materials that were more amenable to the fluent depiction of flowing shapes and blended tones, utilizing oils that had been employed up to that point for decorative, rather than artistic purposes (Meyer, 1969). The transition from tempera to oil was gradual, at first featuring oily ingredients incorporated into tempera paints to create intermediate tempera, before Venetian artists switched fully to oil-based paint in the first decade of the sixteenth century (Steinberg & Wylie, 1990).

Oil paint consists of pigments dissolved in drying oil, usually linseed oil. The pigment is milled with linseed oil, grinding each color by hand. The oil dries by oxidation in a chemical process that occurs as atmospheric oxygen is added to exposed oil. The introduction of oxygen launches a reaction that transforms the linear structure of the fluid into a hardened, complex lattice structure. The slow-drying process (which appeared as alchemy to contemporaries) was a key reason why oil quickly surpassed egg tempera in popularity, allowing for versatility, subtle brushwork, and longer working time. The affordances of oil are rather complex but can be summarized based on past research (e.g., Langlais, 1959) in three categories: visual representation, expressiveness, and durability.

Representation. Since it dried slowly, oil had several major advantages over tempera, which had significant impact on the quality of visual rendering. Critically, the drying time and the superior blending ability of oil paint allowed for more subtle development of tone, capturing the translucency of light by superimposing layers and glazes. The application of paint in very thin layers (glazes) led to the elaboration of new techniques, such as chiaroscuro (contrast of light and dark) and sfumato (a misty or foggy effect). When light strikes a surface built up of glazes, it penetrates to the lower layers, creating the appearance of luminosity. These techniques enabled artists to capture the varying effects of light on textures, enhancing the illusion that viewers are looking at real objects rather than painted imitation (Stokstad & Cothren, 2016: 298). Once applied, the paint has time to smooth out during the drying process, erasing traces of individual brushstrokes.

Furthermore, oils offered an unprecedented intensity and luminosity of color. Oil supports a high concentration of pigment, bringing richness and depth to the color. Blending colors with oils gave the artist a richer palette than ever before. The greater color variety allowed to depict the human figure and natural environment in increasingly realistic visual terms. The oil base facilitated versatility, as paintings were used for a wider variety of social situations and subject matter.

Expressiveness. Oil paint is physically different from other paint, characterized by high degree of viscosity. Depending on the pigment (and its reaction time with oil), oils become dry in a period of two to twelve days, sometimes even longer. As drying occurs through a long, slow breathing process, it allows for extended blending and working time, giving the artist the freedom to come back to a piece and continue working on it days or weeks later. With the introduction of oil paint, artists could rethink and revise as they went, allowing them to be more spontaneous in their work. That changes could be made easily during the drying process encouraged artists to experiment and take greater risks, as it was now possible to come back and revise if the original design was judged inferior to intentions. Oil thus changed the way that artists worked and thought about their methods. They became accustomed to the practice of blending and application, then correcting tones and colors, erasing perceived mistakes or overhauling a full section of the canvass. Furthermore, the controllable density and weight of oil-based paint allowed each stroke to leave a distinctive trace, which could be carefully modeled into a desired form. The freedom to experiment and pursue new, more spontaneous forms of expression on a canvass was a key ingredient in the acceleration of innovation and proliferation of styles in the early sixteenth century.

Durability. The durability of oil paint is why it was originally used for purposes of decoration. When colors are milled with sufficient skill, they remain stable in suspension almost indefinitely. If the correct procedure for blending of pigment and oil is followed, allowing for the oil to dry longer, it would lead to permanence and stability on the painted surface, lasting for many generations (as visible in museums nowadays). The enhanced durability of artworks encouraged artists to project themselves into the future, as the product of their work progressively transcended its utilitarian function as a mere tradable good, to assume the objective of conveying the presence of the artist through the centuries.[5]

Oil-based paint presented several advantages relative to tempera, but what attracted painters to it was the affordance for enhanced visual representation. European culture at the time was undergoing changes that resulted in greater understanding of perspective and depth, and increasing appreciation of veracity, fostering the pursuit of more sophisticated techniques to represent reality (Langlais, 1959). It was Flemish painters who responded the first to the new demand for realism in the culture at the time.

Van Eyck: Art Mirrors Reality

One of the most enduring puzzles in centuries of art history is the sudden and dramatic way in which the dominant visual idiom changed in the beginning of the fifteenth century. As Hockney (2006) observes, there seems to have occurred a revolution in the vicinity of 1420, as art turned radically, inexplicably more realistic within a decade. A staggering leap in verisimilitude in artistic representation resulted in the emergence around 1430 of an "optical look" that practically mirrored reality (Hockney, 2006). No adequate or widely accepted explanation has emerged in art history, but the quick speed at which the change occurred suggests that the catalyst was the adoption of a new technology,[6] of which oil-based paint is the chief suspect.

The oil-based medium allowed painters to reproduce the appearance of the real world with all its variety of textures, nuances of light, and intensity of colors (Ione, 2005). The quest for naturalness and technical perfection defined the new Flemish style, whose earliest manifestations are in the work of Robert Campin, further elaborated by Rogier van der Weyden and Jan van Eyck (1390–1441), who is widely considered as the pioneer of oil painting. The art of Van Eyck is unprecedented in the depth and detail of the visual illusion created on the canvass. The variety of visual effects in his paintings is astonishing—curling locks of hair, woolen weave of oriental carpets, crisp folds of satin brocades, and translucence of hand-blown glass (Harbison, 1995). The faces of his figures look more like a personal likeness than anything since ancient Rome (Stokstad & Cothren, 2016: 293).[7] With his outstanding technical capability, Van Eyck enhanced the prominence of painting, enlarging its representational vocabulary, and contributing to the consecration of oil as the new dominant medium in European art.

Van Eyck's style emerged from a local, Flemish tradition, becoming the founding moment of Northern art (Van Mander, 1994 [1707]). The naturalness of this style reflected the tendency for secularization in the North and the interest in optics, color, and light. Northern artists were within, as well as creating, a culture that was more and more embedded in the material world (Ione, 2005). The early fifteenth century witnessed a deepening shift in people's consciousness, becoming less focused on the heavens and more so on the physical world (Ione, 2005). The growing demand for realism, for art to convey what is observed in everyday life, encouraged artists to paint scenes replicating the material world, to represent the variety of textures or shapes visible around them (Stokstad & Cothren, 2016).

Northern painters were naturally drawn to oil as a more material medium, with its affordances allowing them to adapt to a changing cultural landscape and a new way of seeing that tended to equate reality with physical matter (and not spiritual). The affordance of enhanced representation encouraged technical mastery, scrupulous attention to detail, three-dimensional mass of the figures, and complex rendering of modulated light. Fifteenth-century portraits appear astonishingly lifelike, revealing a growing interest in the individual with her particularities and psychological states. Even in religious paintings, the saints and angels have distinct personalities, based on human models. Rich in detail and realistic in color and proportions, Northern paintings combined the terrestrial and heavenly universe through the increasingly sophisticated medium of oil paint. This form of realism reflected the changing relations between the individual, society, religion, and art.

That the oil paint technology reflected contemporary culture does not mean that it is reducible to it. Its function as an agent of change is most visible in the manner in which it reinforced underlying tensions and contradictions in that culture. By allowing artists to manifest supreme mastery of their trade through the meticulous crafting of objects and rendering of details, this technology contributed to the professionalization of the occupational category of the artist as craftsman. This is manifested in Van Eyck's pride in his achievements and his self-consciousness about his work as a painter. He was the only fifteenth-century Netherlandish painter to sign his canvases, with his motto proclaiming "*As Best I Can.*" As Harbison (1995) observes, this can be read as a somewhat arrogant assertion of the quality of the work, challenging other artists to do better than him. This understanding of art as the arena of competition between professional painters in command of their talents and tools is remarkably modern for its time, presaging the highly developed Dutch art market in the early seventeenth century (Sgourev, 2018).

The assertion of professional excellence through oil painting not only elevated the status of the painter, but also attracted commissions by those who wanted to assert their professional achievement by having their portrait painted by a reputed master (Harbison, 2012). The visible skill of the painter became his trademark—the rendering of numerous details and bright colors made the work instantly recognizable. The more details, the more valuable the painting. That the oil technique served to differentiate painters on the level of skill and make paintings appear as luxury objects had important repercussions in reinforcing the desacralization of art and the increasing recognition of artworks as consumable goods, whose value did not derive exclusively from their (religious) content.

Furthermore, oil painting and the stylistic developments it made possible writ large underlying tensions in societies at the time, such as the need to reconcile the admiration for beauty of the physical world with the notion that beauty must be renounced for a higher goal (Harbison, 2012). Painters were ready to oblige when patrons demanded to have their material belongings portrayed, but this had the unintended effect of reinforcing the belief that the material world is more important than the spiritual one. This is the reason why the new style was not accepted in some parts of Germany, deemed too ostentatious and inconsistent with the Protestant ideology. The practical and realistic orientation of the new style conveyed the growing skepticism about the authority of social and religious institutions. The brilliant and finely rendered objects appealed to the desire of bourgeois patrons for material display of their political and economic ascent. These aspirations were mixed with religious doctrines in the fifteenth century but became increasingly separated from them as the sixteenth century approached (Harbison, 2012).

Improved technical means were instrumental in this process, fostering the growing demand for realism and encouraging artists to create their own reality, which was neither the empirical reality, nor the reality of religious scriptures. Technology thus became implicated in a complicated game within fifteenth-century culture between tradition and innovation, the Church and individual belief, spirituality and materiality, ostentation and austerity. The style pioneered by Van Eyck did not convey only piety, but individual aspirations and professional achievement. It signified the ascendance of technical prowess over abstract ideas, as *What* is portrayed became tangibly less important than *How* it is portrayed.

In this transformation, technology was crucial. It reflected cultural and economic processes, such as the growing prominence of the merchant and his desire for material display. But technology was not a mere cultural product. It was actively used by artists to navigate a complex social landscape by articulating a new professional identity within a conservative society. They used it to give flesh to a conceived reality, convincing viewers that the represented objects (and the aspirations of patrons) were “real.” Oil painting was an agent of change that deepened latent contradictions within the culture, contributing markedly to the desacralization of art and diluting the boundaries between artistic genres.

Venice: Oil, Canvass and a Looser Brush

Although oil emerged as a medium in Northern Europe, it matured as an artistic practice in Venice. Until the late fifteenth century, Italian art was dominated by the schools of Florence and Rome, steeped in the use of the traditional mediums of fresco and egg tempera on wood surface. Both were water-based and dried fast, making them ill-fitted to the humid Venetian climate. Unsurprisingly, the introduction of oil paint in the late 1470s was met with an enthusiastic reception in Venice. Venice contributed to the popularity of oil-based paint more than any other location. This was due not only to its resistance to humidity, but also to the affordance of expressiveness, articulating the Venetian penchant for color. In contrast to Florence and Rome, Venice attributed primary importance to color in the pictorial space, rather than to composition. The greater depth and luminosity of color that oil paint enabled encouraged experimentation and the accumulation of skills by Venetian artists in mixing and using color pigments.

The adoption of oil in Venice occurred in two stages. It started with Giovanni Bellini in the late fifteenth century, using an oil-based variant of the old tempera technique, highlighting the shading and blending qualities of the new medium. As painters were making increasing use of oily ingredients, oil supplanted tempera by the early sixteenth century, as manifested in the work of painters such as Giorgione or Titian (Meyer, 1969). The development of oil-based techniques by Venetian painters contributed to the increasing demand for art and encouraged technical and stylistic innovations.

One of the most important consequences of the adoption of oil related to the working method, as painters began to work *a la prima*—abandoning the meticulous drawing and underpainting of tempera painting and sketching with the paints themselves, using thick, coarse brushes (Steinberg & Wylie, 1990). In stark contrast with tempera painting or earlier Flemish examples, the act of painting proceeded directly on the canvass with little preparation in the form of sketches or drawings (Rosand, 1997). By experimenting, painters became increasingly adept at blending colors by mixing paints of various viscosities, obtaining startlingly rich colors on the canvass.

As the new working method in oil allowed more and larger paintings to be made more quickly the result was a spectacular increase in artistic output in a relatively short period of time. Shifting from tempera to oil allowed painters to meet the increasing public demand for art in the early sixteenth century, related to the extensive renovation of Venice's ecclesiastical and civic buildings (Brown, 1988). As Steinberg and Wylie (1990: 67) attest, the average yearly output in square meters of Venetian painters rose from 2.4 and 2.8 in the 1460s and 1470s to 7 in 1480s, to 12 in the 1500s and 16.9 in the 1510s.

The ability of artists to cover more ground more quickly than before was also due to a related technical development—the adoption of canvass as the main support for painting, replacing walls and wood around 1500. Canvass was relatively inexpensive and lightweight, with its principal advantage being its portability, allowing artists to work in their studios and dispatch their work to near or more remote locations. They could now paint smaller portraits, opening up a wider market for their work. The portability of canvas permitted painters to remain in Venice and to have their production transported to buyers all over Europe.[8] This led to increasing physical distance between producer and buyer, tilting the balance of power between them in favor of the former, by reducing their dependence on courts and the Church, relying more and more on middle-class patrons (Rosand, 1997).

The technical and commercial developments accompanying the adoption of the oil-on-canvass format resulted in important stylistic innovations, such as the pursuit of much broader range of topics, and the greatly enhanced naturalism, depicting objects as perceived by the eye. The representational possibilities of oil paint enabled artists to render reality in such visually convincing manner that the painters were now considered able to "counterfeit" or "feign" nature (Steinberg & Wylie, 1990: 37) by directly working from life itself. The objective of the artist became that of reproducing the vivacity and complexity of observable reality in the most elaborate ways possible. The more lifelike a work of art was and the more convincing the rendition of objects, the more valuable it was considered (Rosand, 1997). Similar to Flemish art in the early fifteenth century, critics and buyers appreciated and encouraged virtuosic depictions of materials (i.e., glass, metal, or clouds), of highlights, shadows and movement, and of figures in unusual postures (Steinberg & Wylie, 1990: 65).

The presence of so much detail in natural painting had a dual function. It served to guarantee to the viewer the veracity of the divine miracle that was represented, enhancing verisimilitude of the rendition (Brown, 1988). But it also strived to respond to the public expectation of demonstration of artistic excellence and skill, reflected in the ability to reproduce or even surpass reality on the canvass through accurate rendition of perspective, light and shadow, through dazzling colors and lifelikeness of objects. The fifteenth-century viewer expected veracity in portraits and technical precision in rendering the clothes and furniture that defined one's social status. The principles of evaluation changed in a way that prioritized difficulty—the performance of difficult things on the canvass was valued in itself, as a demonstration of skills and talent (Baxandall, 1988). Excellence was based on knowledge of materials and techniques and involved doing hard things in a way that appeared seamless and was easy on the eye. Skill was valued when it was conspicuous, manifested in a supremely fine brush that reproduces reality, but leaves no visible trace.

Realism became a standard of quality in Venice but the same technical development that made it possible also helped to lead away from it by reinforcing the expressive (versus representational) properties of art. Venetians initially adopted the Flemish method that mixed tempera and oil, but then started experimenting by modulating the proportions. Consistent use of oil-based paint revealed many of its advantages, such as intense colors, shading, flexibility, and ease of corrections (Ilckman, 2014).

They realized that the quick drying of tempera precluded more expressive brushstrokes, while using predominantly oil afforded a new range of aesthetic effects. For example, in tempera painting, grass had to be painted as a solid field of color, while oil allowed to paint it in strokes of green. Similarly, static clouds gave way to skies blending blues, yellows, and pinks behind cloud masses that featured swirling whites and grays (Steinberg & Wylie, 1990). It became increasingly common for Venetian painters to draw on the blending qualities of oils to suggest, rather than to clearly delineate contours.

In figuring out how to render more convincingly shades or the haziness of distant scenes, the painters learned how to heap up higher viscosity paints thickly (impasto) and enlarged their brush kit to include wider ones for some of the sketching and for impasto, thin brushes for finer details and yet others for wash-like effects (Steinberg & Wylie, 1990). The different effects of these brushes in the application of oil paint started to attract attention to brushwork as an indication not of skill, but of the emotional presence of the artist. The flexibility of oil paint allowed adjustments and corrections over a prolonged period, encouraging artists to alternate brushes and to vary strokes in pursuit of the perfect expression. Thus, they discovered how to make best use of uneven surfaces or how to manipulate paint in order to leave a broken, interrupted mark, lending new vibrancy to the surface itself (Rosand, 1997).

It appears that the Venetians were the first to understand the expressive implications of the oil-canvass combination and that the turning point in the evolution of a new pictorial technique occurred around 1500 (Ilckman, 2014). In aspiring for perfection, artists experimented toward a style of softer contours, complex sequences of paint layers, and newly expressive brushstrokes (Ilckman, 2014). For the first time in the history of art, the personal touch and identity of the artist became manifested in the visible brushstrokes. The choice of brush style by the artist was no longer viewed merely as a technical decision, but an aesthetic one too, a manifestation not of skill, but an identity. If in the fifteenth century the brushstrokes disappeared within a fine style of painting that mirrors nature, the sixteenth century witnessed the reaction to this development, when brushstrokes became important and their thickness increased in an unprecedented manner (Langlais, 1959: 64).

I use the term "bifurcation" to refer to the growing misalignment between the representational and expressive affordances of oil paint in the early sixteenth century. The bifurcation can be observed in the careers of prominent painters, such as Titian. He became famous with the fine style, but his technique evolved considerably over decades, through corrections and reworkings on the canvass that he viewed as a means of expression. Toward the end of his career, Titian went so far as to use the handles of his brushes to mold the thick impasto and apply glazes with his fingers (Hope, 2004). He stopped signing his pictures at a certain point, because, as it changed from smoothness to expressive rawness, his bold handling of paint was identification enough (Langlais, 1959). The expressive function of oil paint was elevated to a higher level with Tintoretto, who found new ways to assert the physical presence of the artist. His brushwork left visible traces; empty and slushy spots dotted the painting, contributing to an impression of incompleteness and ineffability. The idiosyncratic style he developed in the later stages of his career arguably marks the accomplishment of the bifurcation process that oil paint set in motion.

Similar to what occurred in Flanders, the ascent of oil painting also reinforced contradictions and sources of tension in the Venetian culture. As Steinberg and Wylie (1990) document, the technical accomplishments intensified a conceptual predicament inherent in religious painting. Profane objects, such as foliage, flesh, sky, or cloth, could be depicted unproblematically in the new naturalistic style.

Catholic doctrines, however, maintained the separation between a sacred order of reality and a profane one. Depicting a sacred figure with the same level of meticulousness as profane objects threatened to upend the existing order by diluting the difference between the profane and sacred universe. It became apparent to Venetian painters that they had to devise new ways of reintegrating the two, so that the depiction of biblical subjects and the virtuosity with which this was done were not perceived to be in tension. The acceleration of technical and stylistic innovation in the early sixteenth century posed a problem in the sense that it proceeded faster than changes in the surrounding culture from which it evolved. It became a question of scholastic debate whether a painting materialized God's creative faculty or the faculty of the painter to render visible the invisible through sophisticated means and his own talent.

This source of tension was aggravated by and reflected in changes in the social hierarchy of Venice. If painters were traditionally considered as little more than craftsmen, they started to gain in prominence by the early sixteenth century. Technical developments contributed to the perception of the painter as an artist and not a mere craftsman. Painting without extensive preparation (*a-la prima*) in slow-drying, easily adjustable oils not only allowed painters to experiment on the canvass, but also forged a new identity for the artist as an individual endowed with special talent and the ability not just to imitate nature, but to better it with his own designs. The embodiment of this new conception of the artist was Tintoretto, whose expressive liberty on the canvass and a self-determined career trajectory presaged the advent of a new era in the history of art that would come to be known as the Baroque.

Increasing demand for the services of particular painters accorded them status and a level of self-determination that was unthinkable a generation earlier (Steinberg & Wylie, 1990). Naturally, the individualization of careers and artistic practices, where virtuosity was increasingly valued for its own sake and not for its religious function, defied a social ethic that placed the highest value on harmony and order. The established practice of allotting public commissions widely among painters appeared increasingly out of step with tendencies favoring competition, the display of talent through invention and the pursuit of individual careers. Oil-based paint was a key agent in the process of emancipation of the artist that traverses the history of art, culminating with the artist-as-star in the late twentieth century.

Discussion

Scholarship has long identified the relative paucity of research on technology (Orlikowski & Scott, 2008) and the need to better understand and empirically capture the complexity of the co-evolution between technologies, people, and organizations (e.g., Barley, 1986; Orlikowski, 1992, 2000). To avoid cultural and technological determinism in doing so requires that scholars describe not only how users make sense of and apply a technology, but also the concrete ways in which technological affordances propel and condition the evolution of social practices (Clarke & Fujimura, 1992; Knorr-Cetina, 1997).

To disentangle the complex interplay between material and social properties, it is suggested to follow the same technology over time (Leonardi & Barley, 2008). This is the approach adopted in this study, pursuing a longitudinal perspective on the interplay between technology and culture in the fifteenth and sixteenth centuries. Oil-based paint is appropriate to this objective, as it is irreducible to a cultural artefact, constituting simultaneously a product and a process.

Starting with an overview of the affordances of the technology, the analysis recounted how the affordances were activated in two contexts. The new technology enhanced the quality of painting, affording more realistic representation, but also forged possibilities for stylistic differentiation in the application of the brush. Far from a mere product of cultural transformation, the technology reinforced the tendency toward desacralization of art and catalyzed a bifurcation that up to the sixteenth century was only implicit—between representational and expressive functions, between ideas and emotional states.

The analysis demonstrates that the importance of technology lies not simply in facilitating or structuring production or in serving as a means of cultural reproduction, as typically presented in the organizational literature. It can also be an autonomous factor of change and a source of tension within the same cultural context that made possible the emergence of the technology. A deterministic causal chain fails to do justice to the complexity of the trajectory that originated in the north before weaving its way south to Venice. The affordances of the technology were not static or fixed—the ways in which they were activated in Flanders and Venice were similar in some regards, but different in others.

As demonstrated, Van Eyck conceptualized the optical possibility of using systematic glazing to make a painted surface appear more realistic. Oil proved an excellent medium for rendering light. Meticulously representing multiple objects in highly refined detail through superimposed glazes and imperceptible brushstrokes, Flemish and Venetian painters learned how to reproduce nature on the canvass, making figures or objects appear alive. This verisimilitude responded to a growing demand for realism by patrons that valued and demanded manifestations of status and material well-being.

But as oil developed into a sophisticated medium, it afforded new ways of representing matter in all its colors and radiance, encouraging artists to experiment through trial and error with new styles of painting, based on increasingly audacious brushwork. A growing asymmetry occurred between art in Venice and in the North of Europe, between the expressive and representational functions of art.

If the representational affordance attracted initially artists to oil, the expressive affordance loomed larger in the next century, enabling artists to revolt against the logic of precision in representation. Oil paint proved a key protagonist in the congealment of the "fine" and "broad" styles of painting—a fundamental aesthetic divide that spans individual careers (e.g., Tintoretto, see Nicholls, 2015), but also traverses centuries of art history, resurfacing with Impressionism in the nineteenth century. Research rarely discusses such forks in the road, when the affordances of a technology start to diverge, leading in different directions. A key contribution of this study is in highlighting the process of bifurcation of affordances and outcomes, associated with the technology of oil paint. This process is analytically important because it advises against technological or cultural determinism, implying a higher degree of agency (or choice) in the evolutionary trajectories of technologies than is generally recognized.

In agreement with reviews of organizational scholarship on technology (Leonardi & Barley, 2008; Orlikowski & Scott, 2008), this analysis embodies the understanding that technology is both a social product and a source of change or contradiction. Important shifts in the visual culture and the religious practices in the fifteenth century encouraged the pursuit of new technical means for expression, whereas the emergent schism between Protestant and Catholic ideologies affected the ways in which the visual idiom developed in different parts of Europe. The ways in which the affordances of the oil medium were activated were shaped by the Protestant penchant for purity and simplicity or the quest for visual splendor and rich coloration in the Catholic tradition. At the same time, the technology affected the manner in which artists appropriated and reinvented their own pictorial traditions. The affordances of oil reinforced the preoccupation with technical mastery, detail and light in the Northern tradition, and with the predilection for vivid, expressive colors in Venice.

Critically, the new technology deepened a tendency toward materialization and desacralization of art, where the display of technical virtuosity became equated with artistry, pursued and valued for its own sake. Artists learned how to manipulate the religious conventions for personal ends, becoming increasingly responsible for the idea and execution of their works. Technical developments augmented their productivity, enhancing their status relative to craftsmen and promoting individualized career trajectories. These changes were essential in the emergence of a new professional category but were also incongruent with a social ethic that remained religious at its base, prioritizing order and harmony between classes or artists. Technological aptitude established itself as a factor of stratification in the artistic world that was increasingly independent of cultural and religious influences.

Further research is needed to capture convincingly the complex interplay between social and technological factors. The current study is anchored in a historical context and cannot be approached as capturing more than an episode in an ongoing process. A contemporary episode appropriate to the postulated research objective is digital art and the set of possibilities and constraints associated with it.

Consider the example of a digital museum in Paris, presenting exhibitions of digital artworks projected on the walls of a remodeled nineteenth century foundry. The experience is unprecedented, as the viewer is allowed to do something that was unthinkable before—entering the work of art, feeling the intensity of colors or the interplay of composite parts. A quintessentially postmodern spectacle mixes genres (art, music, animation) and centuries (twentieth-century art in a nineteenth-century factory for a twenty-first-century audience). The initiative was successful, attracting 400,000 visitors in the first three months. Beyond the novelty effect, the numbers attest to the recognition by the public of the new museum as legitimate. Whether digitally projected art constitutes "real" art is a question that seems to have received a positive answer (so far).

This question is simultaneously technological and cultural in nature. It harkens back to the form of interplay discussed in the context of oil painting—when contemporary culture made possible a technological development that accelerated changes and reinforced contradictions in the same culture.

The digital museum is a logical development in an era of fast-paced technological change, when much of the cultural economy is migrating online, including books, music, concerts, or performances. But it is also tempting to think of the consequences of the digitalization of art and its experience on practices of art production and consumption. As demonstrated, these consequences are rarely ordered and often unintended. It is expected that digital museums will accelerate the digitalization tendency in traditional museums, but the opposite is also conceivable—that the new technology will reignite the contradiction between the "traditional" and "digital" identities, inciting further differentiation, rather than alignment.

If oil paint contributed to the materialization of art, digital art serves the opposite objective—of dematerialization. But there is a less obvious development that brings them together—the emphasis on the sensory experience of art rather than on intellectual comprehension, on emotions over content. The digital museum seeks to astound visitors in a similar manner to how Flemish and Venetian artists sought to dazzle patrons with rich details and technical wizardry. Brilliant colors, resounding visual effects and intense emotions—five centuries apart, digital art and oil painting have plenty in common.

Notes

1. The words technology, technique, and practice are absent from influential literature reviews (e.g., George, 2007).
2. Thus, German sculptors of the fifteenth and sixteenth century could count on their audience's intimate knowledge of the properties of wood and on their eye for fancy calligraphy (Baxandall, 1980).
3. Mathematicians think about complex problems by way of the "possibility space" of the possible solutions (also called a solution or probability space). Possibility spaces refer to the set of all possible answers to a problem. These answers vary on their degree of complexity or elegance, depending on the number of components and on their arrangements.
4. Langlais (1959) suggests that the importation of Chinese lacquer in the early fifteenth century may have something to do with the resurrection of interest in the oil paint technology in Flanders.
5. As the emphasis in the analysis is on the expressive and representational affordances of oil paint, the durability affordance is mentioned, but not developed further. This is in agreement with scholarship in art history, where durability has received much less attention than other affordances. Furthermore, there is little to indicate that the durability affordance was activated differently in the two contexts—Flanders and Venice.
6. One of the explanations known as the "Hockney and Falco thesis" is that artists resorted to the use of camera obscura (see Hockney, 2006). The debate is ongoing and unresolved. Recent scientific evidence from

computer analyses of paintings from that period has identified slight inaccuracies in the proportions of objects and figures, invisible to the human eye. This testifies against the use of camera obscura.

7. Langlais (1959) surmises that van Eyck must have introduced an ingredient, a volatile diluent, that altered the chemical composition of paint in a very consequential manner.
8. The affordances of canvass are an intriguing research topic in its own right but will not be elaborated further in an analysis that is focused on oil paint. Undoubtedly, canvass as a material surface was more suitable to oil-based paint than a wooden panel and helped bring out the most valuable qualities of oil paint. It is the combination between the two that reorganized art production, but it should be reminded that oil paint preceded the introduction of canvass and had already spurred stylistic innovation when canvass became dominant as a support in the early sixteenth century.

References

Acord, S. K., & DeNora, T. (2008). Culture and the arts: From art worlds to arts-in-action. *The Annals of the American Academy of Political and Social Science, 619*(1), 223–237.

Ambrose, S. H. (2001). Paleolithic technology and human evolution. *Science, 291*(5509), 1748–1753.

Aspers, P. (2001). A market in vogue: Fashion photography in Sweden. *European Societies, 3*(1), 1–22.

Barley, S. R. (1986). Technology as an occasion for structuring: Evidence from observation of CT scanners and the social order of radiology departments. *Administrative Science Quarterly, 31*, 78–108.

Baxandall, M. (1980). *The limewood sculptors of Renaissance Germany*. New Haven: Yale University Press.

Baxandall, M. (1985). *Patterns of intention: On the historical explanation of pictures*. New Haven: Yale University Press.

Baxandall, M. (1988). *Painting and experience in fifteenth century Italy: A primer in the social history of pictorial style*. Oxford and New York: Oxford University Press.

Brown, P. F. (1988). *Venetian narrative painting in the age of Carpaccio*. New Haven: Yale University Press.

Cappetta, R., Cillo, P., & Ponti, A. (2006). Convergent designs in fine fashion: An evolutionary model for stylistic innovation. *Research Policy, 35*(9), 1273–1290.

Cattani, G., Ferriani, S., & Lanza, A. (2017). Deconstructing the outsider puzzle: The legitimation journey of novelty. *Organization Science, 28*(6), 965–992.

Caves, R. (2000). *Creative industries: Contracts between art and commerce.* Cambridge, MA: Harvard University Press.

Clarke, A. E., & Fujimura, J. H. (1992). *The right tools for the right job: At work in 20th-century life sciences.* Princeton, NJ: Princeton University Press.

DeNora, T. (2000). *Music in everyday life.* Cambridge: Cambridge University Press.

Eisenman, M. (2013). Understanding aesthetic innovation in the context of technological evolution. *Academy of Management Review, 38*(3), 332–351.

George, J. M. (2007). Creativity in organizations. *The Academy of Management Annals, 1*(1), 439–477.

Gibson, J. J. (1982). A preliminary description and classification of affordances. In E. S. Reed & R. Jones (Eds.), *Reasons for realism* (Chapter 4.9, Part II) (pp. 403–406). Hillsdale, NJ: Lawrence Erlbaum Associates, Inc.

Gieryn, T. (2002). What buildings do. *Theory & Society, 31*(1), 35–74.

Harbison, C. (1995). *Jan van Eyck: The play of realism.* London: Reaktion Books.

Harbison, C. (2012). *The art of the Northern Renaissance.* London: Laurence King Publishing.

Hennion, A. (2015). *The passion for music: A sociology of mediation.* Oxford: Routledge.

Hockney, D. (2006). *Secret Knowledge: Rediscovering the lost techniques of the old masters.* London and New York: Thames and Hudson.

Hope, C. (2004). *Titian.* London: Chaucer Press.

Hutchby, I. (2001). Technologies, texts and affordances. *Sociology, 35*(2), 441–456.

Ilckman, F. (2014). *Jacopo Tintoretto in process: The making of a Venetian master, 1540–1560* (PhD Thesis). Columbia University.

Ione, A. (2005). *Innovation and visualization: Trajectories, strategies, and myths.* Amsterdam: Brill.

Jones, C., Meyer, R., Jancsary, D., & Höllerer, M. (2017). The material and visual basis of institutions. In R. Greenwood, C. Oliver, T. B. Lawrence, &

R. E. Meyer (Eds.), *The SAGE handbook of organizational institutionalism* (pp. 621–646). London: Sage Publications.

Knorr-Cetina, K. (1997). Sociality with objects: Social relations in postsocial knowledge societies. *Theory, Culture & Society, 14*(4), 1–30.

Langlais, X. (1959). *La technique de la peinture a l'huile*. Paris: Flammarion.

Leonardi, P. M. (2013). Theoretical foundations for the study of sociomateriality. *Information and Organization, 23*(2), 59–76.

Leonardi, P. M., & Barley, S. R. (2008). Materiality and change: Challenges to building better theory about technology and organizing. *Information and Organization, 18,* 159–176.

Meyer, R. (1969). *A dictionary of art terms and techniques*. New York: Crowell.

Moeran, B. (2013). *The business of creativity: Toward an anthropology of worth*. New York: Routledge.

Mokyr, J. (2016). *A culture of growth: Origins of the modern economy*. Princeton, NJ: Princeton University Press.

Munir, K. A., & Phillips, N. (2005). The birth of the 'Kodak moment': Institutional entrepreneurship and the adoption of new technologies. *Organization Studies, 26*(11), 1665–1687.

Nicholls, T. (2015). *Tintoretto: Tradition and identity*. London: Reaktion Books.

Orlikowski, W. J. (1992). The duality of technology: Rethinking the concept of technology in organizations. *Organization Science, 3*(3), 398–427.

Orlikowski, W. J. (2000). Using technology and constituting structures. *Organization Science, 11*(4), 404–428.

Orlikowski, W. J., & Scott, S. V. (2008). Sociomateriality: Challenging the separation of technology, work and organization. *The Academy of Management Annals, 2*(1), 433–474.

Padgett, J. F., & Powell, W. W. (2012). *The emergence of organizations and markets*. Princeton, NJ: Princeton University Press.

Perrow, C. (1967). A framework for the comparative analysis of organizations. *American Sociological Review, 32*, 194–208.

Rao, H., Monin, P., & Durand, R. (2003). Institutional change in Toque Ville: Nouvelle cuisine as an identity movement in French gastronomy. *American Journal of Sociology, 108*(4), 795–843.

Roberts, K., & Grabowski, M. (1996). Organizations, technology and structuring. In S. Clegg, C. Hardy, & W. Nord (Eds.), *Handbook of organization studies* (pp. 409–423). London: Sage.

Rosand, D. (1997). *Painting in sixteenth-century Venice: Titian, Veronese.* Tintoretto: Cambridge University Press.

Sgourev, S. V. (2013). How Paris gave rise to Cubism (and Picasso): Ambiguity and fragmentation in radical innovation. *Organization Science, 24*(6), 1601–1617.

Sgourev, S. V. (2018). Strange Bedfellows: Art and Finance or the Monetization of Art. In C. Jones & M. Maoret (Eds.), *Frontiers of creative industries: Exploring structural and categorical dynamics* (pp. 73–101). Bingley: Emerald Publishing.

Siggelkow, N. (2007). Persuasion with case studies. *Academy of Management Journal, 50*(1), 20–24.

Steinberg, A., & Wylie, J. (1990). Counterfeiting nature: Artistic innovation and cultural crisis in renaissance Venice. *Comparative Studies in Society and History, 32*(1), 54–88.

Stokstad, M., & Cothren, M. (2016). *Art: A brief history*. London: Pearson.

Van Mander, K. (1994 [1707]). *The lives of the illustrious Netherlandish and German painters*. Doornspijk, The Netherlands: Davaco.

Zammuto, R. F., Griffith, T. L., Majchrzak, A., Dougherty, D. J., & Faraj, S. (2007). Information technology and the changing fabric of organization. *Organization Science, 18*(5), 749–762.

4

Industry or Field? The Value of the Field Construct to Study Digital Creative Industries

Santi Furnari

Introduction

Let me start by admitting that this chapter's title is a bit of a teaser to invite readers in. Debating whether a creative industry 'is' an industry or a field is bound to be unproductive because the constructs of industry and field are, as any other construct, tools that we use to organize our thinking about the real world (Martin, 2015). Thus, obviously this chapter will *not* show whether a creative industry really 'is' an industry or a field because this exercise would essentially be meaningless from a philosophy of social science perspective. Rather, this chapter aims at discussing whether and how the constructs of industry and field are *useful* to address important and timely questions about the phenomenon that we conventionally refer to when we talk about creative industries. This phenomenon can be generally described as the activities engaged by a collective of organizations and individuals to produce, distribute, and

S. Furnari (✉)
Cass Business School, City, University of London, London, UK
e-mail: santi.furnari.1@city.ac.uk

J. Strandgaard Pedersen et al. (eds.), *Technology and Creativity*,
https://doi.org/10.1007/978-3-030-17566-5_4

consume products and services whose value is largely inscribed in their aesthetic and symbolic elements (cf. Hirsch, 1972; Jones, Lorenzen, & Sapsed, 2015; Moeran and Pedersen, 2011; Power, 2002).

Starting from this premise, I argue that the conceptualization of a creative industry as an 'industry' is not adequate to understand the blurring of creative industries' boundaries and roles induced by digital technologies, intended here as technologies of digitization and Internet connectivity (Castells, 1996; Dutton, 2013: 9; Lanzolla et al., 2018: 378). The reason for this inadequacy is that the industry construct embeds two key assumptions that do not facilitate understanding how industry boundaries and roles change: (1) the boundaries of industry are defined around a central product/service and its close substitutes (Geroski, 2001; Porter, 1980); (2) the position of an organization in an industry is conceptualized on the basis of the organization's 'attributes' (e.g., type of product/service, cost function, competencies or resources) vis-à-vis the other organizations in the industry. These two assumptions enable researchers to describe changes in industry boundaries and roles *ex-post*, after they have occurred, but have limited power to understand the mechanisms and processes underlying these changes. This is not to say that such assumptions are not useful. Quite the contrary, they have been proven useful to address research questions concerning the relative performance of organizations within a creative industry (e.g., Caves, 2000) *once* an industry structure is established (cf. Porter, 1980: 162). However, they are less well suited to address research questions concerning the blurring of creative industries' boundaries and roles.

These questions are timely and important as digital technologies are shaping in profound ways the dynamics of boundaries and roles in creative industries as diverse as music, book publishing, and film. Thanks to the digitization and connectivity affordances offered by these technologies, traditionally established *roles* in creative industries, such as 'producer,' 'distributor,' and 'consumer,' have now become much more fluid. For example, consumers increasingly take up the role of (co-)producers of creative content by engaging in digitally enabled practices of content's sampling, sharing, or mashing-up (e.g., Troilo, 2015); or serve the role of 'critics' by striving to act as 'influencers' on social media platforms (Etter, Ravasi, & Colleoni, 2019). Meantime, digital distributors such as Netflix have become producers, while local creative producers (e.g., artists) have become distributors of their own content (Hirsch & Gruber, 2015). Digital technologies have also induced changes in creative industries' *boundaries*, which were once relatively clear and now increasingly 'shift from permeable to non-existent' (Davis & Marquis, 2005: 337) as large high-tech firms such as Amazon and Apple enter established creative industries, like music and TV, with specialized digital distribution platforms (e.g., Amazon Music, Apple TV).

I argue that the construct of 'field' (Bourdieu, 1971, 1993; Martin, 2003) is more useful than the industry construct to address research questions related to these important changes in creative industries' boundaries and roles. This is because the field construct embeds three key assumptions that are well suited to inquire into such questions: (1) the boundaries of a field are defined on the basis of a central *activity* or *practice* (rather than product) around which a set of actors form concrete social *relations*; (2) the position of actors in the field is defined *relationally*, vis-à-vis each other, rather than on the basis of actors' attributes; (3) the actors in field are connected through *multiple relations*, which can be *material* (e.g., resource exchanges) or *symbolic* (e.g., participating in a joint debate or using similar language/discourse). While the construct of field has been extensively used in creative industries literature (e.g., Cattani, Ferriani, & Allison, 2014; Mazza & Pedersen, 2004; Moeran & Pedersen, 2011; Townley, Beech, & McKinlay, 2009; Schüßler & Sydow, 2015), the assumptions underlying such construct have not been explicitly compared with those underlying another construct commonly used in this literature, namely 'industry' (e.g., Bilton, 2007; Caves, 2000; Lampel, Shamsie, & Kant, 2006; Towse & Handke, 2013). In addition, previous research has not discussed the usefulness of the field construct to specifically study the effects of digital technologies on creative industries' structure and dynamics.

I address these scope limitations of current research by linking the three distinctive assumptions of the field construct identified above with the blurring of creative industries boundaries and roles facilitated by digital technologies. The gist of my argument is that the industry construct focuses on *outcomes*, such as products, black-boxing the processes leading to those outcomes. Differently, by focusing on actors' *relations* and ongoing *activities*, the field construct enables researchers to analyze the *processes* underlying large-scale dynamics such as the blurring of creative industries' boundaries and roles (cf. Marquis & Davis, 2005). Thus, the assumptions embedded in the field construct enable a more fine-grained understanding of the fluid dynamics characterizing creative industries in the digital era than the assumptions underlying the industry construct.

This chapter is structured in four sections. First, I illustrate the widespread conceptualization of a creative industry as industry, identifying the key assumptions underlying this conception. Second, I identify two main types of changes in creative industries induced by digital technologies (i.e., the blurring of boundaries between creative industries; the blurring of roles within creative industries), explaining why the industry construct is not well suited to address research questions concerning these changes. Third, I unpack three key assumptions embedded in the field construct and point at the specific benefits they provide to explain changes in creative industries' boundaries and roles. Finally, I discuss the theoretical contributions of the chapter and their implications for future research.

The Conceptualization of Creative Industries as 'Industries'

Constructs are 'abstractions of phenomena that cannot be directly observed' (Suddaby, 2010: 346). A construct's definition is important because it embodies a researcher's assumptions about the entities that constitute a phenomenon and these entities' properties (Goertz, 2006). In turn, such 'ontological' assumptions allow researchers to 'see' and analyze some aspects of a phenomenon while at the same time obscuring others (Alford & Friedland, 1985). Thus, definitions are not important because they capture 'real' properties of a phenomenon that exists out there, but because they orient researchers and their audiences toward certain research questions and answers while distracting them from others (Furnari & Marti, 2018).

Multiple definitions of creative industries have been extensively debated in the literature, particularly with reference to whether some industries (such as arts, cultural heritage, and information technology) should be considered as creative industries (e.g., Causte, 2003; Galloway & Dunlop, 2007), whether there are relevant differences between 'cultural' and 'creative' industries (e.g., Cunningham, 2002) and between 'creative' and 'traditional' industries (e.g., Miller, 2001). Within this debate, one widely used definition is more denotative and has been developed by the UK government, identifying the creative industries as 'those activities which have their origin in individual creativity, skill and talent and which have a potential for wealth and job creation through the generation and exploitation of intellectual property, namely: advertising, architecture, art and antiques, crafts, design, designer fashion, film, interactive leisure software, music, performing arts, publishing, software design, TV and radio' (DCMS, 2008).

Another widely cited definition is more theoretical and focuses on key general properties of the phenomenon, identifying a creative industry as the system of economic actors involved in the production of creative products intended as 'non-material goods directed at a public of consumers for which they generally serve as an aesthetic or expressive, rather than clearly utilitarian, function' (Hirsch, 1972: 44). While sharing this product- and consumer-centered definition of creative industries, more recent contributions have also emphasized that creative products have both a symbolic component (i.e., the semiotic codes capturing the relations among the symbols embedded in a creative product) and a material base (i.e., the technologies and materials giving form to a creative product) (Jones et al., 2015).

Whether theory- or policy-oriented, most definitions of creative industries assume that a creative industry is, first and foremost, an 'industry'—intended as a group of firms producing products or services that are close substitutes, thus competing with each other (Bain, 1956; Geroski, 2001; Porter, 1980). This industry-based conceptualization has had an important effect on the academic, practitioner, and policy conversations on creative industries (e.g., Bilton, 2007; Caves, 2000; DCMS, 2008), shaping how several scholars have studied—and still often study—creative industries. Historically, this assumption emerged because of the need of justifying the economic importance of culture in the face of state support's cutbacks for cultural activities occurring in the late 1970s and 1980s (Galloway & Dunlop, 2007: 18). Indeed, casting creative activities through the term 'industry' and its underlying market ideology was helpful to justify the economic value of such activities in the eyes of policy makers and state officials (Causte, 2003). While the historical factors facilitating the diffusion of the industry-based conceptualization of creative industries are interesting for their own sake, my focus here is on the consequences of this diffusion for research on creative industries and digital technologies.

More specifically, I argue that the conceptualization of creative industries as 'industries' may be useful to study creative activities under relatively stable technological conditions or incremental technological changes, but it is less useful to study such activities under more radical technological changes such as those implicated by digital technologies and the Internet. This is because, as any construct, the construct of 'industry' carries with itself ontological assumptions about the entities that constitute the phenomenon captured by the term 'industry'. These ontological assumptions are rooted in the tradition of industrial organization economics (Porter, 1980), which was not primarily concerned with questions about radical technological changes and their implications for the blurring of an industry's boundaries and roles. In particular, there are two assumptions embedded in the construct of industry that are worth highlighting here as they affect the study of creative industries in relationship with digital technologies.

First, an industry typically denotes a set of organizations that produce products or services that are close substitutes (Bain, 1956; Geroski, 2001; Porter, 1980). This definition assumes that the boundaries of an industry are drawn on the basis of a central product/service and its close substitutes (Munir & Phillips, 2002). This assumption is exemplified by the fact that countless industry studies operationalized the construct of industry through the codes of the Standard Industrial Classification (SIC) system, in which a code identifies a different type of product/service and its corresponding organizations. SIC codes—which underlie also the classification and identification of creative industries used by policy makers—assume that, since a group of organizations sell similar products or services, their market share and profitability (i.e., performance) can be reliably compared. This assumption has served well a generation of strategy scholars interested in performance heterogeneity (e.g., Greckhamer, Misangyi, Elms, & Lacey, 2008) but has been challenged even within strategy scholarship (Bettis, 1998; Farjoun, 1994; Sampler, 1998). For example, Sampler (1998) has suggested that industry boundaries can be drawn on the basis of the information that a set of organizations share around the same group of customers, while other scholars have advanced the idea that organizations can be clustered into industries depending on the competencies (Bettis, 1998) or resources (Farjoun, 1994) they share.[1] Whether around similar products or services, critical information or competencies, the industry construct emphasizes that boundaries are drawn on the basis of an 'attribute' that a set of organizations share rather on the concrete social relations that can connect these organizations in different ways.

Second, the industry construct emphasizes that the position of an organization within an industry is typically conceptualized on the basis of relevant 'attributes' of that particular organization, such as, the particular product or service that the organization sells, its cost function, or its competences and resources (Geroski, 2001) and on the degree of similarity/difference of those attributes vis-à-vis the other organizations in the industry. Again, rather than considering directly the concrete relations linking organizations, this conceptualization of positions is more 'attribute-based', being often operationalized with Euclidean distance measures.

While these assumptions have been proven useful to address questions related to performance within a creative industry (e.g., Caves, 2000), I contend that they are less well suited to understand the changes in creative industries' boundaries and roles provoked by the rise of digital technologies. To illustrate this, in the next section I first describe these changes and then explain why an industry construct is not well suited to capture them.

Digital Technologies and the Blurring of Creative Industries' Boundaries and Roles

The relationship between technology and the dynamics of creative industries has always been an intimate one. Technology underpins creative production, which at its core consists of inscribing symbolic content into a technological, material medium (cf. Jones et al., 2015), be it film, television, books, magazines, or Web sites. It is therefore not surprising that the evolution of many creative industries over the course of the nineteenth and twentieth centuries, from small-scale craft systems to mass-scale industrialized sectors, parallels the evolution of the technologies available for producing and distributing symbolic content, such as printing, sound recording, photography, film, and video. As these technologies increasingly allowed for more effective distribution and more scalable 're-production' of symbolic content (cf. Benjamin, 2007 [1937]), the structure of many creative industries evolved toward specialization and concentration, leading, for example, to the emergence of large media conglomerates intermediating the distribution and production of creative content (e.g., Held, McGrew, Goldblatt, & Perraton, 1999). In sum, as for other industries, throughout history technology has crucially conditioned, yet not determined, the structure and dynamics of creative industries (Lampel et al., 2006).

While technology has always been a crucial factor conditioning creative industries' evolution, previous research has highlighted that digital technologies have enabled discontinuous, radical changes in the industry structure characterizing many creative industries over the second half of the twentieth industry (Hirsch & Gruber, 2015; Khaire, 2015; Mangematin, Sapsed, & Schüßler, 2014; Towse & Handke, 2013). At the risk of over-simplifying, such structure typically identified relatively clear roles and boundaries among at least four types of actors: producers (who produced and copyrighted creative content), distributors (who supported the distribution of creative content through marketing and organizing), consumers (who experienced the creative content), and critics (who evaluated and often ranked creative content). In addition to clear roles and boundaries *within* a creative industry, also the boundaries *between* different creative industries were relatively clear as any industry was centrally concerned with a distinctive core product. Using such stylized representation of a creative industry' structure as point of comparison, I organize the industry-level changes induced by digital technologies, according to the literature, in two main theoretical categories.

First, previous research has shown that digital technologies have enabled a substantial *blurring of roles within an industry*. For example, consumers of creative products have been shown to increasingly act as producers, being engaged in co-production of creative content through digitally enabled practices such as sampling, sharing, or mashing-up contents (Troilo, 2015). This new blurred role of prosumers is enabled by digitally mediated, online communities or by hybrid online/off-line spaces (e.g., Parmentier & Mangematin, 2014). In turn, these new roles had also implications for other roles in creative industries, typically undermining the role of media conglomerates and other distributors in extracting value from copyrighted creative content by performing marketing and distribution. Differently, through the new possibilities of interaction afforded by social media, many consumers have taken up the role of critics, sometimes becoming influential evaluators who assess creative products and content in real time on platforms such Instagram. As Etter and colleagues recently argued, 'social media now give voice to actors who previously had limited access to the public domain, and it enables them to bypass the gatekeeping function of traditional news media and reach wide audiences connected through online social networks' (Etter et al., 2019: 4). Relatedly, producers of creative content have often taken the role of distributors of their own content by using new digitally enabled platforms such as soundcloud.com or Spotify, while digital distributors of content like Netflix have also become producers. While roles changes and switching were of course possible also before the digital technologies became pervasive, such technologies have exponentially increased the scale and speed at which role changes have happened and have reduced the cost for switching roles (Khaire, 2017).

Second, previous research has shown that digital technologies have *blurred the boundaries of creative industries*. The more visible example of this phenomenon is the entry of large high-tech firms, such as Amazon and Apple, in the music or TV industries with specialized digital distribution platforms such as Amazon Music or Apple Music. Similarly, new 'born digital' distributors such as Spotify have emerged, effectively re-intermediating the relationship between music producers and their consumers (Hirsch & Gruber, 2015). In both these cases, inherent features of digital technologies (such as platforms' network effects) have facilitated or enabled the entry of new organizations from different industries into a focal creative industry. In addition, creative industries' boundaries have also been affected by new digitally enabled business models which offer consumers 'bundles of creative products' that can be digitally experienced as a seamless whole (such as audiobooks or podcasts now downloadable together with music on the same platform). These new business models have facilitated the blurring of boundaries among two or more creative industries and between creative and 'traditional' industries. In sum, as Mangematin and colleagues argue, digital technologies have 'blur[red] the boundaries and roles between different actors and break up the existing partition of value creation and appropriation' in creative industries (Mangematin et al., 2014: 4).

The industry construct has been used to understand changes in boundaries and roles such as the ones described above, generating important insights to this end. A core insight is the so-called industry-life cycle model explaining industry change and changes in industry boundaries on the basis of patterns of producers' entry and exit (e.g., Klepper, 1997). In this view, the shifting of boundaries is to be expected insofar as new entrants carry with them capabilities/competences that are new to the industry (e.g., when they come from different domains). While these insights are important to understand industry boundaries' changes, they are less well suited to explain the processes and mechanisms underlying such changes. Indeed, by anchoring an industry boundary around a central product, the industry construct focuses attention on *outcomes*, black-boxing the complex, collective, and dynamic *processes* leading to those outcomes. For this reason, when put to work to explain changes in an industry's boundaries and roles, the industry construct conceives these *explananda* as 'outcomes' too, treating them as 'things' or 'entities.' This outcome-focused orientation does not facilitate our understanding of the mechanisms and processes underneath changes in boundaries and roles. A more *relational* and *process-oriented* construct is needed to do that: the construct of field.

The Value of the Field Construct for Studying Creative Industries and Digital Technologies

A field can be generally defined as 'an arena – a system of actors, actions, and relations- whose participants take one another into account as they carry out interrelated activities' (McAdam & Scott, 2005: 10).

The construct of field has a long history in the social sciences (see Martin, 2003 for review) and in organization and management theory (see Zietsma, Groenewegen, Logue, & Hinings, 2017 for review). Bourdieu (1971) was the first to introduce the idea of a fully fledged field analysis of creative industries. This idea has later inspired a stream of studies using field theory and methods to study creative industries (e.g., Cattani, Ferriani, & Allison, 2014; Khaire, 2014; Mazza & Pedersen, 2004; Moeran & Pedersen, 2011; Schüßler & Sydow, 2015; Townley et al., 2009).

Since a review of the important contributions of these field analyses is beyond the scope and space constraints of this chapter, I focus below on three key assumptions underlying the field construct, which are useful to understand the changes in creative industries' boundaries and roles induced by digital technologies. As I summarize in Table 4.1, these assumptions are fundamentally different from the ones underlying the industry construct.

Field Boundaries Are Defined Relationally Around Activities or Practices

A key assumption is that the boundaries of a field are defined around *activities* or *practices* through which actors interact and form concrete social relations. As Bourdieu remarked, 'to think in terms of field is to *think relationally*' (Bourdieu & Wacquant, 1992: 96; emphasis in original). Focusing on activities/practices rather than products (as in the industry construct) matters because an activity is different from a product: The former is a process, the latter is an outcome. Activities identify processes by which actors arrive (or not) at a product (or at other outcomes). Not every activity translates into a product because many activities do not result in 'tangible' or relative durable outcomes such as products. For example, activities may include participation at field configuring events (Lampel & Mayer, 2008; Moeran & Pedersen, 2011), fleeting interactions on social media or blogs (Etter et al., 2019) or transitional interactions such as play and experimentation in 'interstitial spaces' (Furnari, 2014) like hobbyist clubs, creative fab-labs or

Table 4.1 Comparing the industry and field constructs, their assumptions, and usefulness for creative industries research

	Construct definition	Assumptions underlying the construct	Usefulness of the construct in relation to creative industries research	Exemplary studies
Industry construct	An industry denotes a set of organizations that produce products or services that are close substitutes	• Boundaries = industry boundaries defined on the basis of a central product/service and its close substitutes • Positions = organizations' positions in an industry are defined on the basis of organizations' attributes (competencies/resources, cost functions, etc.) vis-à-vis each other	• Useful to address questions concerning the relative performance of organizations within a creative industry *once* the industry has formed and its boundaries/roles are relatively stable • Less useful to address questions concerning mechanisms and processes underlying changes in creative industries' boundaries and roles, such as the ones provoked by digital technologies	• Porter (1980) • Bain (1956) • Geroski (2001) • Caves (2000)
Field construct	A field denotes an arena (i.e. a system of actors, actions, and relations) whose participants take one another into account as they carry out interrelated activities	• Boundaries = field boundaries defined on the basis of a central activity or practice around which a set of actors form concrete social relations • Positions = organizations' positions are defined relationally, on the basis of concrete relations connecting them • Relations = multiple types of relations, material (e.g. resource exchanges) and symbolic (e.g. discourse/debate)	• Useful to address questions concerning the mechanisms and processes underlying changes in creative industries' boundaries and roles, such as the ones provoked by digital technologies • Less useful to address questions concerning the relative performance of organizations in a creative industry under times of relative stability of boundaries and roles	• Bourdieu (1971) • Di Maggio and Powell (1983) • Hoffman (1999) • Fligstein and McAdam (2012)

makerspaces (Browder et al., forthcoming). Drawing boundaries around activities thus implies taking into account a *wider set of actors* than the ones connected by an existing product/service and their close substitutes. In turn, casting such 'wider net' allows researchers and practitioners to study the changes in a creative industry' boundaries differently, as I illustrate below.

Consider the case of Kodak, which has been disrupted by the advent of digital cameras and in particular by early new entrants in the photographic industry, such as Sony. As Munir and Phillips (2002) well illustrate, part of Kodak's problem was that the organization's top managers conceived the photographic industry narrowly defined around its core product (camera and film). Differently, had they considered more broadly which actors were involved in the various activities (such as participation of trade events, conferences, hobbyist clubs) surrounding photography and its related domains, they would have probably realized earlier that representatives from a different industry (i.e., Sony) were participating those activities. By re-defining boundaries around activities rather than products Sony, Adobe, Kodak and Intel would all result members of a broader 'photography activity network' (Munir & Phillips, 2002: 291). This view would allow Kodak managers, or a researcher studying Kodak, to identify whether actors operating in an industry different than photography are getting involved into activities related to photography even *before* they will eventually develop or prototype a photographic product.

Using activities and relations rather than products as 'anchors' to draw boundaries has important implications for how scholars can study changes in creative industries' boundaries induced by digital technologies. For example, the field construct can allow to see whether actors from two or more different industries (i.e., currently producing different products/services) start to engage in similar activities before eventually producing similar products. It can also enable an analyst to see the multiple 'trajectories' that, at any given point in time, a set of activities may take, investigating which of these activities will eventually result into new creative products (cf. Furnari & Rolbina, 2018). Finally, field analysis allows to study the type and intensity of relations between organizations from two or more industries, for example by studying the frequency of events jointly attended by such organizations. This relational lens can provide a more fine-grained understanding of how the boundaries of a creative industry are evolving, investigating the extent to which such boundaries are becoming more or less fluid (Furnari, 2016).

Actors' Positions Are Defined Relationally Vis-à-Vis Each Other

A second important assumption of the field construct is that actors positions in a field are defined relationally vis-à-vis each other. Fields are 'structured spaces of positions' (Bourdieu, 1993: 72). A position's properties are defined on the basis of its relationships to other positions in the field (Bourdieu & Wacquant, 1992). Importantly, since field boundaries are defined broadly, including actors that may produce in other industries but are related in some ways with actors in the focal creative industry under study, a position reflects the patterns of relations of one actor *within and outside its focal industry*. This relational understanding of positions differs from the industry definition of actors' positions based on actors' similarity in terms of their individual attributes. Indeed, whether the attribute considered is the type of product produced by firms in an industry, or the information, competences or resources they share, the industry-based definition of positions is based on similarity measures between actor-level (i.e., node-level) characteristics rather than on properties of their relations.

A relational, rather than attribute-based, understanding of positions has important implications for our understanding of the changes in *roles* occurring in creative industries as a result of the widespread diffusion of digital technologies. Particularly, such relational understanding allows to distinguish roles and positions. A role is an abstract category that allows people to identify similar positions across different structures (Winship & Mandel 1983: 316), while a position identifies a particular location in a [field] structure (Powell, White, Koput, & Owen-Smith, 2005). For example, Baker and Faulkner (1991) identify three key roles in the Hollywood film industry—i.e., producer, director, and screenwriter—and analyzed which individual, with a particular socio-structural position, was more likely to take any of these roles or combine them. This perspective allows an analyst to study how different types of field positions can become 'coupled' with particular roles, thereby better explaining the frequent role changes in creative industries induced by digital technologies. For example, using this perspective we can explain which consumer in a creative industry takes on the additional role of 'influencer' on social media based on her/his position in the field. Or we could address questions such as: Can the position of Netflix in its initial industry (video rental) explain why this organization moved to the role of digital distributor and then producer? More generally, what kinds of positions are more likely to influence the changes of existing roles or the emergence of new roles in a given creative industry? In sum, the fluidity of roles in digital era's creative industries can be better accounted for through a field-based relational understanding of positions than an industry-related, attribute-based view of positions.

Field Actors Are Linked by Multiple Symbolic and Material Relations

The third important assumption of the field construct is that field actors are linked by *multiple* different relations, some of which are *material* (e.g., resource exchanges, alliances), while others are *symbolic* (e.g., joint participation in debates and discourse around an issue). The notion of field emphasizes the crucial importance of taking into account *both* these kinds of relations simultaneously, looking also at how they interact (e.g., Mohr, 2013; Oberg, Korff, & Powell, 2017). While this aspect of the field construct was noted by Bourdieu through his emphasis on different types of capital, it was more explicitly and systematically developed by institutional theorists in organizational sociology, particularly through the work of Hoffman (1999) and more recent multi-relational field analyses (Mische, 2008; Oberg et al., 2017; Padgett & Powell, 2012). The emphasis on the simultaneous co-existence of material and symbolic relations differs from the industry construct's emphasis on material exchanges and outcomes, adding the symbolic layer as an essential component of what constitutes a field. This additional relational dimension has important implications for how digitally enabled changes in creative industries' boundaries can be analyzed.

In fact, this multi-relational lens allows an analyst to see whether the entry of new actors in a focal creative industry can be preceded by past symbolic relations among the new entrants and the actors already operating in the creative industry. In other words, symbolic relations can be an important antecedent of industry entry from outside-industry entrants and thus a factor explaining the blurring of creative industries' boundaries. In fact, since symbolic relations—i.e., such as an organization's participation in a blog or online forum or newspaper—are more transient and initially less consequential (Furnari, 2014), they may signal in advance an actor's developing engagement and interest in the industry. The intensity of symbolic relations and its level of coupling with material relations could thus be useful to unpack the mechanisms underlying the strengthening or weakening of a creative industry's boundaries or the formation of a whole new creative industry (cf. Furnari, 2016).

Although not directly focused on a creative industry, Oberg and colleagues provide a powerful example of the potential of this type of multi-relational field analysis (Oberg et al., 2017). Mapping all the organizations involved in the online debate around the issue of social impact assessment, they analyze the dynamic co-evolution of the discursive and material relations connecting such organizations. They find that the organizations' receptivity to discursive elements of different industries alters the configuration of materials relations in a field. In a similar vein, this approach can allow to analyze new digital entrants from different industries or re-configurations of a focal creative industry as a function of preexisting symbolic relations with other industries. In other words, this key assumption of the field construct affords a more prescient, theoretically driven approach to the study of creative industries' boundary dynamics in the digital era.

Concluding Remarks

In this chapter, I have compared two alternative conceptualizations of creative industries—the industry and the field—and argued that the field-based conceptualization enables researchers to better analyze and understand the blurring of creative industries' boundaries and roles induced by digital technologies. The industry conceptualization—centered on products and actor-based similarities—has not been originally developed to address research questions concerning radical changes in an industry's boundaries and roles. As such, it is better suited to describe such changes *ex-post*, after their occurrence, rather than explaining the mechanisms and processes underlying them. Differently, the relational ontology underlying the field construct better enables researchers to investigate such mechanisms and processes. At its core, the increased explanatory and analytic power of the field construct rests on its focus on multiple types of relations among actors (rather than their attributes) and on activities rather outcomes (e.g., products). Taken together, these inherent features of field analysis can provide a more fine-grained understanding of the fluid dynamics of competition and innovation in creative industries in the digital era.

The arguments advanced in this chapter make the following theoretical contributions to research using field analysis to study creative industries and to research on digital technologies and the creative industries.

Contributions and Future Research

I contribute to the long tradition of research using the field construct to study creative industries (e.g., Bourdieu, 1971, 1993; Cattani, Ferriani, & Allison, 2014; Mazza & Pedersen, 2004; Moeran & Pedersen, 2011; Schüßler & Sydow, 2015; Townley et al., 2009) in two ways.

First, I provide a systematic comparison of the assumptions underlying the constructs of industry and field that is relevant for research on the creative industries given the widespread use of both constructs in this research. Yet, despite its relevance, to the best of my knowledge such a comparison had not been provided so far. In fact, despite the frequent use of both these constructs in creative industries research, their assumptions are rarely made explicit and discussed on the basis of their appropriateness for studying some research questions rather others. Future research on the creative industries could use, and further develop, the comparison developed in this chapter in order to better evaluate the usefulness and analytical potential of the industry and field constructs for different types of questions.

Second, I connect the field construct with important changes in the creative industries that have been induced by digital technologies. While most extant field analyses of creative industries have not specifically link such an analysis to digital technologies' developments, I identify three ways in which the assumptions underlying the field construct can address important changes in creative industries enabled by digital technologies. By doing so, I link conceptually the relational ontology underlying field research with relevant and current developments that have deeply affected the structure and dynamics of creative industries in the digital era. Future research could further develop the conceptual links identified in this chapter, leveraging the wide availability of digital data to empirically investigate creative industries' blurring boundaries and roles through field analyses.

While there is an emerging stream of research on the relationship between digital technologies and the creative industries (e.g., Hirsch & Gruber, 2015; Khaire, 2015; Mangematin et al., 2014; Towse & Handke, 2013), it is fair to say that the 'effects [of digital technologies] on established forms of creative product and consumption is rarely explicitly addressed' in creative industries research (Mangematin et al., 2014). My contribution to this conversation is the identification of two salient types of changes in the creative industries that have been enabled by digital technologies: (1) the blurring of roles within a creative industry; (2) the blurring of boundaries between creative industries. These changes constitute a starting point for developing a more refined typology of digitally induced changes in the structure and dynamics of creative industries. For example, different creative industries could be compared depending on the intensity (e.g., low vs high) of their changes on the two dimensions of 'roles blurriness' and 'boundaries blurriness' identified in this chapter. Future research can further build on the literature on industry emergence and convergence (e.g., Agarwal, Moeen, & Shah, 2017; Lanzolla & Anderson, 2010) and leverage more refined conceptualizations of digital technologies (e.g., Castells, 1996). In particular, an interesting area for future research would be to link more closely the changes in a creative industry structure and dynamics with different types of affordances and uses of digital technologies, thereby unpacking the 'micro-foundations' of the digital transformation of creative industries.

Despite the limitations of the conceptualization of digital technologies used here due to the space constraints, the two types of industry-level changes identified can provide practical insights for policy makers and practitioners of creative industries, highlighting the need of a broader conceptualization of a creative industry, one that includes different types of actors from different fields as well as the multiple symbolic and material relations connecting them. Much remains to be done to develop this 'wider lens' to effectively study creative industries dynamics in the digital era. My hope is that this chapter will sensitize other researchers to continue developing this important research agenda.

Acknowledgements I thank the editors Mukti Khaire, Jesper Strandgaard Pedersen and Barbara Slavich, as well as Simone Ferriani, Gino Cattani and Denise Falchetti, for valuable comments on a previous version of this chapter, I also thank Hans Frankort and Gianvito Lanzolla for their help and comments during the development of the chapter.

Note

1. A more fundamental criticism of the traditional notion of industry has been brought forward by the socio-cognitive view of industries (e.g., Porac, Thomas, & Baden-Fuller, 1989), which argues that industry boundaries are cognitively and socially constructed by industry participants. While this view shares some commonalities with the field view illustrated in this chapter (e.g., its social constructionist approach), it also differs from it by devoting less attention to the patterns of activities and practices connecting actors into networks of concrete social relations.

References

Agarwal, R., Moeen, M., & Shah, S. K. (2017). Athena's birth: Triggers, actors, and actions preceding industry inception. *Strategic Entrepreneurship Journal, 11*(3), 287–305.

Alford, R. R., & Friedland, R. (1985). *Powers of theory: Capitalism, the state, and democracy.* Cambridge: Cambridge University Press.

Bain, J. S. (1956). *Barriers to new competition*. Cambridge, MA: Harvard University Press.

Baker, W. E., & Faulkner, R. R. (1991). Role as resource in the Hollywood film industry. *American Journal of Sociology, 97*(2), 279–309.

Benjamin, W. (2007 [1937]). *Illuminations: Essays and reflections*. New York: Schocken.

Bettis, R. (1998). Commentary on 'redefining industry structure for the information age' by J.L. Sampler. *Strategic Management Journal, 19,* 357–361.

Bilton, C. (2007). *Management and creativity, from creative industries to creative management*. Malden, MA: Blackwell.

Bourdieu, P. (1971). Intellectual field and creative project. In M. F. D. Young (Ed.), *Knowledge and control: New directions for the sociology of education* (pp. 161–168). London: Collier Macmillan.

Bourdieu, P. (1993). *The field of cultural production*. Oxford: Polity Press.

Bourdieu, P., & Wacquant, L. (1992). *An invitation to reflexive sociology*. Chicago: University of Chicago Press.

Browder, R. E., Aldrich, H. E., & Bradley, S. W. (forthcoming). The emergence of the maker movement: Implications for entrepreneurship research. *Journal of Business Venturing*.

Castells, M. (1996). *The rise of the network society: The information age: Economy, society and culture* (Vol. 1). London: Wiley.

Cattani, G., Ferriani, S., & Allison, P. D. (2014). Insiders, outsiders, and the struggle for consecration in cultural fields: A core-periphery perspective. *American Sociological Review, 79*(2), 258–281.

Caust, J. (2003). Putting the "art" back into arts policy making: How arts policy has been "captured" by the economists and the marketers. *International Journal of Cultural Policy, 9*(1), 51–63.

Caves, R. E. (2000). *Creative industries: Contracts between art and commerce*. Cambridge, MA: Harvard University Press.

Cunningham, S. (2002). From cultural to creative industries: Theory, industry and policy implications. *Media International Australia Incorporating Culture and Policy, 102*(1), 54–65.

Davis, G. F., & Marquis, C. (2005). Prospects for organization theory in the early twenty-first century: Institutional fields and mechanisms. *Organization Science, 16,* 332–343.

Department for Culture, Media and Sport (DCMS). (2008). *Creative Britain—New talents for the new economy*. London: DCMS.

DiMaggio, P. J., & Powell, W. W. (1983). The Iron cage revisited: Institutional isomorphism and collective rationality in organizational fields. *American Sociological Review, 48,* 147–160.

Dutton, W. H. (Ed.). (2013). *The Oxford handbook of internet studies*. Oxford: Oxford University Press.

Etter, M., Ravasi, D., & Colleoni, E. (2019). Social media and the formation of organizational reputation. *Academy of Management Review, 44*, 28–52.

Farjoun, M. (1994). Beyond industry boundaries: Human expertise, diversification and resource-related industry groups. *Organization Science, 5*(2), 185–199.

Fligstein, N., & McAdam, D. (2012). *A theory of fields*. Oxford: Oxford University Press.

Furnari, S. (2014). Interstitial spaces: Microinteraction settings and the genesis of new practices between institutional fields. *Academy of Management Review, 29*(4), 439–462.

Furnari, S. (2016). Institutional fields as linked arenas: Inter-field resource dependence, institutional work and institutional change. *Human Relations, 69*(3), 551–580.

Furnari, S., & Marti, E. (2018). Umbrella constructs and problem-driven research: A pragmatist approach. In *Academy of Management proceedings* (Vol. 1, p. 12726). Briarcliff Manor, New York: Academy of Management.

Furnari, S., & Rolbina, M. (2018). Brokerage styles and interaction rituals in creative projects: Toward an interactionist perspective on brokerage. In *Frontiers of creative industries: Exploring structural and categorical dynamics* (pp. 17–45). Bingley: Emerald.

Galloway, S., & Dunlop, S. (2007). A critique of definitions of the cultural and creative industries in public policy. *International Journal of Cultural Policy, 13*(1), 17–31.

Geroski, P. A. (2001). Exploring the niche overlaps between organizational ecology and industrial economics. *Industrial and Corporate Change, 10*, 507–540.

Goertz, G. (2006). *Social science concepts: A user's guide*. Princeton: Princeton University Press.

Greckhamer, T., Misangyi, V. F., Elms, H., & Lacey, R. (2008). Using qualitative comparative analysis in strategic management research: An examination of combinations of industry, corporate, and business-unit effects. *Organizational Research Methods, 11*(4), 695–726.

Held, D., McGrew, A., Goldblatt, D., & Perraton, J. (1999). Global transformations: Politics, economics and culture. In *Politics at the edge*. London: Palgrave Macmillan.

Hirsch, P. M. (1972). Processing fads and fashions: An organization-set analysis of cultural industry systems. *American Journal of Sociology, 77*(4), 639–659.

Hirsch, P. M., & Gruber, D. A. (2015). "Digitizing fads and fashions". In C. Jones, M. Lorenzen, & J. Sapsed (Eds.), *The Oxford handbook of the creative and cultural industries* (pp. 421–438). Oxford: Oxford University Press.

Hoffman, A. (1999). Institutional evolution and change: Environmentalism and the U.S. chemical industry. *Academy of Management Journal, 42*(4), 351–371.

Jones, C., Lorenzen, M., & Sapsed, J. (2015). Creative industries: A typology of change. In C. Jones, M. Lorenzen, & J. Sapsed (Eds.), *The Oxford handbook of the creative and cultural industries* (pp. 3–32). Oxford: Oxford University Press.

Khaire, M. (2014). Fashioning an industry: Socio-cognitive processes in the construction of worth of a new industry. *Organization Studies, 35*(1), 41–74.

Khaire, M. (2015). Art without borders? Online firms and the global art market. In O. Velthuis & S. B. Curioni (Eds.), *Cosmopolitan canvases: The globalization of markets for contemporary art* (pp. 102–128). New York: Oxford University Press.

Khaire, M. (2017). *Culture and commerce: The value of entrepreneurship in creative industries*. Stanford, CA: Stanford University Press.

Klepper, S. (1997). Industry life cycles. *Industrial and Corporate Change, 6*(1), 145–182.

Lampel, J., & Meyer, A. D. (2008). Field-configuring events as structuring mechanisms: How conferences, ceremonies, and trade shows constitute new technologies, industries, and markets. *Journal of Management Studies, 45*(6), 1025–1035.

Lampel, J., Shamsie, J., & Lant, T. K. (Eds.). (2006). *The business of culture: Strategic perspectives on entertainment and media*. London: Lawrence Erlbaum Associates.

Lanzolla, G., & Anderson, J. (2010). The digital revolution is over. Long live the digital revolution! *Business Strategy Review, 21*(1), 74–77.

Lanzolla, G., Lorenz, A., Miron-Spektor, E., Schilling, M., Solinas, G., & Tucci, C. (2018). Call for special issue: Digital transformation: What is new if anything? *Academy of Management Discoveries, 4*(3), 378–387. https://doi.org/10.5465/amd.2018.0103.

Mangematin, V., Sapsed J., & Schüßler, E. (2014). Disassembly and reassembly: An introduction to the special issue on digital technology and creative industries. *Technology Forecasting and Social Change, 83*, 1–9.

Martin, J. L. (2003). What is field theory? *American Journal of Sociology, 109*, 1–49.

Martin, J. L. (2015). *Thinking through theory*. New York and London: W.W. Norton.

Mazza, C., & Pedersen, J. S. (2004). From press to E-media? The transformation of an organizational field. *Organization Studies, 25*(6), 875–896.

McAdam, D., & Scott, W. R. (2005). Organizations and movements. In G. F. Davis, D. McAdam, W. R. Scott, & M. N. Zald (Eds.), *Social movements and organization theory*. New York: Cambridge University Press.

Miller, D. (2001). *Consumption*. London: Routledge.

Mische, A. (2008). *Partisan publics: Communication and contention across Brazilian youth activist networks*. Princeton: Princeton University Press.

Moeran, B., & Pedersen, J. S. (Eds.). (2011). *Negotiating values in the creative industries: Fairs, festivals and competitive events*. Cambridge: Cambridge University Press.

Mohr, J. (2013). Bourdieu's relational method in theory and in practice: From fields and capitals to networks and institutions (and back again). In F. Dépelteau & C. Powell (Eds.), *Applying relational sociology* (pp. 101–135). New York: Palgrave Macmillan.

Munir, K. A., & Phillips, N. (2002). The concept of industry and the case of radical technological change. *The Journal of High Technology Management Research, 13*(2), 279–297.

Oberg, A., Korff, V. P., & Powell, W. W. (2017). *Culture and connectivity intertwined: Visualizing organizational fields as relational structures and meaning systems*. Research in the Sociology of Organizations (Vol. 53, pp. 17–47). Bingley: Emerald.

Padgett, J. F., & Powell, W. W. (2012). *The emergence of organizations and markets*. Princeton: Princeton University Press.

Parmentier, G., & Mangematin, V. (2014). Orchestrating innovation with user communities in the creative industries. *Technological Forecasting and Social Change, 83*, 40–53.

Porac, J. F., Thomas, H., & Baden-Fuller, C. (1989). Competitive groups as cognitive communities: The case of Scottish knitwear manufacturers. *Journal of Management Studies, 26*(4), 397–416.

Porter, M. (1980). *Competitive strategy*. New York: Free Press.

Powell, W. W., White, D. R., Koput, K. W., & Owen-Smith, J. (2005). Network dynamics and field evolution: The growth of interorganizational collaboration in the life sciences. *American Journal of Sociology, 110*(4), 1132–1205.

Power, D. (2002). 'Cultural industries' in Sweden: An assessment of their place in the Swedish economy. *Economic Geography, 78*(2), 103–127.

Sampler, J. (1998). Redefining industry structure for the information age. *Strategic Management Journal, 19*, 343–355.

Schüßler, E., & Sydow, J. (2015). Organizing events for configuring and maintaining creative fields. In C. Jones, M. Lorenzen, & J. Sapsed (Eds.), *The Oxford handbook of creative industries* (pp. 208–300). Oxford: Oxford University Press.

Suddaby, R. (2010). Editor's comments: Construct clarity in theories of management and organization. *Academy of Management Review, 35*(3), 346–357.

Townley, B., Beech, N., & McKinlay, A. (2009). Managing in the creative industries: Managing the motley crew. *Human Relations, 62*(7), 939–962.

Towse, R., & Handka, C. (Eds.). (2013). *Handbook on the digital creative economy*. Bingley: Edward Elgar.

Troilo, G. (2015). *Marketing in creative industries: Value, experience and creativity*. London: Macmillan International Higher Education.

Winship, C., & Mandel, M. (1983). Roles and positions: A critique and extension of the blockmodeling approach. In S. Leinhardt (Ed.), *Sociological Methodology 1983–1984* (pp. 314–345). San Francisco: Jossey-Bass.

Zietsma, C., Groenewegen, P., Logue, D., & Hinings, C. (2017). Field or fields? Building the scaffolding for cumulation of research on institutional fields. *Academy of Management Annals, 11*(1), 391–450.

5

The Internet as Liberating Space for the Visual Arts: Political Hopes and Sociological Realities

Mia Rosa Koss Hartmann

Introduction

In Western societies, art is often attributed great liberating potential, at least ideologically, in the sense that artistic forces are associated with unrestrained creativity and critical voice. Much of this potential lies in art's ability to foster critical reflection, to provoke established ways of seeing and thinking and speaking truth to power in favour of social justice and equality (e.g., Deleuze, 1988; Deleuze & Guattari, 1972; Mouffe, 2007, 2008; Mouffe, Deutsche, Joseph, & Keenan, 2001). The Internet is persistently associated with similar potential

M. R. K. Hartmann (✉)
MIT Sloan School of Management, Cambridge, MA, USA
e-mail: mkh.msc@cbs.dk

Copenhagen Business School, Frederiksberg, Denmark

J. Strandgaard Pedersen et al. (eds.), *Technology and Creativity*,
https://doi.org/10.1007/978-3-030-17566-5_5

(although imaginaries of dystopias have also entered debates) in that it provides structures, such as global networks and platforms for free dialogue and the sharing of ideas and digital material, without centrally controlled or mediated limitations on access.

In principle then, the marriage of art and Internet could—perhaps even ought to—create a particularly vivid and liberating space for artistic, creative freedom that becomes powerful in challenging dominant hegemonies (Lillemose & Recke, 2008). Since the infancy of the Internet in the 1990s, dedicated visual artists have experimented with the media as platform for new forms of materiality, communication and distribution to explore that space. Exemplary of this is the Danish group of artists, *Artnode*, which will serve as empirical point of reference in this chapter.

In a continuous effort to offer a non-commercial, open structure for contemporary visual art online, six young artists seized the dawn of the Internet and, in the decade following the group's 1996 founding, worked to create an Internet-based platform for a production and display of art. The group included the artists Christian Heide, Nikolaj Recke, Martin Pingel, Niels Bonde, Kim Borreby and Mogens Jacobsen (later also Morten Schjødt), all individuals with very different approaches to art and media. Sporadic activities in the latest decade indicate that the Artnode bond still exists to this day.

What united the artists was a set of quite disturbing questions that were introduced together with the Internet. What if art could be radically free without restrictions imposed by the selection criteria of elitist institutions and society? In a radically open and democratic world, what and who is to determine the appropriateness of art in public space? When, for example, the Danish artist Jes Brinch's planned exhibition at a town hall was censored because it featured a figure of a man who had hanged himself, Artnode published the entire project description and the rejection from the municipality on their site (Kristensen, 2017). Or when female artists are struggling to find outlets for their art and messages, suddenly digital versions of their work are freely accessible online, as we will revisit later in the case of the first Danish online book *Inserts* (Landgreen, Hinnum, & Olsen, 1997).

An important part of the attraction was the democratizing and creative potential of the technology enabling online spaces parallel to the traditional art institutions, i.e., who and what conventionally defines "art" in terms of its cultural and economic value and thus determines the social stages and roles of the different actors in the visual art world arenas. Such conventional restraints include limitations of creative artistic autonomy and career trajectories and therefore limit how freely art can be expressed, exhibited and experimented with within a given normative setting.

That such constraints operate in at least physical art worlds is well established. Seminal studies on the sociology of art have carved out how both "art" and "artist" are social constructs subject to limitations imposed by the very conventional traditions from which they are defined and valued (e.g., Becker, 1974, 1982; Bourdieu, 1984b). But new technologies, such as the Internet, seem to persistently give rise to hopes that call for re-examination: To what extent is cyberspace freed from the dominant hegemonies that rule convention in the established visual art world? Or, to frame the curiosity that motivates this chapter differently: How free are the freeing forces of art when artists enter the socio-technological realm of the Internet, which supposedly would be a space of unrestrained artistic creativity and critical voice? The chapter thus responds to recent calls in the sociology of art seeking research that engages not only with the context of creative productivity but also on the creative products per se with respect to their interaction with social life (e.g., De La Fuente, 2007; Prior, 2011).

More specifically, the attention here is the synergetic potential of visual art and Internet as creating a space for creativity and critical reflection as exemplified in the hopes of the Artnode group, taking this group as exemplary of early efforts to make use of digital technologies for creative purposes and how, or if, such hopeful efforts have been realized over time. Hope is considered here in terms of the sociological notion of "hopeful practices" (Alacovska, 2018), treating hope as an engaging, forward-looking response to the precarious conditions that often characterize the endeavours of creative workers. "Hope entails finding purpose and a reason to act in precarious conditions" (ibid.: 6), and by exploring artists' motivational endurance (facing both disappointments and accomplishments) in retrospect and up until the present, we may cut to the core of just how freeing conditions that the Internet offers for visual artists and their art.

At the dawn of the World Wide Web, the Artnode group played a pioneering role in shaping Danish net art as a practice and a category.[1] The synergetic, liberating potential that the chapter examines is acknowledged both in political theory and within the theoretical and practical fields of visual art, but there are surprisingly few examinations of the actual limitations and possibilities of such synergy. Based on in-depth interviews, the chapter offers a phenomenological exploration of the extent to which the exemplary hopes of two prominent Artnode members have been fulfilled over the past three decades (in the view of the artists themselves). These experiences are related to hopes of other international net artists and historians as they are being expressed in a Danish anthology on the matter (Lillemose & Recke, 2008). Two categories of hopeful practices are identified and examined.

One hope surrounds the synergetic power of art and Internet as *transformative*. It refers to the Internet as a freeing space for experimenting with the content, form and role of visual art that not only paves the way for net art as an innovative genre per se but also as disruptor of the conservatism and conventionality upheld by members of the "established" visual art world. The other hope that stands out is concerned with the *antagonist* possibilities of the Internet. It is rooted in critical reflections on power and constraints with the ambition to free voices both in the world of the visual arts and in society in general that the artists wish to challenge. These hopes are rooted in liberating values that are very similar to the political hopes expressed in the political and philosophical literatures.

What stands out from the analysis is the striking disappointments faced by net artists as regards the genre's actual influence within and beyond the art world. From a sociological perspective, these disappointments entail important consequences for moderating political ideologies that embrace the liberating power of visual art on the Internet. With reference to Becker's sociology of art, it becomes apparent how cyberspace does *not* operate as a free haven independent of the traditional and physical art world. It is then discussed how elaborate understanding and acknowledgement of the sociological realities that inhabit virtual spaces for visual art are crucial in adjusting political hopes for the fusion of the Internet and art. In closing, some ideas for what can be done to support its potentials as liberating space for the visual art and society are modestly proposed.

Art and the Internet: A Hopeful Synergy to Evade Convention?

In Western societies, art occupies a unique place within cultural production. From sociological, philosophical and political points of view, art earns an honorific status because it is often associated with large degrees of economic and political freedom. Sociologists, such as Howard Becker, have long been advocated a more moderate view of the actual independence of art from the cultural context in which it is created. Yet, political and philosophical thinkers such as Chantal Mouffe and Gilles Deleuze, view art as central to critical reflection and subversion of power relations in democracies. Despite the more dystopian prophecies made for the Internet, it is still today surrounded by such hopes.

The Sociological Entanglement of the Visual Arts

In his seminal sociological analysis of *Art as Collective Action* (1974) and *Art Worlds* (1982), Becker demonstrates how our conceptualizations of "Art" and the "Artist" are social constructs. An art piece, in this view, is shaped through collaborative production, not solitary genius or skill. "Art" functions as a label that is assigned to a work, rather than the being the somewhat exalted result of an extraordinarily talented individual (the artist) and individualized vision. Art worlds still tend to subscribe to some version of these imaginations (Becker, 2008/1982), but art can also be understood as a social process of production and consumption; a myriad of activities within a network of people, who organize knowledge and conventions around an extensive division of labour. "Art" and "artist" are artefacts nominated by people who are in a privileged position to honour a piece of work as such on the basis of shared values within the particular network (Becker, 1974, 1982; Bourdieu, 1984a/1979).

Conventions set the scene for every piece of work that becomes honoured as "art". They determine for instance what *means of distribution* are appropriate, leaving artists disadvantaged should they wish to use alternative forms of distribution or none at all. But established distributive infrastructures are at the same time what make art worlds efficient and enabling for the art and artists. Conventions act as *sorting mechanisms* controlling what gets exhibited where by whom, and what constitutes proper size, shape and level of abstraction of an art piece, etc. Such expert selection is also crucial for maintaining the exclusiveness of art and for cultivating the shared knowledge and experience of an audience. As Becker puts it, "[o]nly because artist and audience share knowledge of and experience with the conventions invoked does the artwork produce an emotional effect" (2008/1982: 30).

Conventions are *embodied* in, for example, training, language materials of choice and facilities available to the successful artist. So ingrained and interconnected are these intricate conventions that deviant experiments and innovations within an art world often become a drag. "In general, breaking with existing conventions and their manifestations in social structure and material artifacts increases artists' trouble and decreases their freedom to choose unconventional alternatives and to depart substantially from customary practice" (Becker, 2008/1982: 34). Attempts to challenge hegemonies by changing one component, e.g., a material of choice to the artist, involve changes throughout the system.

What becomes labelled as "art" and how art is produced and experienced is therefore intrinsic to societal and (sub-) cultural hegemony. In effect, visual art, its performers and audiences are subjected to certain pre-determinations in how they explicitly and implicitly shape the space for autonomy, creativity and critical voices of the visual arts. But while art and artists are not granted unconditional creative and critical autonomy, Becker emphasizes that the idea of the exception—the gifted artist with extraordinary vision—still reserves a unique position for the arts to experiment and voice silenced issues. In fact, innovative and/or critical characteristics are highly valued both within the art worlds as well as in a more layman appreciation of the arts, although the visual arts have to a far greater extent become subject to market mechanisms.

The Political Dimension of Art in Fostering Critical, Democratic Dialogues

Political theorist, Chantal Mouffe, develops a substantive analytical framework for understanding the challenges of contemporary democracy and art plays a key role in that framework (e.g., Mouffe, 1991, 2000). Mouffe argues that people no longer organize politically around a substantive common good in Western postmodern democracy. Instead, dispersed citizens' ideals and identities are being cultivated around multiplied forms of collective ideals as well as a myriad of participative forums or "discursive surfaces" in which people partake as collectives of subject positions (Mouffe, 1991: 80). To embrace the heterogeneity of contemporary democracy means to politically recognize and orchestrate the cacophony of critical voices—voices that are outside and *antagonist* to a given hegemony and therefore crucial for challenging dominant order, power relations and inequalities.

Art may serve a central function in escaping capitalist totalitarianism by in its capacities to facilitate *antagonist public spaces* where conflict and division can be voiced and potentially challenge hegemonic order (Mouffe, 1991, 2000). Art reserves truly critical dialogical spaces in favour of democracy qua its crucial antagonist qualities (Mouffe et al., 2001, 2007, 2008). "Every form of art has a political dimension", Mouffe et al., (2001: 100) claims, referring to how critical art potentially spurs "... dissensus and makes visible what the dominant consensus tends to obscure and obliterate" (Mouffe, 2007: 4). In its autonomous abstraction, art facilitates collective, societal self-reflection while contributing directly to challenging, constituting or maintaining a given hegemonic order: "What is needed to widen the field of artistic intervention, by intervening directly in a multiplicity of social spaces in order to oppose the programme of total social mobilization of capitalism. The objective should be to undermine the imaginary environment necessary for its reproduction" (Mouffe, 2008: 7).

Mouffe's positioning of art as potentials seeds of (self-)critical reflection in society resonates strongly with philosopher Gilles Deleuze's focus on the crucial function of art to raise critical consciousness (Deleuze, 1992/1988; Deleuze & Guattari, 1972; see also Sauvagnargues, 2013/2005), and their perspectives nuance Becker's strong emphasis on conventions in the art world, suggesting that unconventional artistic production has indeed successfully subverted various hegemonic arenas across history and national borders. Examples include subtle and yet powerful forms of cultural revolutions during wartime occupation (Greaves, 2014; Ilchuk, 2017), "unsanctioned interventions" in public space by street artists successfully subverting urban planning (Bengtsen, 2013), etc.

It is this tension—between political ideals of subversive forces and sociological convention—that this chapter explores. The Internet could be a distinct social space with particular potential for enabling plural voices and antagonist confrontation, but could also remain subject to convention stifling that potential, as will now be elaborated.

Liberating Promises of the Internet

Almost a century ago philosopher Walter Benjamin anticipated the democratizing potential of technological reproduction in respect to imagery, hoping that such developments would help cultivate democratic values and exorcize Fascism (Benjamin, 1936). Today, the Internet offers a unique infrastructure for Mouffe's suggestion of plural, antagonist spaces because of its extensive possibilities for accessing and mobilizing social spaces parallel to the physically bound places. It has therefore also been attributed great democratizing potential in line with Katz' *digital citizen*, referring to Americans that were eager to first connect to the Internet and use it to create a decentralized World of growth and opportunity as opposed to centrally prescribed and fixed ideology (Katz, 1997).

Activists and scholars have suggested that the Internet might hold a far greater potential to revolutionize political activity than other communication technologies, such as the telephone or television, because it provides unmediated interaction between citizens and politicians. "One of the most striking effects of the Internet, however, has been its ability to spread ideas and products across national boundaries. It is one of the most effective forces of globalization" (Ferdinand, 2000: 11). Others take a contrary position, warning against the paradoxical situation that while the web reduces communication costs, it has also become a commercial machinery "devoid of interactive 'public' spaces", such that "[i] nstead of democracy's din, the Internet seems to be creating a hyper-speed cacophony of dissonant shouting voices" (Noveck, 2000: 19).

In spite of such reservations, the technological advancements of the Internet and the cultural creation of art are both arenas infused with beliefs in their capacities for creating exceptional conditions for creative and genuinely critical capacities in today's fragmented democracies. But just *how* does the Internet enable such liberating space for the visual arts while bringing the critically reflective capacities of art to public conscience?

Visual artists rapidly made use of digital media both as an instrument for creating their art and as a platform for displaying and sharing it (Ekman, 2013; Shanken, 2009). Curating and sale of visual art have to a large extent moved from the traditional physical displays in galleries and showrooms to the digital media, in recent years, especially social platforms. The grounds on which the art industry and its communities operate are thus expanding. But to understand the liberating potential of the Internet for the visual arts and democratic society more broadly we need to dig below the commercial surface that the Internet provides for the visual arts and unfold the creative and critical synergy, as well as the tensions, between technology and art. As an analytical entry point, hopeful practices have recently been emphasized as a key to further our understanding of creative worker's moral fuelling and existential coping when dealing with the hardships and uncertainties of precarious work (Alacovska, 2018).

For this purpose, interviews with two members of net artist group Artnode, Nikolaj Recke and Mogens Jacobsen unfold the hopes and lived experiences on nearly three decades experimenting with art on the Internet. The phenomenological accounts of engaging in these experiments reflect, I suggest, how ideals and hopeful practices operate in tension with conventionality when art encounters the Internet.

Artnode and the Dream of Cyberspace as "Other"

As one of the most influential Danish artist-driven online communities, Art node formed in the mid-1990s as a space for experimenting with and voicing the potential "other" created by advancements in computational technology and the World Wide Web. Together with artists across the World, the Artnode members envisioned the Internet as a parallel world separate from the art world (Berry, 2008/2001). The group of young men organized themselves around their fascination with what the new technology could mean for how art was created, understood and distributed. While some of the Artnode members, such as Nikolaj Recke, were particularly dedicated to experimenting with the Internet as an "instant voice" and channel of communication for the visual arts, others, for example, Mogens Jacobsen, were more intrigued by the new aesthetic qualities of art through interactive media. The two artists have been selected for interviews given their respective professional backgrounds in visual arts at the Royal Danish Art Academy (Recke) and computational technology (Jacobsen).

The Dream of a Transformative "Free Space" for Artists and Their Art

In the early days of Artnode and other net artists, a series of hopes surround the idea of the Internet as transformative in the sense that it is capable of changing the ways in which artists work (Schreiber, 2001). What particularly seems to have infused net artists with hope was the idea of the Internet as an online "free space" independent of commercial selection mechanisms, popularized demands and other conventionalities embedded with the established art institutions (Berry, 2001). The novel space that the Internet offered, in other words, was interpreted as a space potentially free of convention. One dimension of this free space was connected to increased globalization and various "open" approaches (i.e., open source, open platforms, etc.) that picked up speed with the general availability of computers and World Wide Web

(Baumgärtel, 2008/1999). As Mogens Jacobsen exemplifies: "*What happened in the early 1990's was that the art scene became democratised. Suddenly, we were able to see art online that was not accessible before, particularly from Eastern Europe. The Internet created access to an entire new geographical art scene*".

In line with these principles of openness and access, Artnode programmers developed one of the first Danish artist-driven online platforms in the hope that it would partly or completely substitute the traditional practice among young artists creating their own information channels and forms through artist-driven galleries in support of their up and coming work and profiles. Net art was specifically born from the availability and fascination of online technologies as artists across the World experimented with the new digital immateriality, materiality (in the form of hardware, software applications, code [programming], etc.), visual formats and distribution networks (e.g., Baumgärtel, 2008/1999; Berry, 2008/2001; Greene, 2008/2000). Nikolaj Recke explains: "*I believe that an artist-driven place will always be in opposition to the established institutions of art. It may not necessarily be born from an oppositional drive but also from the need to create a platform to communicate your message. It is in the artist's DNA to have something at heart. It is not so much about having a critical voice but about the possibility of having a voice. And as an artist you just know that you need to create your own space or "language" in order to be heard. You are interested in having loud and wide ranges of communication*".

By basically moving the traditional basement exhibition room of young artists online, the Artnode site provided an alternative place, or rather online space, for the creation, display and distribution of net art hereby expanding an artistic space for a new art form and artists beyond what was more narrowly defined as contemporary art by the elitist art institutions.[2] This movement carries a utopian reminiscence from the avant-garde idealism to change and subvert the art system from within by creating fluid boundaries between how art is being produced and received (Schreiber, 2001). When visual artworks are not reserved for the eyes of their typical audiences, the antagonist confrontation of visual art that Mouffe envisages is possible *across* the heterogeneity of discursive surfaces that characterize of postmodern democratic participation. An image can pass in and out of multiple social and political spheres as a prism creating multiple reflections and meanings around it.

The opportunities afforded by the Internet extended beyond increased access and visibility. The Artnode site changed from being an early version of an online gallery where art could be downloaded by entering a long code and into a digital "canvas" as the Mosaic browser and increased Internet access made it possible to create distinctive online art exhibitions as well as the fusion of genres. Artists were invited to experiment with the "new digital paint palette", in Recke's words, i.e., the fast-growing range of technological applications and potentials of the media. For the Artnode members and other net artists, the Internet became a transformational portal for renewing and transcending conventional ideas of art through inexpensive and pioneering experimentation with new and unexplored digital materiality and changing social interaction patterns fostered through online infrastructures. Illustrative of how Artnode invented a new platform for the voice of artists is when they spent two months coding a programme for publishing a book online called *Inserts* (Landgreen et al., 1997). The book was about feminist art and art history and was written by 67 female artists who had made several attempts to publish it with no luck. At the time, no publishers wished to publish a book featuring only women artists. The book had received an ISBN number but the authors did not have enough funding to publish it themselves. With help from the Artnode programmers, the book was published as the first Danish e-book in 1997.

As excited as many net artists were about the potential of the Internet to create openings of and for art from within, as disappointing were the reactions from a hesitant art world. Although Artnode was particularly active in the first ten years, the project remained pretty much non-commercial. Net art as a category did not attract sufficient attention and because Artnode, in their interpretation, did not fit into any existing categories on the Danish art scene their applications for financial support were often declined. This is exactly Becker's (2008/1982) point when he explains how the adventurousness of artists experimenting with alternative forms of distribution of their art, etc. leaves them disadvantaged. They simply put themselves out of the game defined by central players of the art world. Recke's interpretation is that their applications for funding were typically rejected because the online art did not look good enough when printed on paper. If art did not have a physical form that could somehow be claimed or owned, it simply could not, in Becker's sense, be honoured with the label of government-funded art, at least not then. Creative autonomy in a given art world is not unconditional, as Becker suggests: "… art worlds provoke some of their members to create innovations they then will not accept. Some of these innovations develop small worlds of their own; some remain dormant and then find acceptance from a larger art world years and generations later; some remain magnificent curiosities of little more than antiquarian interest" (Becker, 2008/1982: 36).

Paradoxically, Artnode's production was acknowledged by some of the most prestigious museums in Copenhagen, but Recke and Jacobsen both emphasize how the only adjustments that were made to integrate net art in the art world were in the commercial interest of the art institutions now digitalizing art portfolios online or scouting for new "products" to promote. "*In spite of the attention they* (the net artists) *may achieve, the* (art) *institutions have not been really challenged by it*", Recke concludes. "*The system is often very commercial. Particularly when you look at the big Internet arenas there is a trinity between museums, galleries and the curators. If they want they can produce a star* via *online media. The Internet reinforces this big, strong commercial system. In this sense it has produced commercial highways*", he continues.

Perhaps Artnode and other examples of net art emerged in a time of technological milestones so polarized from, and potentially disruptive of, the conventional body of the traditional genres of visual art that the herding of the Danish net artists into a group was welcomed and even encouraged by the local art world. Artnode was a conveniently comprehensible flirt with the new digital technologies and as long as "it" stayed collected, it could be subjected to a sufficient othering to preserve it in a non-canonical category. Perhaps wholehearted appreciation of net art required equal enthusiasm for art and Internet and their combined potentials—a fascination that just did not fashion the majority of actors in the art world (Berry, 2008/2001). It may also be that the non-commercial space surrounding the marginalized position of artists and their art created the impetus for critical reflectivity and creativity.

With the economic independence and lack of institutional acceptance that characterized Artnode and other net artists came opportunities for autonomous experimentation with no obligations to "please" anyone or anything but their own curiosity. As already mentioned, the Artnode members were interested in using the new materiality, speed, movement and free distribution of videos and images. With skilled programmers, they could transition new advancements in technology into online art. What particularly excited the artists was not only the introduction of new artistic tools and forms, but also the potential for transcending genres. However, while the Artnode artists found, and still find, great attraction in the undefined and transcending "other", they experienced that the traditional art world called for the opposite: "*I really wish that it would be possible to break down the traditional boundaries for which materials that belong to what art form in order to mix them more. Art institutions want to preserve the genres because it makes it easier for them to communicate about things. But it also becomes a clear-cut path that it is hard to break free from. To me, art becomes interesting when it is difficult to place within a category*", Jacobsen explains.

Such eclecticism is not appreciated within the conventional normative framework of visual arts but as a non-profit online "laboratory", Artnode could experiment more freely with conventional boundaries. From this experimental space, the Artnode members were met with what they saw as inertness and misunderstandings from the art world in how actors related to the new media: "*When I was invited to teach at the Royal academy of art it was to teach the students about creating homepages not to teach them about what the media can actually do in relation to art*", Recke exemplifies.

In an attempt to foster, a theoretical ground for the appreciation of the potentials of the Internet in relation to visual art, the Artnode group therefore collected and selected texts from international artists and art historians on the topic and published them in the anthology "Vi elsker din computer" ("English: We love your computer")[3] in 2008. Whether the book ever made it into the educational institutions of art is not clear to the Artnode editors. But again, it was an act to, as artists, manage a task conventionally performed by art theorists in order to speed up the integration of a genre into the legitimate art world and be recognized for their originality. With their persistent attempts to mobilize art on the Internet as transformative space expanding the boundaries for creativity, what the Artnode experiences demonstrate is how there is no technological escape from convention. But the Internet and its distributive forces it has mobilized for the visual art does prove some extent liberating potentials for the arts and contemporary democracy as framed by Jacobsen's reflection: "*The greatest victory from experimenting with art on the Internet has nothing to do with the art but everything to do with the institution of art. Today, no one has a monopoly on acting as a gallerist or a museum. A young artist can have just as many followers on Instagram than an art museum. Our idea of the Internet as a free exhibition space has become a reality, although it has become very commercial in many respects. But it has proven to have an absurd range. The Internet offers a supplementary and distributed, and not only parallel, space for the visual arts*". In this way, irrespective of whether net art as a genre is extinct or dormant, net artists' experimentation with the Internet has demonstrated the potential of "a creative explosion" (Baumgärtel, 2008/1999: 40) of multiplied spaces and networks for creating, displaying and distributing art globally and have inspired traditional art institutions to make use of the new media.

The Dream of an Antagonist Space Reinforcing "Critical Voices"

Another driving force among artists attracted to the potential of the Internet is characterized by more direct engagement and confrontation with societal issues. One such hope concerns artistic abstraction and its crucial role in critical reflection. Recke explains: "*Abstraction can create because it opens these spaces from where you can communicate and say something completely unexpected in unexpected ways. You become a critical voice, a voice that comes from another place, from a self-defined form of production and not from a gallery where your purpose is to sell stuff. Art often speaks a universal language that immediately makes sense and potential impact. Art may achieve more than a politician will ever do in his or her entire career. Although a minister of foreign affairs, for example, may have achieved a privileged platform to speak from, he or she may not be able to voice or bring across the kind of messages that a powerful piece of art can do*".

Visual art may reinforce disruptive and (self-) critical thinking at individual and collective levels (Deleuze, 1988; Mouffe et al., 2001, 2007, 2008). Combined with the multiplicity of spaces and channels offered by the Internet, the technology may further amplify critical art as antagonist force both in terms of its content (message), its propagation and potential challenge of hegemonies. "*Art is good when it feeds doubt*", Jacobsen states. However, Artnode has according to the members been met with too limited efforts both from audiences to fully digest a level of abstraction necessary to engage with critical reflection. In spite of Artnode's current status as iconic on the Danish net art scene, several of their exhibitions in the large museums rarely succeeded in bringing across the groups' messages to the audience, not least in the eyes of critics.

Consider the example of their installation *User's Club* at the National Gallery of Denmark in 2001 (see Fig. 5.1). User's Club references Aleksandr Rodchenko's format for a *Worker's Club* in 1925 Paris as a post-revolutionary space where the public could actively engage with and debate political issues thus maintaining a critical spirit. The Artnode version of a public meeting ground for the freedom of speech combined physical and virtual spaces. An eight meters long table with four microphones was installed like a megaphone at the National Gallery of Denmark in Copenhagen and connected to Artnode's Internet site, basically as what we today would recognize as a chat room. People could openly share their messages in verbal or written form via the Internet or the microphones at the museum and their messages would be projected in words on the museum walls. *User's Club* materializes Mouffe's positioning of art as a central antagonist actor in public spaces with voice being open, free and unhindered. Everyone could exhibit his or her statement on the museum walls (see Fig. 5.1).

The installation, however, was too disturbing for the museum to host and was shut down before planned. The night watchmen, for example, complained that they were scared when people from across the Globe suddenly announced their statements in the closing hours in the middle

Fig. 5.1 "Users' club" from 2001 (Close-up of the open communication table from the Interactive installation by Artnode at the National Gallery of Denmark)

of the night. "*It was a really central and foresighted piece at the time. It was Skyping before Skype and Facebook live streaming before Facebook. But it was also too abstract, people did not know how to relate to it*", Recke explains. This mirrors Schreiber's (2001) problematizing of museums and galleries' practices of exhibiting net art in ways that enforce traditional conventions and thereby deflate net art's ambitions for public intervention.

Irony was a persistent feature of the group's experience. In the winter of 2017, Artnode was invited to exhibit at *Den Frie* Centre of Contemporary Art in Copenhagen. They named their exhibition *404 Not Found* to, on the one hand, investigate manifestations of digitalized society, and on the other hand, ironize about the very limited status that net art had achieved over the past decades (hinting how much net art now existed only as dead links prompting "404 not found" error messages). And, as an example, the group exhibited their retrospective work called *Museum* featuring a digital version of 100 drawings that Artnode had to produce for an exhibition on Charlottenborg Art Centre in Copenhagen in 1998 to visualize their homepage because the centre's Internet connection kept failing. Based on the drawings, Artnode received funding from the National Gallery of Denmark that then bought the artwork and now stores it in their collection of cobberplate engravings, ironically enough the first technological invention of mass production methods from the 1400s. And as yet another ironic feature in the 2017 exhibition, it was not possible to borrow the actual drawings from the National collection due to safety measures. According to the group, few critics got the irony that the Charlottenborg exhibition of net art was not online, and instead of directing their critique against the lack of technological advancement of the museum institution, Artnode's 2017 show was criticized for being Internet art without the Internet.

It is not uncommon that audiences and artists disappoint one another in such ways (Becker 2008/1982). What is illustrative here, however, is how Artnode's attempt to change hegemonies within the art world is met by layers of direct and indirect resistance from the traditional art world, including ignorance of their core critical messages. Lovejoy (1997) has observed how electronic media are indeed challenging to more traditional forms of representation. And for Artnode's exhibition in 1998, the Internet had not been set up although this was only a reasonable expectation given their status as net artists. As soon as the Artnode artists translated their art into physical drawings, State funding and acquisition honoured Artnode's productivity but without recognizing net art as such. For the artists, this was a subtle disciplining to comply within the boundaries of existing conventions.

Although an expert audience will be more open to artistic challenges of hegemonies (Becker 2008/1982) than the broader category of people with a more limited knowledge of art, openness and willingness to critical reflection are not given. This is central to the dynamics of net art, because it means that actualizing the political hopes for art as Mouffe's *antagonist force* is as dependent on facilitation as is the Internet in general if antagonist public spaces are to be arise. In fact, the computer screen individualizes experience, a condition that contributes to why Mogens Jacobsen, and other net artists with him, have chosen to move from net art and into other subgenres of the visual arts: "*What still fascinates me about the Internet as an artist is that it enables presence in multiple places at the same time. But when the interaction with art becomes an individualised experience, it is really a problem. It focuses the observer rather than the connectedness of art. Art has the potential to produce a sense of connectedness to what it means to be a human being. That things are not necessarily easy but troublesome and incomprehensible and that this is okay*", Jacobsen says. Paradoxically then, the increased public exposure of art that has become possible with the Internet does not per se ensure the sociability, or collective relatedness, of art. In Jacobsen's view, the visual preferences of Internet users are more that of a decorative, easy to digest kind of imaging fostered by commercialization. Technologies of production and reproduction have opened the gates for a "... flooding of daily life with objects and images" (Shanken 2009: 22) causing a visual overload that may habituate or numb our receptiveness to visual art requiring patient and deep levels of reflection.[4]

In the genre of electronic art, Jacobsen finds the combination of the virtual and the physically manifest more influential in challenging hegemonies. Illustrative of this is, for example, his installation *Crime Scene* in 2003 (see Fig. 5.2) questioning legal and moral issues surrounding copyright and intellectual properties in respect both to data software and as a comment to artistic production. Two computers are positioned next to each other in an infinite act of data files swapping. According to Danish law at the time, defining how it was the actual action of copying a file that was illegal. The title of the work ironizes on that.

The Danish Ministry of Culture's Rights Fund asked if they could run the Crime Scene artwork as a legal case to test the sensibility of the formulation in the law and Jacobsen agreed on the condition that he would not be charged with a sentence. "*After a long time, I received a strange letter saying that according to existing law the art piece was in its full right to exist as conceptual art, but it was illegal to exhibit*", Jacobsen laughs.

Fig. 5.2 "Crime scene" from 2003 (Installation by Mogens Jacobsen at Electrohype ROM, Malmoe, Sweden)

"*The installation was a method, an examination of the relation between what was defined as legal and illegal. It was absurd because when you install a program on your computer you are copying a file. Now the law has changed*", he continues. In this case, the physical presence of an art piece becomes a fundamental legal issue of the State: If the act of a technological object has become illegal (in this case copying of files), to what extent is the existence of that object then illegal? When art becomes physical it may become more intrusive. Eventually, the law was updated.

On the other hand, the Internet still makes it possible to operate in a public, non-commercial space (at the expense of official recognition) that is tolerant of complexity: "*With the Internet, I am not forced to streamline and reduce my art. People have often asked me why I don't just make more simple art. But I do not need to specify in three sentences what it is that I am doing. I am free to make things as crooked and inaccessible as I want to*", Jacobsen explains. Thus, although the Internet tends to individualize the experience of art and trivialize critical reflection, the technology still reserves important potential for occupation of online spaces by art that is outside and antagonist to existing hegemonies. As Mouffe (2008: 10) states, "[a] given hegemony results from a specific articulation of a diversity of spaces and this means that the hegemonic struggle also consists of the attempt to create a different form of articulation among public spaces".

As a result, the diversity of antagonist spaces, whether physical or virtual, are essential when confronting hegemony because such diversity multiplies the discursive surfaces on which antagonist struggles play out "… between opposing hegemonic projects which can never be reconciled rationally" (Mouffe, 2007: 3). When artists such as Jacobsen insist on certain layers of complexity in his artistic messages that he is then free to display on the Internet, it is not a question of whether or not critical art is being cultivated in spirit of democracy; what seems to be more of an issue is the degree to which a critically reflective audience will actively seek out such *outside* and *antagonist* visual abstractions via "other" spaces as enabled by the Internet as well as how such critical art is being engaged with through pluralist civic participation.

Discussion: What Critical Potential Could We Hope for?

Now that the political ideals of art and Internet as synergetic, democratizing forces seems to be entangled with quite influential sociological factors, what may we make of whatever liberating leeways that may actually be? The experience of the Artnode group represents an interesting quandary. On the one hand, the Internet functions as a transformative space for the visual arts to the extent that it provides an autonomous free space for play and experimentation. Artists can freely create and develop artistic innovations online. But for the artist, the price for doing so is limited recognition from the established art world in the sense that they may be encapsulated in a financial vacuum and receive limited attention from a half-hearted audience, if any at all. As in the example of the persistent experiments performed by the Artnode group, some artists are willing and able to pay the price of being a non-profit "shadow operator", at least for some time, primarily because being creatively "other" from the conventional art world fuels the artistic ethos. On the other hand, however, the serial disappointments that the group has been facing demonstrate how the conventionalism of the established art world limits the antagonist potential of art by holding new art forms at an arm's length and hereby minimizing its power to challenge existing hegemonies in the art world and beyond. Following Khaire (2015), it appears the lack of an online art ecosystem in the online world renders this genre hard to sustain. In other words, the antagonist forces of art, however, critical they may be, are far from autonomous to constraints imposed by societal conventions but are heavily subjected to intricate hegemonies themselves.

The degree to which individual and collective liberating forces will succeed in expanding creative and critically reflective art on the Internet will vary according to many factors, for example, personal and collective ingenuity of actors in communicating a message, mobilization of skills, tactics, resources, receptiveness of an audience, etc. This chapter merely scrapes the surface of the complex interrelations of visual art worlds and the way their artworks are being distributed and engaged with on the Internet. However, in extracting and illuminating the interplay between hopeful practices of the Danish net artists, I hope to offer an indicative idea of the openings that after all do seem to exist for the Internet to serve an as enabler of *transformative* and *antagonist* "other" spaces for the creative and critical-reflective potentials of art, respectively.

In terms of *transformative* capacities, the Internet's primary benefit lay, in the experience of the artists studied here, in multiplied online spaces where artists could experiment with content, form and the role of art. Structurally, the technology facilitates Mouffe's envisioned ensemble of critical voices through pluralist civic participation. But commercialization of both art and the Internet combined with omnipresent conventional hegemonies of the art world *also* pave the paths for opportunity and recognition in cyberspace. This makes it reasonable to moderate Mouffe's belief in art's unique position as force of autonomous abstraction and challenger of hegemonies. The space for artistic autonomy is guarded by boundaries of conventionality determining how artists and their art will be labelled and appreciated by the art world and a more general audience. Herein lies a catch. While art is inherently "other" in its capacity to insist on innovation, its experiment cannot be too subversive, too alien or "other", to conventional standards since this will result only in a starving artist (deprived of elitist attention and profit) or dormant attempt to transform hegemonies from within.

Still, the Internet does enable marginal(ized) artistic experiments, such as net art, that would otherwise probably be limited to transient dreams and basement play, to be heard and seen. This raises the question whether art in itself should necessarily be *transformative* in order to serve as instrument for democratizing ideology. In case of Artnode's experiences, the creative potential of art seems inseparable from its critical potential in the sense that the artists' potentially subversive message may take radically new forms of expression, manifests itself in new materials and insists on new art forms (genres) or merging of forms to be a "free" voice. On such an optimistic note, virtual spaces might very well be where we find the most autonomous forms of dissonant voices—outside and antagonist to a given hegemony—and their artistic expressions, but we cannot necessarily expect such alien innovations to diffuse into more popular online spheres.

This leads to reflections on the Internet's *antagonist* capacities. The Internet may foster the critical and dialogical potential of art essential to pluralist democracy, but only given certain conditions. In line with the relatively limited space for creative-transformative artistic practices that the Internet actually enables, antagonist spaces are not *given*, neither in cyberspace nor in physical space. Mouffe's identification of the numbing effect of capitalist forces on critical reflexivity very evidently extend onto the World Wide Web (see also Noveck, 2000), despite the hopes of the artists. And, as Mouffe (2000) emphasizes, public antagonist spaces are actively *made*, insisted on and persistently nursed for (Mouffe, 2000), something that may particularly apply to cyberspace: "In the same way that we consciously construct buildings with space for public displays of art or with handicapped access or that we design rooms for acoustic panels to facilitate conversation and musical performance, we must also purpose-build public chat rooms and cyber fora. the absence of politically relevant discussion spaces on the net is not surprising given that we are trying to force our public debates into spaces designed for private and commercial interaction" (Noveck, 2000: 21). More concretely, Mouffe's notion of critical, polyphone dialogue through the cultivation of manifold antagonist public spaces becomes challenged in the short-span attention characteristic of Internet users as well as individualized experience, where the audience is more likely to find pleasure in entertaining and decorative visual graphics rather than in critical reflectivity.

This means that a curious and critically reflective audience of visual art on the Internet is far from given. Critical awareness, as well as patient and informed analytical skills, is cultivated, for example, through general education. Darts (2004), for example, argues that since visual culture has become ubiquitous, we are bombarded with politically charged symbolism in our everyday lives. And to critically relate to such visual exposure, critical mindsets should be educated from an early age. Critical-reflective citizens must learn to know when and why to be emotionally touched by a critical message in an artwork rather than being numbed by *habitualisation* (with reference to Russian critic Viktor Shklovsky, 1988), i.e., unaware of critical aspects in what has become "natural" to us. People need to be visually shakeable and shaken for the distributive channels and dialogical platforms of the Internet to be activated as antagonist forces. In other words: we have the technology for supporting the critical potential of art in pluralist democracy, but perhaps the Internet has not been here long enough for us to learn to use it properly and develop ways to appreciate the art that it enables.

In addition, the Artnode experiences suggest that in order to catch critically reflective attention of an audience, critical visual art can benefit from complementing its online representation with a physical manifestation, thereby making the statement for invasive to people's awareness. Immersive artistic practices that engage audiences socially "… by inviting those audiences to participate, act, work and create together; observe one another; or simply be together" (Harvie 2013: 1) may be a promising path to pursue and integrate into online lives of people in order to ignite social engagement and "fair democratic opportunity" (ibid.: 2). It may therefore be constructive to further explore the synergies of representational spaces in engaging people with visual art. Recently, scholars within communication studies emphasize the importance of recognizing and mobilizing social dimensions through the materiality of communication technologies (Lievrouw, 2014). At MoMA, for example, experiments with online technologies (a MoMAR Gallery smartphone app) have been conducted with what appears to be success, having "... opened up new possibilities for activists and art enthusiasts eager to have a part in shaping the museum-going experience" (Katz, 2018).

Schreiber (2001) points out how a subtle feature of net art is how net artists and commercial web designers draw on the same qualifications and use the same software which makes artistic interventions truly subversive because one cannot tell the difference between the visual presentation of critical art and its commercial counterpart. Consider, for example, the artist group ®TMark's subversive hack of George W. Bush's presidential campaign, where the artists owned the domain "gwbush.com" that was almost identical to the official Bush homepage, but instead parodied the presidential candidate and his party while publishing Bush-critical articles. The site caught the attention of several news media and eventually led Bush himself to threaten legal action (Neal, 1999; Schreiber, 2008/2001). In this regard, however, the subtle tactics at net art's disposal can make the art slide into the everyday public sphere unnoticed (Greene, 2008/2000) and have lead, e.g., Schreiber (2008/2001) to ascribe it greater subversive prospects than video art. We may understand this potential in the light net art's capacity as "art activism" which is "... positioned at the intersection of art and political activism, empowered by new forms of social organization, enabled by the Internet" (Bradley & Esche, 2007: 11).

Conclusion

In order for the Internet to successfully elevate the liberating potentials of the visual art both as a transformative, creative force and an antagonist democratizing actor in society, political hopes need to be adjusted to the sociological realities in which they are embedded. Visual artists and their art are not unconditionally autonomous actors but are deeply embedded within, and dependent on, societal hegemonies, such as the legitimizing conventions of the art world. Further, when relying on the Internet as a given "free space" that is completely other, or parallel, to the existing social world, the critical voice of art quickly becomes undistinguished from commercial noise or disintegrated with the established art world and thus deprived of its subversive potentials. Therefore, transformative and antagonist synergies between visual art and the Internet must be carefully attended to, reinforced by supplementary forms of representation as well as socially engaging and immersive practices facilitated, for example, through physically manifest interventions, interactive technologies and/or cultivation of critical reflectivity of present and future Internet users.

Notes

1. Here, "net artists" refer to "artists producing (…) art works for the World Wide Web" (Schreiber, 2008/2001, orig. language); Particularly in Europe, several artists use the name "net.art" which can be read as an ironic reference to the conventions of the art world, such as its use of definition of genres and group formations (Baumgärtel, 2008/1999).
2. The artistic fascination with the Internet as open portal for art and/as information is well illustrated in one of the first online media artworks by Spanish Antoni Muntada, called *The File Room* (1994). In a physical installation, Muntada created an open-ended online database as records of artistic and cultural censorship around the World. Any user could then re-publish repressed and deleted material in an online public record (see Baumgärtel, 2008/1999).
3. With reference to the title of Tilman Baumgärtel's interview with the artists behind the net art site *jodi* in 1997 published in *Intelligent Agent*.
4. A condition that is well illustrated in the New York artist Mark Napier's artwork *The Digital Landfill* (1998), an online landfill storage for indigestible data as an ironic note to our time's data trash (see Baumgärtel, 2008/1999).

Literature

Alacovska, A. (2018). Keep hoping, keep going: Towards a hopeful sociology of creative work. *The Sociological Review, 1*(19).

Baumgärtel, T. (2008/1999). Netkunst. Historisk rids over det kunstneriske arbejde med telekommunikationsmidler. In J. Lillemose & N. Recke (Eds.), *Vi elsker din computer. En antology om netkunst redigeret af Artnode*. Det Kongelige Danske Kunstakademis Billedkunstskoler (Originally published in English in 1999 with the title: Net art. On the history of artistic work with telecommunication. In T. Druckrey & P. Weibel (Eds.), *Net condition: Art and global media*. Cambridge: MIT Press).

Becker, H. S. (1974). Art as collective action. *American Sociological Review, 39*(6), 767–776.

Becker, H. S. (2008/1982). *Art worlds*. 25th anniversary edition published by the University of California Press (Originally published in 1982 by The Regents of the University of California).

Bengtsen, P. (2013). Beyond the public art machine: A critical examination of street art as public art. *Konsthistorisk tidskrift/Journal of Art History, 82*(2), 63–80.

Benjamin, W. (1936). The work of art in the age of mechanical reproduction. In H. Arendt (Ed.) & H. Zohn (Trans.), *Illuminations: Essays and Reflections* (pp. 217–252). New York: Schocken.

Berry, J. (2008/2001). Re-materialiseringen—blot en gentagelse? In J. Lillemose & N. Recke (Eds.), *Vi elsker din computer. En antology om netkunst redigeret af Artnode*. Det Kongelige Danske Kunstakademis Billedkunstskoler (Originally published in English in 2001 with the title: Re-dematerialisation of the object & the artist in biopower. *Nettime*, February 5).

Bourdieu, P. (1984a/1979). *Distinction*. London and New York: Routledge (Originally published in 1979 with the French title: *La Distinction* by Editions de Minuit).

Bourdieu, P. (1984b). *The field of cultural production: Essays on art and literature*. New York: Columbia University Press.

Bradley, W., & Esche, C. (2007). *Art and social change: A critical reader*. London: Tate Publishings.

Darts, D. (2004). Visual culture jam: Art, pedagogy, and creative resistance. *Studies in an Education: A Journal of Issues and Research, 45*(4) (2004), 313–327.

De La Fuente, E. (2007). The new sociology of art: Putting art back into social science approaches to the Arts. *Cultural Sociology, 1*(3), 409–425.
Deleuze, G. (1992/1988). *The fold: Leibniz and the baroque*. Minnesota: University of Minnesota Press (Originally published in French in 1988 with the title: *Le Pli: Leibnitz et le Baroque* by Les Éditions De Minuit).
Deleuze, G., & Guattari, F. (1972). *Anti-oedipus*. Trans. R. Hurley, M. Seem, & H. R. Lane. London and New York: Continuum, 2004. Vol. 1 of *Capitalism and Schizophrenia*. 2 vols. 1972–1980. Trans. of *L'Anti-Oedipe*. Paris: Les Editions de Minuit.
Ekman, U. (Ed.). (2013). *Throughout: Art and culture emerging with ubiquitous computing*. Cambridge, MA, USA: MIT Press.
Ferdinand, P. (Ed.). (2000). *The internet, democracy and democratization*. Abingdon: Frank Cass Publishers.
Greaves, K. (2014). Hell-horse: Radical in Nazi-occupied Denmark. *Oxford Art Journal, 37*(1), 47–63.
Greene, R. (2008/2000). Webarbejder: en historisk oversigt over Internetkunsten. In J. Lillemose & N. Recke (Eds.), *Vi elsker din computer. En antology om netkunst redigeret af Artnode*. Det Kongelige Danske Kunstakademis Billedkunstskoler (Originally published in English in 2000 with the title: Web work: A history of internet art. *Artforum*).
Harvie, J. (2013). *Fair play—Art, performance and neoliberalism*. Performance Interventions. Basingstoke: Palgrave Macmillan.
Ilchuk, Y. (2017). Hearing the voice of Donbas: Art and literature as forms of cultural protest during war. *Nationalities Papers, 45*(2), 256–273.
Katz, J. (1997). The digital citizen. *Wired*, pp. 68–82.
Katz, M. (2018, April 23). Augmented reality is transforming museums. *The Wire, Culture*. https://www.wired.com/story/augmented-reality-art-museums/.
Khaire, M. (2015). Art without borders? Online firms and the global art market. In O. Velthuis & S. B. Curioni (Eds.), *Cosmopolitan canvases, the globalization of markets for contemporary art*. Oxford: Oxford University Press.
Kristensen, J. T. (2017, January 14). En note om Artnode. *Idoart.dk*.
Landgreen, M., Hinnum, S., & Olsen, S. K. (Eds.). (1997). *Inserts. 67 kvindelige kunstnere i Danmark*. Artnode Production.
Lievrouw, L. A. (2014). Materiality and media in communication and technology studies: An unfinished project. In T. Gillespie, et al. (Eds.), *Media technologies: Essays on communication, materiality, and society*. Cambridge, MA, USA: MIT Press.

Lillemose, J., & Recke, N. (Eds.). (2008). *Vi elsker din computer. En antology om netkunst redigeret af Artnode.* Det Kongelige Danske Kunstakademis Billedkunstskoler.

Lovejoy, M. (1997). *Postmodern currents: Art and artists in the age of electronic media.* Upper Saddle River, NJ: Prentice Hall.

Mouffe, C. (1991). Democratic citizenship and the political community. In The Miami Theory Collective (Ed.), *Community at loose ends* (pp. 70–82). Minneapolis: University of Minnesota Press.

Mouffe, C. (2000). *The democratic paradox.* London and New York: Verso.

Mouffe C. (2007). Artistic activism and agonistic spaces. *Art & Research: A Journal of Ideas, Contexts and Methods, 1*(2), 1–5.

Mouffe, C. (2008). *Art and democracy: Art as an agnostic intervention in public space.* Open 14. Rotterdam: NAI Publishers.

Mouffe, C., Deutsche, R., Joseph, B. W., & Keenan, T. (2001). Every form of art has a political dimension. *Grey Room, 2*(Winter), 98–125.

Neal, T. M. (1999, November 29). Satirical web site poses political test. Facing legal action from Bush, creator cites U.S. tradition of parody. *Washington Post Staff Writer*, p. A02.

Noveck, B. S. (2000). Paradoxical partners: Electronic communication and electronic democracy. In P. Ferdinand (Ed.), *The Internet, democracy and democratization.* Abingdon: Frank Cass Publishers.

Prior, N. (2011). Critique and renewal in the sociology of music, Bourdieu and beyond. *Cultural Sociology, 5*(1), 121–138.

Sauvagnargues, A. (2013/2005). *Deleuze and art.* London: Bloomsbury Academic (Originally published in French with the title: *Deleuze et l'art* by Presses Univesritaires de France).

Schreiber, R. (2008/2001). Net.kunst: efter det utopiske øjeblik? In J. Lillemose & N. Recke (Eds.), *Vi elsker din computer. En antology om netkunst redigeret af Artnode.* Det Kongelige Danske Kunstakademis Billedkunstskoler (Originally published in English in 2001 with the title: Net.Art: Shredding the Utopian moment. *A Critical Journal of the Arts in Baltimore and the World*, Issue 7).

Shanken, E. A. (2009). *Art and electronic media.* London: Phaidon Press Limited.

Shklovsky, V. (1988). Art as technique. In D. Lodge (Ed.), *Modern critic is mandatory: A reader* (pp. 15–30). New York and London: Longman.

6

Evaluation and Producers' Attention to Ratings in the Chocolate Confectionery Markets

Thomas Collas

Introduction

Consumer guides which select producers and rank them by a small number of criteria, when seen as "judgement devices" (Karpik, 2000), have been described as salutary beacons for consumers—and also producers—exposed to uncertainty in the thick fog of the markets.[1] This "functional" approach (Dodier & Barbot, 2016), which infers the market function of a critical guide from its content, has been complemented and enriched by studies of the "reactivity of rankings" (Espeland & Sauder, 2007: 12), i.e. the "mechanisms" (ibid.) that generate, in the producers evaluated and in the other participants in the markets, behaviours that are oriented towards the guides—in particular behaviours aimed at conforming to the quality standards they promote. The restaurant market (Fantasia, 2010; Lane, 2013; Rao, Monin, & Durand, 2005; Surlemont & Johnson, 2005) and the wine market

T. Collas (✉)
IACCHOS, UCLouvain, Louvain-La-Neuve, Belgium
e-mail: thomas.collas@uclouvain.be

J. Strandgaard Pedersen et al. (eds.), *Technology and Creativity*,
https://doi.org/10.1007/978-3-030-17566-5_6

(Chauvin, 2011; Fernandez, 2004; Jamerson, 2009) have provided case studies of the role of quantified evaluations in market activities and have underpinned a description of such guides as *taste makers*, bringing production and consumption behaviours into line with the quality standards they define and promote.[2]

The evaluation of food products and their producers by guides covers a much broader territory than the specific markets of restaurants and wine: it extends to other specialist foods, with reviews of sausages, baguettes, ice creams, etc. This chapter focuses on one such publication, the *Guide des croqueurs de chocolat* ("The Chocolate Eater's Guide", hereafter "GCC"), and brings to light the distance between the work performed by the guide of rating and of promoting a set of quality standards and the registers in which the producers show themselves attentive to it, i.e. take account of it and make use of it in their commercial activity.

The GCC is devoted to *bonbons de chocolat*, confectioneries weighing a few grams and containing cocoa (cocoa butter and/or mass), which can be transported and kept for a few weeks, and may be made either in series of a few sweets or through large-scale automated production. The guide was initiated by the *Club des croqueurs de chocolat* (hereafter "the Club"), an association founded in 1981 by a group of happy few—two restaurant critics and businessmen, the CEO of a champagne firm and a CNRS researcher—after a dinner rounded off with a chocolate cake said to have revealed the diners' shared enthusiasm for products derived from the roasted cacao bean (Pessis, 2011). The association, limited to 150 members who are admitted after verification of their knowledge of cacao products, was described in 1996 as one of the "25 most influential clubs, circles and business networks" of the Paris region (Marty & Ivanoff, 1996: 21). It meets several times a year for tasting sessions in the salons of grand hotels in Paris.

The GCC was first published in 1988, at a time when the suppliers of raw materials and producer collectives were promoting a "craft" tradition in chocolate sweets (Terrio, 2000).[3] As is still the case today, these producers were mostly trained in pastry and confectionery and made the product in the backrooms of specialist shops displaying the sign "*pâtisserie-confiserie-chocolaterie-traiteur*", which might also offer cakes and pastries, fancy breads, ice creams, savoury appetisers and other confectionery. That period of institutionalisation of the French chocolate world saw the emergence of associations (of professionals or amateurs), initial training courses in chocolate, pastry and confectionery (Casella & Shapiro, 1991), raw materials with a high cocoa content and professional chocolate-making competitions.[4] The GCC is the only multi-edition guide entirely devoted to comparing chocolate confectionery producers in France. It gives a score—from 1994 in the form of a number of "chocolate bars"—to the firms it reviews, which have voluntarily supplied a sample of their production.

The GCC's ratings are based on a defined set of standards for chocolate confectionery, which have remained unchanged for over twenty years (section "Behind the Chocolate Bars: Rating System and Quality Standards"). However, although producers show themselves to be attentive to the guide, this does not lead them to conform to the standards promoted, but rather to denigrate the ratings procedure, to withdraw from assessment when they are rated poorly, or to invoke the scores of the guide as proof of superiority within geographically circumscribed markets while detaching them from the context of comparison (section "Producers' Attention to the Guide: Disputed, Dispensable and Malleable Ratings").

Materials

The study is based on two types of materials.
First, the content of the seven editions of the GCC published between 1988 and 2012 was examined. Subsequently in this text, these editions are referred to by "GCC" followed by their year of publication (GCC, YEAR). The prefaces were closely studied. The reviews of two editions (1988 and 2011), chosen because of the length of time between them, were lexicometrically analysed. For all the editions, the rates of participation in the next edition were compared in relation to the score obtained.
Secondly, 33 interviews were carried out—one with an editor of the guide, the others with chocolate producers. For the latter, when the subject turned to confectionery and the interviewee did not mention the GCC, she or he was asked: "Do you send chocolates to the *Guide des croqueurs*?" This made it possible to discuss the uses made of the GCC and of participation in the guide's ratings. The names attached to the interviews have been changed.

Behind the Chocolate Bars: Rating System and Quality Standards

This section sets out two aspects of the production of scores by the GCC: the rating system, which generates these scores and the—stable—quality standards on which it is based. The scores were given out of 20 in 1988 and in numbers of "chocolate bars" from the second edition (Table 6.1).

Publicisation of a Tasting Procedure to Underpin Expert Evaluation

Blank (2006) distinguishes two types of reviews: "connoisseurial" ones are based on the reviewer's legitimacy to evaluate, whereas "procedural" ones rely on codified evaluation procedures. The GCC has progressively published an evaluation procedure presented not as a substitute for but as an underpinning of the members' judgements.

The first edition of the guide states that "all the chocolates were tested in Paris under the same conditions by a jury of at least four members" (GCC, 1988: 5). The confectioneries were rated independently of their context of sale and were subject to the risks of transportation to Paris, two characteristics retained in the subsequent editions. The next three

Table 6.1 Ranking systems in the successive editions of the editions du GCC

Edition	Firms	Rankings
1988	171	22 scores on a scale (with half-points) up to 20 (ranging from 7 to 19), synthesised in 6 levels (from "Top Score" to "Could do better")
1994	138	6 levels (0–4 bars and 4 gold bars)
1998	141	6 levels (0–5 bars)
2003	142	Idem
2010	156	6 levels (1–5 bars and 5 bars + "award") and a "heart" (a symbol partially independent of the number of bars)
2011	151	Idem
2012	167	5 levels (2–5 bars and 5 bars + "award") and a "heart"

editions gave details of the samples judged and the conditions in which this was done. Producers were contacted—320 in 1994 (p. 6), 200 in 1998 (p. 11)—and invited to send chocolates (3–5 varieties depending on the year) including at least one with a ganache centre and one with a *praliné* or gianduja centre.[5]

In these earliest editions, the expertise of the judges is guaranteed by their membership of the Club and the "professional" capacity of some of them who were chocolate confectioners.

In 1988, the judges' evaluation sessions were not clearly distinguished from plenary meetings of the Club, in which confectionery producers were invited to present their work: after describing the Club's "tasting sessions", the chairman then explained that it had "seemed to them useful to publish this guide and so enable a greater number of chocolate-lovers to benefit from the findings of (their) tests" (GCC, 1988: 5). The ambiguity of the distinction between the Club and jury is reinforced by the extensive references to the history of the Club and its distinguished members in the prefaces of the first editions. The names of some participants in the judging session were given in 1988 (notably food critic Claude Lebey, fashion designer Sonia Rykiel and businesswoman and essayist Sophie de Menthon). In 1994, the chocolates were rated by a jury of "amateurs and professionals" (p. 6). In the 2003 edition, the mention of "professionals" as a mark of expertise was replaced by length of membership of the Club, and the jury was described as made up of "long-standing members" (p. 14).

Since 2010, the guide has been published every year and gives rise to an "awards" ceremony at the *Salon du chocolat* in Paris. The evaluation now takes a more procedural form. It is made clear that the judges do not know the producers' names. This commitment is accompanied by a detailed description of the sessions on the Club's website.[6] Here the exclusion of "professionals" is presented as fundamental to the panel's legitimacy to express a consumer's judgement. The material conditions of the evaluation are also set out in detail—the number of judges (16 in two groups), the scheduling of the tastings (once or twice a week), the number of producers whose confectioneries are rated each time (4 per session), the foods accompanying them (bread and water), the temperature at which the products are kept before tasting (20 °C), the means of anonymisation, and also the aspects rated (appearance, texture, taste, balance of flavours, length on the palate). Each judge writes "a personal opinion and gives a score between 1 and 5".

The scoring retains a strong element of expert justification: unlike other ratings (Mallard, 2000), it is based not on objectifiable criteria (e.g. density or proportion of sugar, cream or cocoa), but on a judgement, through tasting, of the quality of the confectioneries. The standing of the tasters is thus reaffirmed at the beginning of the text ("informed, passionate chocolate-lovers"). The element of expert critique is increased by the lifting of anonymity before the final score is decided: the average of the judges' scores gives rise to a score for each producer which is discussed by a select committee, including in particular the editors of the guide, the chairman of the Club, and the organiser of the *Salon du chocolat*. This committee takes care to smooth the score trajectories so as to avoid abrupt "ups and downs" and avoid displeasing the participants, as one of the editors explained in an interview. Through this smoothing operation, the committee produces a score based on but not limited to the evaluation procedure. The editor who was interviewed mentioned for example the score of a producer who enjoyed great visibility in the media, who in the course of this smoothing was moved from four bars to five bars and an "award", thus regaining the distinction assigned in the previous edition. This smoothing was presented by my interlocutor as a correction of "blips" in the procedure so as to come closer to the quality of the confectioneries "actually" sold by the producer, a quality presumed to be revealed over time and known to the expert independently of the quality of the products judged. The discrepancies are attributed by this editor to incidental production faults (raw materials, machines, etc.) or damage in transport, and not to any—even rare or occasional—shortcomings on the part of the panel.

Between expertise and procedure, this description is close to what Bonnet (2004) calls "layman's expertise" in the area of restaurant criticism, an expertise, which combines "the pursuit of objectivity […] with the claim to a certain subjectivity. […] The reviewer then presents himself as a consumer like any other (albeit better informed)" (ibid.: 153). The procedure here provides a basis for an expert judgement, which prevails in the last instance.

The spelling-out of the procedure in the 2010s was accompanied by a radical shift in the score distribution (Fig. 6.1). On the one hand, the progressive increase in the average of the scores observed between 1988 and 2003 continued from 2010 to 2012 with a shift of more than one point. On the other hand, the disparity of the distribution was strongly reduced and is concentrated around the highest scores. The proportion of firms awarded four or five bars thus rose from five out of 141 (3.5%) in 1998 to 95 out of 167 (57.1%) in 2012. This may be seen as the mark of a new scoring policy for a guide now presented in a *Salon* for a wide audience and concerned to limit the number of producers, sometimes exhibiting in the *Salon*, who are awarded no bars or only one. The scores nonetheless indicate an order among producers. To make the editions of the guide comparable in the light of this, the remainder of the chapter distinguishes three bands: "low", "middle" and "high".[7]

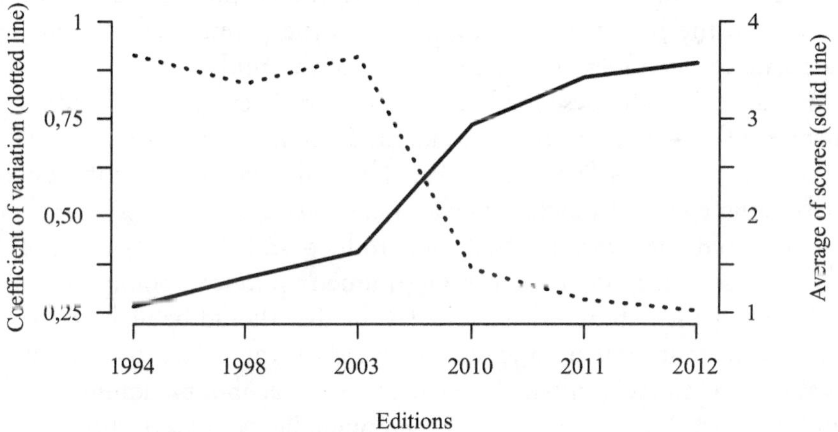

Fig. 6.1 Average (right-hand scale) and coefficient of variation (left-hand scale) of scores in the GCC (*Nota Bene* The editions compared are those for which the scores are expressed in bars [from 1994]. The score "4 gold bars" in 1994 was regarded as equivalent to 5 bars in the subsequent editions)

Opposition to Sweetness, Fat and Thickness: Genesis and Maintenance of a Single Set of Quality Standards

Espeland and Stevens (1998) state that commensuration transforms distinct qualities into *quanta* in a single dimension. When such an operation takes the form of a critical evaluation, the scores assigned present themselves as the most visible reflection of a benchmark scale that is implicitly or explicitly implemented. Through the notes and comments associated with the firms, there thus emerges the definition of a quality chocolate confectionery according to the GCC, one that has been maintained despite several changes of editors.

The highest level[8] of the scale constructed in the first three editions is occupied by just one firm: *La Maison du chocolat*, then run by Robert Linxe, himself a member of the Club and creator of the chocolate cake eaten in the dinner for the first members and described as a founding element (cf. above). Beyond this monopoly of the highest position, there is a strong proximity between what Linxe presents as a radical break with the production of the time and the criteria defining quality chocolate confectionery in the comments of the guide.

As Linxe himself described it fifteen years later (Linxe, 1992), the opening of a first shop under the name *La Maison du chocolat* in 1977 (in the eighth *arrondissement* de Paris) was driven by the ambition of establishing a clear distinction between chocolates and "sweets" [*confiserie "sucrée"*] (ibid.: 48), through both the products and the retail outlets. The principles set out in the book can be summed up in four points: cocoa—"*bel amer*" ["bitter beauty"]—is the flavour that should be highlighted in a chocolate confectionery and should linger on the palate; consequently, "sweets" ["*friandises*"] in which sugar, cream or alcohol predominate cannot be regarded as chocolates, and these ingredients, if used, should only be used to set off the value of the cocoa; the centre—for which ganache should be favoured, in particular over *praliné*—is the main element of a confectionery, so the enrobing should be as fine as possible; finally, the confectioneries should be sold in packages and places stripped of the customary infantile codes of "sweets" or "candies" [*confiserie*].

A lexicometric analysis of the comments in the 1988 and 2011 editions of the GCC (171 and 151 comments respectively) confirms the proximity of the editors' scoring criteria to this definition of a chocolate confectionery.[9] The tourist-oriented comments accompanying each firm in the 1988 edition are excluded from the analysis. The words are lemmatised, i.e. brought together in a single canonical form: the verbs are reduced to their infinitive, demonyms to toponyms and other words to their masculine singular. The analysis is applied to lemmatised terms found in at least five comments. In order to study the object of the evaluation and not its customary procedures, depreciatory or laudatory terms (poor, perfect, etc.) and the quantifying terms (less, more, too much, etc.) are excluded.[10] This is also the case with verbs, first names (Jean, Michel), place names (Paris) and other terms, which have no particular significance for the object. For the 1998 edition, 160 terms are studied, 120 for the 2011 edition.[11] In view of the limited number of comments, the words are then replaced in their evaluation context (appreciation/depreciation of lack/excess) so as to make the results intelligible and interpret them, since a comment associated with a low or medium score often contains appreciative passages.

The terms typical of each band—low, middle, high, cf. above—(Table 6.2) in 1988 partly echo the oppositions put forward by Linxe. For example, as recurrent supports of low scores, one finds components whose excesses are deplored—sugar, liqueur, butter—and others whose small presence is regretted (cocoa, chocolate), and numerous remarks on the over-thickness of the enrobing and the lack or excess of imagination shown by these efforts at "*création*" (the term is then used to emphasise what is judged to be the unsuccessful character of some recipes). The term "*friandise*" is sometimes brought in to round off the rejection of "treats" ["*bouchées*"] which have little appeal for the judges' palates and whose presentation sometimes involves other colours than chocolate brown (in particular, white). The agreeable reception in the shop is several times mentioned to nuance a severe judgement.[12] It is sometimes suggested that the products do not travel well, although this does not affect the procedure in subsequent editions. By contrast, the high band is characterised by comments on the balance (*équilibre*) and freshness (*fraîcheur*) of the compositions, the thinness of the enrobing,

Table 6.2 Typical terms of each band (GCC, 1988)

Term	Residual	Band/Term (%)	Term/Band (%)	Term/All (%)
Low				
Sucre	3.83	51.4	54.3	43.3
Boîte	3.03	77.8	10.0	5.3
Chocolat	3.03	43.4	75.7	71.3
Liqueur	2.98	69.2	12.9	7.6
Blanc	2.69	75.0	8.6	4.7
Aimable	2.37	80.0	5.7	2.9
Voyage	2.37	80.0	5.7	2.9
Palais	2.31	66.7	8.6	5.3
Bouchée	2.28	46.7	30.0	26.3
Friandise	2.18	56.3	12.9	9.4
Saveur	2.01	50.0	17.1	14.0
Patisserie	1.98	60.0	8.6	5.8
Beurre	1.92	62.5	7.1	4.7
Épais	1.92	62.5	7.1	4.7
Imagination	1.92	62.5	7.1	4.7
Production	1.92	62.5	7.1	4.7
goût	1.87	44.2	27.1	25.1
présentation	1.77	41.3	37.1	36.8
Cacao	1.72	42.6	28.6	27.5
Creation	1.57	45.8	15.7	14.0
Praline	1.53	40.4	32.9	33.3
High				
Equilibre	4.87	63.2	50.0	11.1
Cannelle	3.98	83.3	20.8	3.5
Maîtrise	3.50	50.0	41.7	11.7
Sobre	3.44	80.0	16.7	2.9
Parfum	2.75	42.9	37.5	12.3
Pâtissier	2.54	57.1	16.7	4.1
Emballage	2.47	50.0	20.8	5.8
Gianduja	2.31	60.0	12.5	2.9
Enrobage	2.20	50.0	16.7	4.7
Monsieur	2.20	45.5	20.8	6.4
Arôme	1.94	32.4	45.8	19.9
Finesse	1.93	31.0	54.2	24.6
Thé	1.85	37.5	25.0	9.4
Amer	1.76	38.5	20.8	7.6
Adresse	1.66	40.0	16.7	5.8
Fraîcheur	1.58	42.9	12.5	4.1
Tablette	1.58	42.9	12.5	4.1

(continued)

Table 6.2 (continued)

Term	Residual	Band/Term (%)	Term/Band (%)	Term/All (%)
Middle				
Métier	2.67	100.0	9.1	4.1
Cadeau	2.26	100.0	6.5	2.9
Gourmand	2.22	76.5	16.9	9.9
Bouche	2.14	81.8	11.7	6.4
Douceur	1.93	80.0	10.4	5.8
Originalité	1.93	80.0	10.4	5.8
Réputation	1.93	80.0	10.4	5.8
Accueil	1.92	72.2	16.9	10.5
Charme	1.91	85.7	7.8	4.1
Proportion	1.91	85.7	7.8	4.1
Tradition	1.84	73.3	14.3	8.8
Soin	1.76	75.0	11.7	7.0
Produit	1.65	68.4	16.9	11.1
Truffe	1.56	64.3	23.4	16.4
Fabrication	1.54	72.7	10.4	6.4
Noisette	1.54	68.8	14.3	9.4

Note The terms are identified on the basis of the adjusted residuals (Haberman, 1973) from a table of three rows (bands) and 160 columns (terms); the terms retained are those for which this residual is positive (the index of an attraction, i.e. over-representation of the term in the band) and belongs to the highest quintile of the absolute values of the residuals. Band/Term: proportion of comments including the term contained in the band (the percentage base is the total number of comments including the term). Term/Band: proportion of comments in the band including the term. Term/All: proportion of comments (for the whole edition) including the term
How to read: "*sucre*" is over-represented in the low band. This band contains 51.4% of its occurrences and appears in 54.3% of the comments in the band, as against 43.3% of all comments

the "sobriety" of the presentation and packaging, bitterness—here a positive quality—and the daring use of certain ingredients such as tea or cinnamon (*cannelle*). Another important difference between these two bands is the more frequent use, in the comments on high scores, of terms designating an individual producer ("*Monsieur*", "*pâtissier*") whose "mastery" is underscored. The middle band also contains remarks about the thickness of the enrobing or an excess of sugar,[13] but is chiefly characterised by the use of markers of respect for the firm's "craft" [*métier*], "tradition" and "reputation" in making chocolates that are now more frequently described as "*douceurs*" (meaning "sweets" but offering here a positive counterpart to "friandises"), and whose originality is saluted.

In 2011 (Table 6.3), in the low band one again finds the markers of denigration of excess sugar and fat, of enrobings judged to be too thick, and the use of alcohol (including wine) in spite of ideas that are sometimes judged to be good and of work, which is often mentioned, on the appearance of the confectioneries. The overuse of cinnamon, which "overwhelms" the cocoa, is now denigrated, as are the use of coffee and tonka bean.[14] While imbalances and thickness are grounds for denigration, their opposites, in contrast to 1988, are no longer explicit grounds for valorisation. In the high band, the judges now look for the quality of the raw materials, the visual pleasure of the beauty and brilliance of the confectioneries, and the density, power and length on the palate of the ganaches. Here too, there are many references to the individual producer, rare in the other bands, and inferred from the tasting ("*passion*", "*talent*", "*chocolatier*"). It is a sign of a greater one-dimensionality of the comments that the middle band appears more than in 1988 as an in-between, albeit characterised by some terms used positively ("*intense*", "*crémeux*", "*delicatement*", "*raffinement*", "*subtil*").

This comparison brings to light the stable aspects of the set of standards implemented by the GCC and its proximity to an elite definition of chocolate confectionery, in particular because it privileges the most expensive ingredient (cocoa, compared to sugar and cream), and also because, in its rejection of sugar and alcohol and its appeal to "sobriety", it is not without echoes of the symbolic struggles theorised by Bourdieu (1984) as characteristic of 1960s France. This definition, developed in a wealthy *arrondissement* of Paris, is presented as a break with the generality of the chocolate market in the early 1980s. By making the rejection of the "sugary sweet" [*friandise*] the metronome of the confectionery market in France, the GCC linked up with the tradition of the earliest restaurant and hotel guides (Bertho-Lavenir, 1999): a Parisian clientele seeking in its provincial holiday retreats the confectioneries it enjoyed in Paris. From the appetite for the work of Linxe, presented as a founding element of an association of enthusiasts, the aim became to create a quality standard that could be used to describe all chocolate confectionery producers in France.

Table 6.3 Terms typical of each band (GCC, 2011)

Term	Residual	Band/Term (%)	Term/Band (%)	Term/All (%)
Low				
sucre	5.10	81.5	58.7	35.8
saveur	3.58	70.0	56.0	39.7
épais	3.09	91.7	14.7	7.9
vin	2.36	100.0	6.7	3.3
papille	2.30	81.8	12.0	7.3
idée	2.28	87.5	9.3	5.3
cannelle	2.04	85.7	8.0	4.6
apparence	1.93	70.6	16.0	11.3
gras	1.77	83.3	6.7	4.0
café	1.69	72.7	10.7	7.3
discret	1.57	75.0	8.0	5.3
tonka	1.57	75.0	8.0	5.3
texture	1.51	57.4	41.3	35.8
alcool	1.47	80.0	5.3	3.3
High				
noble	4.28	80.0	20.0	3.3
passion	3.92	50.0	35.0	9.3
matière	2.99	60.0	15.0	3.3
beauté	2.96	50.0	20.0	5.3
ingrédient	2.74	37.5	30.0	10.6
brillant	2.66	44.4	20.0	6.0
puissant	2.24	31.6	30.0	12.6
long	1.95	33.3	20.0	7.9
talent	1.95	33.3	20.0	7.9
dense	1.94	37.5	15.0	5.3
œil	1.94	37.5	15.0	5.3
bouche	1.93	25.8	40.0	20.5
fruit	1.86	29.4	25.0	11.3
aromatique	1.69	33.3	15.0	6.0
cacao	1.64	22.2	50.0	29.8
chocolatier	1.51	23.3	35.0	19.9
Middle				
intense	3.17	83.3	17.9	7.9
crémeux	2.83	87.5	12.5	5.3
raffinement	2.81	100.0	8.9	3.3
délicatement	2.55	85.7	10.7	4.6
travail	2.42	58.3	37.5	23.8
subtil	2.40	77.8	12.5	6.0
confection	2.10	75.0	10.7	5.3

(continued)

Table 6.3 (continued)

Term	Residual	Band/Term (%)	Term/Band (%)	Term/All (%)
léger	2.03	70.0	12.5	6.6
bicouche	1.89	80.0	7.1	3.3
doux	1.89	80.0	7.1	3.3
frais	1.72	66.7	10.7	6.0

Note See note to Table 6.2. Here the Band/Term table has three rows and 120 columns

Producers' Attention to the Guide: Disputed, Dispensable and Malleable Ratings

While the quality standard that is promoted is stable, the concentration towards the highest scores (Fig. 6.1) does not seem to reveal a widening acceptance of this standard and the structuring of a market around it. The three main registers of producers' attention to the GCC presented in this section depict evaluations ill-adapted to their object, which they may ignore or may also make use of in the conduct of their commercial activity.

Denigration of a Procedure

Like the hotel trade when TripAdvisor® was launched (Cardon, 2015), chocolate confectionery production is the object of other benchmarks, defined by other guides (non-specialised or published only once), and also by peers in the context of associations and competitions. The most current register of attention to the GCC is criticism of its procedure and of the standards it applies in comparison with these other benchmarks.[15] Two grounds for denigration are recurrent among the producers who are rated.

The first is the establishment of a score independently of the experience of purchasing in a shop. For a number of producers interviewed, the GCC mimics the behaviour of an imaginary purchaser who asks a producer whose shop is hundreds of kilometres away to send confectioneries to Paris, telling him that they will be given a rating there. According to them, rating producers' daily work on the basis of the quality standard that is promoted, i.e. that which is constructed in the pages of the GCC, would on the contrary require an unannounced visit and purchase of products really offered for sale, along the lines of other evaluations. A *pâtissier-chocolatier* in a town of 40,000 inhabitants, who had his score downgraded and then decided to stop submitting his chocolates to the GCC, describes the distance of the GCC from the *Guide Michelin* (anonymous rating of a meal eaten in the restaurant) and from admission to the professional association to which he belongs, which depends in particular on peer assessment of the sensory quality and presentation of the products in the shop. According to him "when you write a guide, […] you have to visit the place, see how they do things, […] how they wrap the chocolates, what they wrap them in, how they are presented". To underline the inadequacy of the procedure for proper evaluation, he gave the example of a neighbouring producer (Dumont), who had won a score of 4 in the latest edition, but whose day-to-day offer in his shop was, in his view, both irregular (with "striped" and "lousy" chocolates in his words) and remote from the GCC standard.

The possible submission of chocolates not sold in the shop is an argument often used against the GCC. Some entrants do indeed see its procedure as a way to get a small panel to sample their new creations. Others clearly distinguish the articles submitted from those they actually sell or intend to sell. This was the case with a *chocolatier* that was given five bars and an award. He justifies the fact that he does not sell the chocolates that were submitted, on which his rating was based, by his clientele's preference for what he calls his "classic" products. For him, the guide above all recognises his capacity for creation in composing centres. That was how he explained to me why he submitted a chocolate containing a centre he had never seen among his competitors in order to "stun" the jury.

The GCC procedure is then denigrated for using quality standards that appear sometimes amnesic, sometimes too conservative.[16] On the first aspect, a *pâtissier-chocolatier* and holder of the "One of the best craftsmen of France" (MOF) title in the category *Chocolaterie-confiserie* complained that the GCC gave too little importance to the work of the *praliné* in favour of ganache, whereas *praliné* is a classic component of chocolate confectioneries, as demonstrated, in his view, by its inclusion in professional competitions: "Yet, every time you offer a confectionery [with a *praliné* centre], you feel there is some resistance, they would rather have a ganache, that drives me crazy!" He deplores the "unacceptable forgetting" of a "traditional" chocolate-making product and a distorted vision of ganache as the only criterion of a confectioner's virtuosity. In his view, "there are products that are just as hard to balance and bring off, that call for similar technical, technological know-how". That apparent rejection of *praliné* in a time "when the *Croqueurs* set themselves up and started their club, their tastings and the books that followed on" brought him to "go against the flow" and to "concentrate" on ganache.

Others see the primacy given to the most delicate enrobings as proof of the conservatism of the GCC. A restaurant *pâtissier* who used to work in the workshops of *chocolatiers* describes the recent downgrading of a Parisian *pâtissier* (Jean) as the penalisation of an avant-garde (which plays on the thickness of its enrobings). He nonetheless sees this downgrading as of little consequence for Jean's future sales:

> Jean's chocolates are far from being the most beautiful; you can find much better-looking ones. But not many that are so good. […] He tries to work on his confectioneries with complex ganaches, spices, fruits, original textures […] whereas chocolates up to now have been finer-grained *ganache* in the classic style of the *Maison du chocolat*, and so on. And then there are people who say 'Yeah, Jean's enrobing is a bit too thick.' […] And he says 'I don't give a damn. You know what, I like thicker enrobing; that way, when you bite into it, it's a bit like eating a slice of *foie gras*, there are real textures there.' […] It only took four or five people who said: 'Really, the enrobing is too thick, it makes me sick.' […]. And so he lost a bar. But Jean couldn't care less whether it's one bar, zero, whatever… Jean's is business is above all that.

The charge of conservatism also extends to the fact that the GCC benchmark turns its back on some production methods introduced in the last two decades. A producer running a firm employing twenty people in a city of 200,000 inhabitants adopted a "one-shot" method in which the centre is simultaneously moulded and enrobed. In his view, this method offers significant gains in productivity and hygiene and also the possibility of many variations in the structure of the confectionery. What he calls the "traditional" method, used by Linxe in particular, consists in running a ganache into a frame, letting it harden for a day or two, cutting it into bite-sized pieces and then enrobing them with chocolate. The appearance of one-shot confectioneries, in particular the thickness and the shininess of their enrobing, differs radically from those. The interviewee attributed the drop in his score solely to his adoption of this method. Looking back after some years, he nonetheless thinks that this downgrading, and then his disappearance from the GCC after he stopped sending samples, have not affected his sales. Other producers using the one-shot technique also regret too what they see as conservatism on the part of the GCC. To adapt, they sometimes hide this innovative method. One explained me that he enrobes his chocolates a second time so as to give them the matt appearance of "traditional" craft candies and then to skirt the initial reluctance of tasters for shiny candies that look like mass-produced ones.

The distance from the definitions of confectionery quality applied by peers, some which have been set out above (the whole range of products offered, the importance of *pralinés*, innovative techniques), is often attributed to the GCC's declared amateurism. Its judges are not thought to have either the rigour or the evaluation skills of the producers or even of other reviewers. As regards rigour, one participant criticised the opacity of the scoring criteria. As he sees it, the evaluation seems to be limited to conformity with the taste of each judge and does not follow any protocol urging judges to "forget themselves" while evaluating the products, he exemplifies: "If it's a chocolate with aniseed, 'Shit, I don't like aniseed, so I'll give it two'? No!". He underlines the jerky career of some producers' notations: "How come one year a *chocolatier* gets four bars and the next year only two? Has the guy forgotten how to do his job?"

The distance from the definitions of quality shared by the producers can also be expressed in a vehement rejection of ratings given by a Parisian club of amateurs. For example, a holder of the title MOF (see note 4), whose scores had varied widely over the years, saw this oscillation as the sign of the judge's incompetence, which had also led the editors of the GCC to treat as equivalent producers whom the interviewee saw as belonging to two distinct worlds of production.

> I told them: '[...] Your scoring system makes no sense. It's not for pet-it-bourgeois Parisian women to give lessons on chocolate to *chocolatiers* like us.... You think you can teach me about materials I've worked with for 25 years? [...] People like Palmier [a producer in the region], he turns out factory-made shitty chocolate just for the money, it's... everything I hate, he's a disgusting character, his products are disgusting, and he gets three bars.' [I said to them:] 'Look, you hand out three bars to a guy like that and three bars to someone like me?'

These comments also indicate that in spite of shared disparagement of the procedure, the scores published are consulted by the evaluees and their peers, who are attentive to a formalised evaluation of chocolate confectioneries offering one of the few scales of comparison that might be mobilised.

Withdrawal After a Low Rating

A second register of attention, encountered several times in the previous sub-section, consists in no longer submitting samples after receiving a poor score. This is reflected in the differing rates of disappearance from one edition to another, according to the score obtained: firms that are given a low rating reappear in the next edition much less often than the others (Fig. 6.2). Between 1988 and 2010, the variations in these rates also seem to depend partly on the length of time between editions. In this period of sporadic editions, the average annual evaporation rates are stable, ranging between 11.4 and 12% overall.

This first comparison does not, however, take account of possible cessation of confectionery production by the firms in question. One way round this pitfall is to study the reviews of these firms in one of the categories associated with *pâtisserie-confiserie* in the other guide listing chocolate confectionery producers over the same period as the GCC, namely the *Guide des gourmands* (GG). This guide differs from the GCC in two ways. On the one hand, it presents itself essentially as a selection of producers. The scoring is therefore more rudimentary and is not presented as the editors' main activity: most of the firms are simply

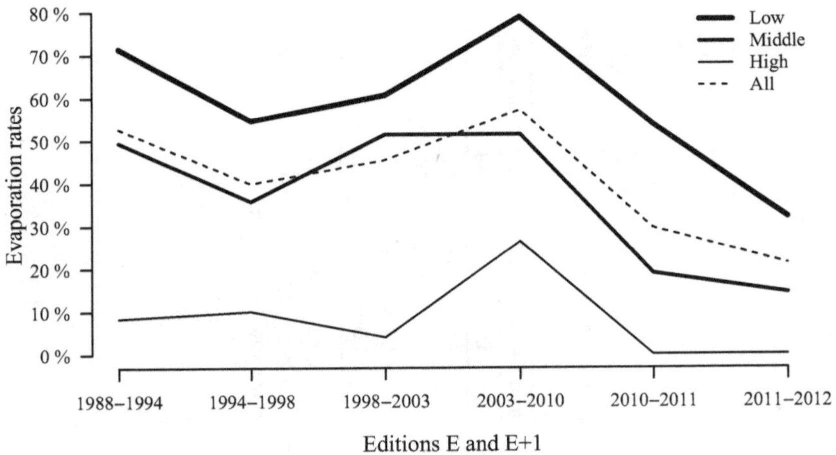

Fig. 6.2 Proportion of firms absent from edition E+1 by band of aggregate score in edition E ($N = 899$. Perimeter: All reviews in the six editions published between 1988 and 2011. How to read: About 9% of firms in the "High" band in 1988 do not appear in the next edition [1994]. This is the case for about 50% of the firms in the "Middle" band.)

listed; "*coq*" (cockerel) and "*coq d'or*" (golden cockerel) are associated with a minority of firms, which, with a few exceptions, retain this distinction from one edition to another.[17] On the other hand, this guide's selection is not based on voluntary participation. Presence from one edition to another is therefore more stable.[18]

For each edition E of the GCC, the firms that retain their presence in the GG between this edition E and the next edition E+1 of the GCC form coherent subsets to study the relationship between score and evaporation.[19] The distribution of evaporation rates by scoring band in the GCC for firms also listed in the GG (Table 6.4) shows regularities similar to those observed for the whole set of firms: the rate is always highest for the lowest-scoring firms (although these are under-represented in the GG) and always weakest for the highest-scoring firms. In three periods out of four, more than half the low-scoring firms did not renew their participation, although they are still running. Among middle-band firms, more than a third do not renew their participation. With the

Table 6.4 Proportion of firms absent from GCC edition E+1 by aggregate score band in edition E among firms maintaining their presence in the GG

Editions of GCC		Editions of GG	Evaporation rate between E and E+1 (Percentage base in brackets)			
E	E+1		High	Medium	Low	All
1988	1994	1989–1995	0% (18)	34.1% (44)	52.4% (21)	31.3% (83)
1994	1998	1995–1999	0% (8)	29.2% (48)	31.6% (19)	26.7% (75)
1998	2003	1999–2003	0% (16)	50% (38)	54.5% (11)	38.5% (65)
2003	2010	2003–2011	8.3% (12)	39.3% (28)	60% (10)	36.0% (50)

Perimeter: Firms present in GCC edition E and maintaining presence in GG between GCC editions E and E+1
How to read: Of the 83 firms listed in the GCC in 1988 and maintaining their presence in the GG between 1989 and 1995, 31.3% do not appear in the 1994 edition of the GCC. This proportion rises to 52.4% for the 21 firms in the "low" band

exception of one firm, which disappears from the GCC between 2003 and 2010, all the highest-scoring firms that can be confirmed as still running renewed their participation.

This comparison supports the hypothesis, which emerges from several interviews, that in many cases low scores lead *chocolatiers* to withdraw from further participation in the ratings.[20] The third register of attention sheds light on this high rate of withdrawal.

Working to Transform the Ratings: Used, but Detached from Their Benchmark

Who uses the GCC to buy confectioneries? When a producer in an interview addresses the question, it always leads more or less to the same supposition: no one, or hardly anyone. Foreign retailers—purchasers who are very attentive to guides and other recurrent forms of evaluation (especially competitions and membership of professional associations)—were often mentioned as an exceptional counter-example. For instance, an "MOF" running two shops in which he mainly sells chocolate confectioneries considers that his listing in the GCC in the early 2000s with a score of four bars was one of the factors arousing the interest of a Japanese importer and a retailer specialising in Internet sales of boxes of chocolates. A producer in a town of 15,000 inhabitants whose chocolates are sold in several Japanese department stores believes that his ranking in the "Top Ten" of *chocolatiers* listed in Japan, published in a Tokyo magazine, compensates, in the eyes of his importer, for his relatively low score of three bars in the GCC.

Except for this very restricted readership, the fiction of a mobile customer, choosing a chocolate shop on the basis of critical reviews, gives way to the image of an archipelago of niche markets with a narrow perimeter around each producer, within which he competes with only a few other chocolate confectioners, despite the possibilities of transporting and conserving these products. In this regard, the Michelin restaurant guide serves as a recurrent contrast. For example, when the GCC was mentioned to a *pâtissier* who had been in business, with ten employees, for 40 years and had appeared in the first edition, interrupted himself to explain how little interest his clientele, mainly from his town and its surroundings, had in that type of ranking, contrary to a restaurant rated in the Michelin guide that welcomes international customers.

This shared understanding sheds light on a third register of attention: when producers for their self-description use GCC scores, they are generally detached from their benchmark.

GCC reviews may support the flattering descriptions of a producer's work on a circumscribed market where there are only rarely competitors who are also listed. Like the distinctions deployed by craftsmen, they are "perceived by the producers as tools for singularisation" (Jourdain, 2010: 28). The rating obtained is then set in contrast with the absence of listing, not with the other ratings of the GCC.[21] Two uses of scores illustrate the dissimulation of the benchmark of comparison.

First, as a guide dedicated to chocolate, the GCC is cited as proof of identity as a *chocolatier*. A confectioner [*pâtissier*] with ten employees in a town of 50,000 inhabitants saw his appearance in the guide, which was then envisaged, as a chance to be identified as a *chocolatier* standing out from his local competitors. At the time of our interview, he is also considering entering the MOF competition in the category *chocolaterie-confiserie* and, following the example of a *pâtissier* in a nearby town, he planned to open a second shop dedicated to chocolate, with his name on the front and the description "*Chocolatier*", like his competitors who specialised only in chocolate confectioneries. In the next edition, on his first listing, he was given a below-average score of 3. This listing was nonetheless directly integrated in his advertising, playing on a confusion between the Club and the guide: "Dinny Paille has recently joined the very select 'Club des Croqueurs de chocolat,' with three bars!" Thus, a rating which can be seen as mediocre, even weak, by an observer who consults the guide and reads some sometimes unflattering comments, can be the basis of a laudatory narrative for the local clientele, highlighting the producer's membership of a "very select" group whose name includes the product with which he seeks to be identified.

Secondly, GCC ratings are often described as substitutes for other credentials in evidencing the producer's superiority over his competitors, whether they be ratings given by other guides, awards from associations of peers, or taking part in competitions. One of the privileged channels for diffusion of laudatory narratives, complementary to shop signs, is the local press, through articles reporting a listing in a guide or a prize won in a competition. A village *chocolatier* explained that his access to the local press was dependent on gaining such distinctions. He thought there was confusion among—and on—these distinctions in the minds of his customers, and that any credential conferred by a third party could allow a commercial relationship to be set up if it was reported in the local press:

> You know, in the newspapers here they don't talk about us as they do in Paris, we can't get big articles with our cakes. A few years ago, I sent [to the local daily paper] photos of the *bûches de Noël* [Yule logs] I was making that year. They replied: 'Mr Kafelnikov, if you would like to advertise, these are our rates.' To get into the papers, you need to win competitions or get prizes. [...] In my youth I won the *Coupe de France* [a sugar craft competition, here in the junior category], I wrote it on my shop front and there were newspaper articles about it. Well, from time to time an older client congratulates me on my title of '*Meilleur ouvrier de France*'. The general public don't have much idea. One of my apprentices won the '*Meilleur apprenti du monde*' ['World's best apprentice'] competition, and they congratulated me on having the world's best craftsman. The customers don't really know what it is and I don't think they care. If that brings them into the shop, so much the better; if they didn't like what they ate, they won't come back.

Contrary to what Sauder (2006) observes for American law schools, the ranking proposed by the GCC does not radically change the claims that producers may make to their customers; on the contrary, it arms them, nurturing and renewing narratives of eminence constructed by them and the local press. The reproductions of newspaper articles displayed in the shop windows or inside the shops can thus feed new narratives (X won such-and-such a competition *and* the press talked about it). This third register of attention, which reveals the importance of the commercial context in which reviews are deployed, highlights the indexicality of negative ratings, which appear as such only in relation to other scores. Detached from the initial benchmark, each of them can be a solid basis for declaring a producer's superiority in a restricted market.

Conclusion

Since 1988, the *Guide des croqueurs de chocolat* has implemented a stable scoring system, based on a regime of expert evaluation, progressively armed with a codified tasting procedure and aimed at promoting elite quality standards. While the guide is the pastime of a few enthusiasts convinced of the justification of their enterprise, confectionery producers do not make it their metronome but see it as an object open to criticism, one which they can dispense with but also exploit in their commercial activity by playing on the meanings assigned to the scores it awards.

Far from there being a consensus among the practices of the producers, the consumers and the judges, this case brings to light parallel and dissonant efforts at description of the markets by their participants. The registers through which the producers show themselves attentive to the guide underpin the conclusion that, for them, the great centralised market described by the GCC, organised around a set of quality standards, on which a mobile purchaser moves in deep uncertainty, is a far from relevant concept for understanding most purchase and production decisions. The producers more readily invoke a territorially very circumscribed notion of the markets in which their shops operate, where critical reviews are one of the tools they deploy, not simply as objects of evaluation but as transformers of a malleable written material that is available to them.

Identifying these registers does not exhaust the range of practices that are deployed around the guide and shape its role in the markets, beyond the intentions of its founders and sometimes in contradiction with them. Without restricting the study to their functions or their supposed effects, this chapter has thus aimed to describe the multiple participation of quality ratings in the markets, by examining the ways in which meaning is given to them by those who produce them and those who make use of them.

Notes

1. A previous version of this chapter was published in French in *Revue française de socio-économie* (© Editions la Découverte). The author thanks La Découverte for authorizing this publication, Richard Nice for translating the piece into English and Pierre François, Camille Herlin-Giret and the referees of *Revue française de socio-économie* for their comments.
2. In this vein, François (2011) offers an alternative framework of analysis to the functional approach to market institutions; he aims to identify these institutions through the regularities that are set up in market practices.
3. Terrio (2000) describes the work of promoting a local chocolate tradition in South-West France.
4. Several patisserie contests used to include tests in chocolate, without specialising in it. From the first edition (1933) of the category Pâtisserie-Confiserie of the examination for Un des meilleurs ouvriers de France ("One of the best craftsmen of France," MOF), the skills evaluated included "making or presenting (...) chocolate confectioneries" (Archives of the Comité d'organisation des expositions du travail, Challenges of the 1933 edition). In the 1980s, competitions exclusively dedicated to chocolate appeared. The Grand prix international de la chocolaterie, launched by a cacao processor and a professional association, has run since 1984. The Chocolaterie-Confiserie category of the MOF contest dates from 1990. These competitions dedicated to chocolate then proliferated in the 1990s.
5. According to this definition, a chocolate confectionery consists of a centre coated in chocolate (enrobing). Ganache is an emulsion of cream and chocolate. Praliné is a mixture of roasted shell fruits (hazelnut, walnut pistachio, etc.) and sugar, sometimes with added cocoa. Gianduja is a mixture of roasted shell fruits and milk chocolate, very finely ground.
6. Source: http://www.croqueurschocolat.com/guide-cote-coulisses, accessed 14 April 2014.
7. For 1988, "low" groups the first two rankings, "middle" the next two, "high" the two highest. For 1994 and 1998, "low" corresponds to 0 bars, "middle" to 1 or 2, "high" to 3 and above. For 2003, "low" corresponds to 0, "middle" to 1–3 and "high" to 4 and above. For 2010, "low" corresponds to 1 or 2, "middle" to 3 or 4, "haut" to 5. For 2011 and 2012, "low" corresponds to 1–3, "middle" to 4 and "high" to 5.

8. "Top Score" ("Le sommet") in 1988, then 3 gold bars in 1994 and 5 bars in 1998.
9. The tm package (Feinerer, Hornik, & Meyer, 2008) of the R software (R Core Team, 2013) was used to construct the corpus and the document-term matrix. The 1988 edition is compared with the 2011 edition, the most recent available at the time of data input.
10. The analysis would otherwise have been polarised by these oppositions.
11. This difference is partly due to the larger number of comments in 1988 and their greater average length (520 characters vs. 387 in 2011).
12. Although the chocolates were judged in Paris, in a large number of reviews the 1988 edition assesses the places where they are sold, although this is not an explicit scoring criterion. These elements may derive from observations made by the members of the Club in the course of their travels.
13. "Sucre" is the third most frequent term in the band—as against second in the low band and fifteenth in the high band. The term "proportion," which appears in Table 6.2, is mainly associated with the description of an excess of sugar.
14. The fruit of the Brazilian teak (tonka in the Tupi language), characterised by its smell of freshly cut hay due to its high coumarin content.
15. Studies of ranking in higher education have shown how common this reaction is (Espeland & Sauder, 2007; Mignot-Gérard & Sarfati, 2015).
16. Linkage to a historical context is a characteristic of quality standards as soon as they are made explicit and codified. See for instance, Stanziani (2005) on the legal norms of food quality or Naulin (2015) on the succession of quality standards in restaurant reviewing.
17. 14% of the firms in the pâtisserie-confiserie category were associated with one of these distinctions in 1988, 37.5% in 1997. The "cockerels" then disappeared and only 7% of the firms were formally separated from the 93% that were simply mentioned.
18. The average rate of evaporation is around 2%.
19. To remove all doubt as to the anteriority of appearance in the GG (often published several months before the GCC), equivalence between an edition of the GCC and the following year's edition of the GG is privileged when possible. For example, a listing in the GCC in 1994 is compared with a listing in the GG in 1995. In the archive consulted, the 2004 edition of the GG was not available. The 2003 edition

of the GCC is therefore compared with the 2003 edition of the GG, published a few months earlier. The GG was not published in 2012 (except for addenda). The last movement considered is therefore that between 2003 and 2010.

20. A nuance to be noted here is that it may be that some producers who are listed do not appear in the GCC because of the selection performed before the evaluations so to retain only the "best." However, the numerous cases of stable trajectories in the low scores (on average, from 1994 to 2012, over half the firms in the "low" category that were also listed in the previous edition had already appeared in this category) and the high evaporation rate of firms given intermediate scores (Fig. 6.2) suggest that this nuance need not concern us too much.
21. We see the primacy of "visibility" (the fact of being reviewed) over "modality" (the positive or negative tone of the review) identified by Shrum (1991).

Bibliography

Bertho-Lavenir, C. (1999). *La roue et le stylo: comment nous sommes devenus touristes*. Paris: Odile Jacob.

Blank, G. (2006). *Critics, ratings and society: The sociology of reviews*. Lanham, MD: Rowman & Littlefield.

Bonnet, E. (2004). Les critiques gastronomiques: quelques caractéristiques d'une activité experte. *Sociétés contemporaines, 53*, 135–155.

Bourdieu, P. (1984 [1979]). *Distinction: A social critique of the judgment of taste*. Cambridge, MA: Harvard University Press.

Cardon, V. (2015). La guerre des étoiles. La réputation hôtelière à l'épreuve du web contributif. *Revue d'anthropologie des connaissances, 9*(1), 39–61.

Casella, P., & Shapiro, R. (1991). *Chocolatier*. Noisy-le-Grand: Éditions de l'ANDEP.

Chauvin, P.-M. (2011). Extension du domaine de la note: Robert Parker comme saillance du marché des grands vins de Bordeaux. In P. François (Ed.), *Vie et mort des institutions marchandes* (pp. 39–77). Paris: Presses de Sciences Po.

Dodier, N., & Barbot, J. (2016). La force des dispositifs. *Annales, Histoire, Sciences sociales, 71*(2), 421–450.

Espeland, W., & Stevens, M. (1998). Commensuration as a social process. *Annual Review of Sociology, 24,* 313–343.
Espeland, W., & Sauder, M. (2007). Rankings and reactivity: How public measures recreate social worlds. *American Journal of Sociology, 113*(1), 1–40.
Fantasia, R. (2010). Cooking the books' of the French gastronomic field. In E. Silvva & A. Warde (Eds.), *Cultural analysis and Bourdieu's legacy* (pp. 28–44). London: Routledge.
Feinerer, I., Hornik, K., & Meyer, D. (2008). Text mining infrastructure in R. *Journal of Statistical Software, 25*(5), 1–54.
Fernandez, J.-L. (2004). *La critique vinicole en France: pouvoir de prescription et construction de la confiance*. Paris: L'Harmattan.
François, P. (2011). Puissance et genèse des institutions: un cadre analytique In P. François (Ed.), *Vie et mort des institutions marchandes* (pp. 39–77). Paris: Presses de Sciences Po.
Haberman, S. J. (1973). The analysis of residuals in cross-classified tables. *Biometrics, 29*(1), 205–220.
Jamerson, H. (2009). Intoxicators, educators, and gatekeepers: The enactment of symbolic boundaries in Napa Valley wineries. *Poetics, 37,* 383–398.
Jourdain, A. (2010). La construction sociale de la singularité: une stratégie entrepreneuriale des artisans d'art. *Revue française de socio-économie, 6,* 13–30.
Karpik, L. (2000). Le Guide rouge Michelin. *Sociologie du travail, 42*(3), 369–389.
Lane, C. (2013). Taste makers in the 'fine-dining' restaurant industry: The attribution of aesthetic and economic value by gastronomic guides. *Poetics, 42,* 342–365.
Linxe, R. (1992). *La Maison du chocolat*. Paris: Robert Laffont.
Mallard, A. (2000). La presse de consommation et le marché: enquête sur le tiers consumériste. *Sociologie du travail, 42,* 391–409.
Marty, A., & Ivanoff, G. (1996). *Cercles et réseaux d'influence: le guide des clubs, cercles et réseaux d'affaires en Île-de-France*. Paris: Les Presses du management.
Mignot-Gérard, S., & Sarfati, F. (2015). Dispositif de jugement sur la qualité ou instrument de construction de la réputation? *Le cas d'un classement universitaire, Terrains & Travaux, 26,* 167–185.
Naulin, S. (2015). Se faire un nom: Les ressorts de la singularisation des critiques gastronomiques. *Sociologie du travail, 57*(3), 322–343.
Pessis, J. (2011). *Le petit roman du chocolat*. Monaco: Éditions du Rocher.

R Core Team (2013). R: A language and environment for statistical computing, Version 3.0.2, Vienna.

Rao, H., Monin, P., & Durand, R. (2005). Border crossing: Bricolage and the Erosion of categorical boundaries in French Gastronomy. *American Sociological Review, 70*(6), 968–991.

Sauder, M. (2006). Third parties and status position: How the characteristics of status systems matter. *Theory and Society, 35*(3), 299–321.

Shrum, W. (1991). Critics and publics: Cultural mediation in highbrow and popular performing arts. *American Journal of Sociology, 97*(2), 347–375.

Stanziani, A. (2005). *Histoire de la qualité alimentaire (xixe–xxe siècles)*. Paris: Seuil.

Surlemont, B., & Johnson, C. (2005). The role of guides in artistic industries: The special case of the star' system in the haute-cuisine sector. *Managing Service Quality, 15*(6), 577–590.

Terrio, S. J. (2000). *Crafting the culture and history of French chocolate*. Los Angeles: University of California Press.

7

Alone or in Concert? Creative Entrepreneurs and the Role of Multiple Institutional Logics in Crowdfunding Pitches

Raissa Pershina and Birthe Soppe

Introduction

The rise of digital technologies has fostered profound changes in the creative industries. Digital technologies not only catalyze novel products, service innovations, and business models (Benghozi & Salvador, 2016; Rüling & Duymedjian, 2014) but also offer novel forms of resource acquisition and new digital platforms and tools to interact with a large audience. Crowdfunding platforms are among those tools that aspiring entrepreneurs increasingly rely on to attract financial resources from the public, i.e., the "crowd," in order to realize, grow, and sustain a business idea or project (Mollick, 2014). The number of crowdfunding platforms has rapidly been growing in recent years (Massolution, 2015), and pitching ideas and projects online has become increasingly

R. Pershina (✉) · B. Soppe
University of Oslo, Oslo, Norway
e-mail: raissa.pershina@sfe.uio.no

B. Soppe
University of Innsbruck, Innsbruck, Austria

J. Strandgaard Pedersen et al. (eds.), *Technology and Creativity*,
https://doi.org/10.1007/978-3-030-17566-5_7

important for creative entrepreneurs, that is, individuals and small firms pursuing entrepreneurial activities in the hopes of attaining both artistic freedom and fame as well as financial gain and profit (Henry, 2007; Svejenova, Slavich, & AbdelGawad, 2015).

Given the novelty and lack of proven entrepreneurial track records on the one side and the largely unknown crowd of investors on the other, the creation of a persuasive and appealing pitch seems to be a crucial first step if not an asset for nascent entrepreneurs seeking to gain traction. A business pitch is used by an entrepreneur (i.e., the pitcher) to persuade an investor to provide (financial) resources (Pollack, Rutherford, & Nagy, 2012). Whereas traditional business pitches involve face-to-face interviews or presentations in front of a specific group of investors, crowdfunding platforms replace face-to-face pitching with a project webpage where aspiring entrepreneurs post text, images, and short videos to pitch their projects to a large, often unknown crowd for financial support. Carefully selecting a persuasive pitching strategy may be worthwhile as the stakes are high, with some projects raising millions of dollars, even on reward-based crowdfunding platforms such as Kickstarter (Kerr, 2017; Parker, 2017).

However, pitching is not as straightforward as it may seem, particularly for creative entrepreneurs who typically straddle multiple and conflicting institutional logics (Greenwood, Raynard, Kodeih, Micelotta, & Lounsbury, 2011). Logics are taken-for-granted practices and rules that define how individuals and organizations "reproduce their material subsistence, organize time and space, and provide meaning to their social reality" (Thornton & Ocasio, 1999: 804). Stemming from distinct social institutions, social actors are often exposed to conflicting logics available to them (Friedland & Alford, 1991). The two contradicting logics that have been repeatedly demonstrated to work on members of the creative and cultural industries are the aesthetic logic and business logic (Eikhof & Haunschild, 2006; Jones, Livne-Tarandach, & Balachandra, 2010). The aesthetic logic refers to the professional identity of creatives anchored in art and aesthetics (Glynn & Lounsbury, 2005; Thornton, Jones, & Kury, 2005). In contrast, the business logic emphasizes managerial and efficiency aspects and an economically oriented setup (Jones et al., 2010; Reay & Hinings, 2009).

This conflict of logics is reflected in business pitches within the realm of the creative industries. Creative entrepreneurs often face the trade-off of whether to abide by requirements dictated by the business world emphasizing elements such as likely commercial success, efficiency, and effective processes in managing and completing new projects, or to follow guidelines prescribed by the aesthetic logic and highlight the creative skill and artistic potential of their ideas.

While much of the previous research has recognized that straddling multiple logics involves tensions and contradicting prescriptions for action inside organizations (Battilana, Sengul, Pache, & Model, 2015; Glynn, 2000), we know little about how external constituencies such as investors deal with contradicting logics in their evaluation of entrepreneurial ideas. This lack of research is surprising given that not only entrepreneurs but also investors may have difficulties in interpreting conflicting logics. We therefore ask the following research question: *What role do multiple logics play in crowdfunding pitches crafted by creative entrepreneurs seeking to mobilize backers to financially support their projects?*

We believe that this is an important question to investigate because institutional logics play an important role in legitimacy-seeking efforts and meaning-making and may thus influence the propensity for resource support. Indeed, prior research has suggested that institutional aspects are critical cultural and symbolic resources for entrepreneurs seeking to leverage resource flows from external audiences (Lounsbury & Glynn, 2001). However, it has also been suggested that straddling multiple logics and social categories creates confusion among potential investors that may reduce legitimacy (Doblinger, Soppe, & Huber, 2019; Zuckerman, 1999). Thus, in this ambiguous and nascent setting with no clear institutional template to draw on for creative entrepreneurs, which logic should be emphasized to garner support from investors? Does the use of multiple logics in concert add to the ambiguity or reduce it? Or is one logic alone more relevant to potential investors than another, and if so, which one and under what conditions?

In this paper, we focus on the aesthetic and business logics in crowdfunding business pitches and analyze their role alone as well as in concert in mobilizing backers to financially support ideas in the creative industries. The empirical setting for our study is the crowdfunding platform

Kickstarter, which was launched in 2009 and has become the largest reward-based platform for crowdfunding entrepreneurs (Barnett, 2013). We focus on analyzing business pitches for digital games. Digital games are a highly relevant empirical context given the purpose of our study because they are complex creative products that represent an important part of the creative and cultural sector (Flew, 2012). We specifically concentrate on the indie-development scene and analyze a sample of almost 500 digital game projects on Kickstarter, including video pitches as those have been widely recognized as one of the most important components of crowdfunding campaigns (Almerico, 2014).

Using multiple linear regression analysis to analyze our data, in contrast to our hypothesized relationship, we find that a hybrid approach to pitch creation, that is, two contrasting logics in concert, discourages potential backers from supporting creative entrepreneurs. Instead, for game creators whose projects are at an early stage of development, emphasizing the business logic seems most appealing to investors, while those at an advanced stage are more likely to garner resources by employing the aesthetic logic.

Overall, the findings of our study advance insights at the intersection between the literature on entrepreneurship and institutions and hold important implications for the literature on creative industries and crowdfunding. First, studying creative entrepreneurship in the crowdfunding setting is intriguing because it makes it possible to investigate entrepreneurial efforts and institutional processes that occur during the earliest stages of new venture formation. Although these emerging stages have been highlighted as particularly important (Aldrich, 1999; Lounsbury & Glynn, 2001), they have received only scant attention from entrepreneurship scholars, probably given the difficulties in data access. Our study offers insights into nascent entrepreneur-investor interactions. Second, although business pitches and resource acquisition represent prominent topics in the entrepreneurship literature (e.g., Balachandra, 2011; Brush, Greene, & Hart, 2001; Chen, Yao, & Kotha, 2009; O'Connor, 2002; Zimmerman & Zeitz, 2002), little research has examined the role of institutional aspects in business pitches. Our study advances existing insights by investigating how several logics in concert or alone have an impact on social evaluation by crowdfunding investors at distinct stages of project development.

Theoretical Orientation

Business Pitches and Entrepreneurial Resource Acquisition

To bring new ideas to life and grow and sustain them, entrepreneurs often engage in activities such as business pitches that are focused on securing support and attracting financial resources. During a business pitch, an entrepreneur (i.e., the pitcher) seeks to persuade an investor to provide resources (e.g., financial capital) (Pollack et al., 2012). Traditionally, pitching involved face-to-face interviews or presentations. In the creative industries, a key example would be Hollywood pitch meetings, in which screenwriters pitch their ideas about a new film screenplay to a producer or studio executive in ca. 20 minutes (Elsbach & Kramer, 2003). The rise of digital platforms such as crowdfunding circumvents face-to-face pitching but allows online pitching of a business idea to gather money for a project from the public, i.e., the unknown crowd.

In the entrepreneurship literature, business pitches and resource acquisition represent prominent topics (e.g., Balachandra, 2011; Brush et al., 2001; Chen et al., 2009; O'Connor, 2002; Zimmerman & Zeitz, 2002). Much of this literature has explored a variety of factors determining successful business pitches and associated resource acquisition. One line of work revolves around the personality attributes of the presenter, that is, entrepreneurs' characteristics and traits, including their perceived coachability and competence (Balachandra, 2011), communication (Clark, 2008) and social skills (Baron & Markman, 2003), preparedness (Galbraith, McKinney, DeNoble, & Ehrlich, 2014; Pollack et al., 2012), body language and facial expressiveness (Chen et al., 2009), gender (Balachandra, Briggs, Eddleston, & Brush, 2013), and even physical attractiveness (Brooks, Huang, Kearney, & Murray, 2014). Another line of work centers on what aspects of pitches affect funding outcomes. For instance, researchers have looked at the impact and characteristics of language utilized

(Gorbatai & Nelson, 2015; Pietraszkiewicz, Soppe, & Formanowicz, 2017) and narrative styles (Maiolini, Cappa, Leone, & Pinelli, 2018; O'Connor, 2002). It has been investigated how these various factors ultimately affect decision-making by providers of key financial resources, including venture capitalists (Chen et al., 2009), angel and informal investors (Balachandra, 2011; Erikson & Sørheim, 2005), clients (Baron & Markman, 2003), the government (Jones et al., 2010), and the larger unknown crowd (Pietraszkiewicz et al., 2017).

Overall, the existing literature suggests that the chances of successful resource acquisition can be increased by putting considerable effort in the construction and style of a business pitch. Specifically, symbolic management and the adoption of winning presentational techniques and strategies may help individuals to gain legitimacy and influence audiences' reactions and judgments (Aldrich & Fiol, 1994; Jones et al., 2010). Although an ample body of work has been dedicated to investigating these critical topics, surprisingly little attention has been devoted to the role of institutional aspects in business pitches (for a notable exception, see, Jones et al., 2010).

In this paper, we examine institutional logics in crowdfunding business pitches and the role they may play in mobilizing backers to financially support the ideas of creative entrepreneurs. We believe that this is important to investigate because creative entrepreneurs have a variety of logics to draw from to obtain legitimacy and financial support. Indeed, it has been argued that judgements over resources "typically involve dynamic processes that are strongly dependent on context, that is, they are subject to localized and situated norms and expectations" (Elsbach & Kramer, 2003: 285). Thus, investigating the use and impact of multiple institutional logics in efforts related to mobilizing backers to provide resources seems critical, as logics are central for being recognized and viewed as legitimate and trustworthy.

Conflicting Institutional Logics in the Creative Industries: Aesthetic and Business Logics

Institutional logics may play an important role in increasing the propensity for resource acquisition through business pitches, including pitches via novel digital platforms such as crowdfunding. Particularly in the situation in which the audience and the aspiring entrepreneurs are (largely) unknown to one another and in which assessments are made before an actual product or service is being produced, institutional logics may provide important cues for meaning making and legitimacy in the eyes of potential backers. Logics provide meaning to the audience and guide social evaluation by offering a set of principles, values, and beliefs regarding how to interpret and act (Greenwood et al., 2011; Thornton, 2004). Logics may thus contribute to overcoming the high level of uncertainty associated with entrepreneurship in general and crowdfunding in particular.

Organizations and entrepreneurs in many contexts have been shown to straddle multiple, often conflicting institutional logics. In the creative and cultural industries, one most prominent and frequently encountered set of competing logics involves the aesthetic logic and business logic (Eikhof & Haunschild, 2006; Glynn, 2000; Jones & Livne-Tarandach, 2008; Pershina & Soppe, 2017). The business logic refers to elements such as commercial success, efficiency, and effective processes in managing and completing new projects, while the aesthetic logic becomes visible in references to creativity, originality of design, artistic work, and the professional identity of the creator. Existing research has looked at the nature of the relationship between these logics and how they inform creative production (Eikhof & Haunschild, 2007), the mechanisms behind managing the involved tensions (Alvarez, Mazza, Pedersen, & Svejenova, 2005) and the strategies that creative organizations utilize to create value opportunities despite conflicting logics (Dalpiaz, Rindova, & Ravasi, 2016; Pershina & Soppe, 2017).

Previous literature has identified various types of responses to institutional pluralism by organizations (e.g., Greenwood et al., 2011; Oliver, 1991; Pache & Santos, 2010) as well as individuals (e.g., Smets, Jarzabkowski, Burke, & Spee, 2015), which can be summarized under two archetypal responses to multiple logics. Logics in concert emphasize the coexistence (Goodrick & Reay, 2011; Smets et al., 2015), hybridization (Pache & Santos, 2013; Pershina & Soppe, 2017), and bricolage (Rao, Monin, & Durand, 2005) of multiple logics, while focusing on a single logic alone highlights the avoidance of blending logics, including prioritizing, filtering, and selecting one dominant logic over another (Goodrick & Reay, 2011; Oliver, 1991; Pache & Santos, 2010). We argue that this set of responses to multiple logics is also evident in business pitches. In the context of our study, we suggest that a business pitch by an aspiring creative entrepreneur is predominantly guided by either (1) the aesthetic logic, (2) the business logic, or (3) a blend of both logics. We seek to illuminate which way of handling multiple institutional logics in business pitches supports resource acquisition.

Recently, both the business and aesthetic logics have been recognized as salient in business pitches as well as in influencing audiences' judgments within the creative industries (Glynn & Lounsbury, 2005; Jones et al., 2010). For instance, Jones et al. (2010), in their study of entrepreneurial architecture firms' pitches to win state construction projects, found the business logic to be the least effective in obtaining clients, with the professional logic (anchored in the aesthetic logic, see Thornton & Ocasio, 2008) being the most effective. While these findings were observed in the context of obtaining critical resources through project acquisition and interaction with professional peers, it has been suggested that the effects may be different in different settings, especially when the "mass-market audience" takes on the role of a disposer of financial capital (Jones et al., 2010: 205).

On the one hand, mass-market audiences on crowdfunding platforms, as opposed to professional peers, may indeed take a different stance on evaluating pitches and lend more value to the business logic. Research has indicated that crowdfunding is highly skewed, with a majority of campaigns failing (see Agrawal, Catalini, & Goldfarb, 2014). Those that manage to reach the goal frequently delay the delivery of rewards, sometimes canceling product implementations altogether, with funders obtaining "neither promised rewards nor their money back" (McKenny, Allison, Ketchen, Short, & Ireland, 2017: 295). Therefore, adopting a business logic, addressing the crowd's pragmatic concerns and offering a certain degree of reassurance might positively affect crowdfunding outcomes.

On the other hand, creative entrepreneurs heavily rely on the patronage and loyalty of fans that are both followers and consumers of cultural products and are driven by an appreciation of artistic and skillful product ideas, including the feelings and emotions they induce (Frey & Eichenberger, 1995). As Throsby (2001) writes, "the idea of art as mystery, a riddle whose secrets are not easily unlocked, has a wider appeal than we might think" (p. xi). Thus, foregrounding creativity and alluring potential fans and funders with the promise of an aesthetic experience could lead to positive crowdfunding outcomes.

Creative entrepreneurs who draw on both logics simultaneously may thus be likely to appeal to both types of potential investors and their legitimacy requests and concerns, including lay investors as well as fans of artistic projects and ideas. Therefore, we expect that creative entrepreneurs who at least partially satisfy the demands of both logics (Pache & Santos, 2013) and employ a hybrid approach to crowdfunding pitches by blending the aesthetic and business logics are more likely to attract funders to support their creative projects via crowdfunding:

Hypothesis 1 A creative project will obtain a higher number of crowdfunding backers if a hybrid approach (blend of aesthetic and business logics) is used to pitch the project.

Idea Development Stage and Institutional Logics

Entrepreneurs routinely underestimate the amount of time, efforts, and resources required to bring an idea to life (Brush et al., 2001; Dailey & Mumford, 2006), which commonly creates uncertainty for evaluators. Therefore, considerations about where in the development process an idea stands—at the very beginning or more advanced—and how much effort and resources have already been invested in it may play an important role in making the decision to fund or not (Mason & Stark, 2004; Pindyck, 1993). This is applicable not only to the context of business ventures and traditional investors such as venture capitalists but potentially also to the creative and cultural industries and the context of crowdfunding. An example from the movie industry demonstrates that potential buyers of movie scripts are reluctant to even meet with sellers of early-stage movie ideas, especially in cases when the sellers are unknown and have no strong track record (Luo, 2014).

Building on these insights, we argue that the development stage of an idea or project presented via crowdfunding affects backers' decision to pledge for a creative project or not. Specifically, we suggest that entrepreneurs who seek to acquire funding for projects at an early stage of development, a situation in which uncertainty is especially high for investors, can mitigate the high level of uncertainty by employing the business logic in their pitching. Highlighting potential commercial success and outlining an effective plan and process in managing and completing a proposed project may be likely to address crowd investors' main concerns related to early-stage projects. We thus hypothesize as follows:

Hypothesis 2a A creative project at an early stage of development will obtain a higher number of crowdfunding backers if the business logic is used to pitch the project.

In turn, we hypothesize that for creative projects at an advanced stage, a situation with lower uncertainty surrounding the completion of the project, the aesthetic logic emphasizing the novelty, creativity, and artistic design aspects of the soon-to-be-finished product may be more likely to appeal to backers interested in helping the project to finally "come to life."

Hypothesis 2b A creative project at an advanced stage of development will obtain a higher number of crowdfunding backers if the aesthetic logic is used to pitch the project.

Methods

Empirical Setting

The empirical setting for our study is business pitches for digital games on the crowdfunding platform Kickstarter. Kickstarter was launched in 2009 and has become the largest platform for crowdfunding entrepreneurs (Barnett, 2013), visited daily by approximately 1 million people. Digital games are a highly relevant empirical context given the purpose of our study because, first, they are complex, creative products, and represent an important part of the creative and cultural sector (Flew, 2012). Second, logic multiplicity seems deeply ingrained in the development of these games. On the one hand, digital games "are an intrinsic part of contemporary global flows of cultural goods," while on the other hand, they are "merely commodities, created as cheaply as possible whose value is dependent on what the customer is willing to pay for them" (Kerr, 2006: 1). Consequently, creators of digital games are guided by both the aesthetic and business logics.

In this study, we specifically focus on the indie-development scene. While large corporations and creators of massive titles (e.g., Blizzard, Electronic Arts) are equipped with large development teams and have access to significant financial resources, indie (i.e., independent) studios are small (sometimes a one-man show), having little or no financial support from a game publisher or investors. In the indie-game community, crowdfunding has become an increasingly prominent way to raise money. The growing importance of this type of funding is reflected in both the amount of game projects posted on large main crowdfunding platforms such as Kickstarter and the emergence of specialized equity crowdfunding platforms for game projects (e.g., Fig.co).

By nature, indie game developers prioritize and enjoy their creative freedom and follow their original ideas and visions in designing the games. Therefore, indie game development is clearly rooted in the aesthetic logic. However, like any other entrepreneur or organization, indie studios need to meet the bottom line to survive and address financial and market considerations. Table 7.1 provides a detailed overview of

Table 7.1 Comparison of the aesthetic and business logics in digital games

Characteristics	Aesthetic logic	Business logic
Source of identity	Game creation as art	Game creation as business
Sources of legitimacy	Reputation of game designer and aesthetics of game design	Scale of the firm and market position, strong game portfolio
Mission and goals	Building reputation, development of game design skills	Building profitable firm with a strong market position
Basis of attention	Incarnation of designer's vision and resolving development problems	Resource competition and profit generation
Basis of strategy	Maintaining creative freedom and independence	Satisfying market and partners' expectations, building strong portfolio of commercially successful products
Guiding principle in product design	Creative vision and intuition, values, and beliefs revolving around originality, creativity, and artistic freedom	Stakeholder demands, monetization, utilization of previously commercially successful design ideas and proven game mechanics
Product identity	Games as art and craft, and a part of cultural production, which serves as a source of artistic pride	Games as commodities
Focus of attention	Emphasis on creating games with original gameplays and creative, novel stories	Emphasis on creating games that are profitable
Basis of attention in resource acquisition (pitching strategy)	Appeal by addressing emotions and create excitement about the game through aesthetics of the game idea, e.g., by showing cinematic and gameplay trailers	Appeal to pragmatic considerations of the decision makers by adopting business-like pitching templates, e.g., by highlighting the reason for the funding request, the timeline, the team

the conflicting logics for the production of (indie) digital games and explains what both logics mean for the basis of attention in business pitches.

While these two logics may be complementary to some degree, they prescribe different paths for action during various stages of the product life cycle (Ross, 2011; Takahashi, 2017; Tschang, 2007) and target a divergent basis of attention in regard to the design and evaluation of pitches. As we elaborate on in more detail subsequently, in pitch construction, the business logic means that a creator tries addressing the pragmatic concerns of potential investors, while the aesthetic logic emphasizes the affective appeal of the idea, primarily stimulating the emotions of potential investors.

Logic Multiplicity in Crowdfunding Video Pitches

Crowdfunding requires the creation of a pitch, that is, the presentation of a detailed project description of the planned venture. This represents the main part of the webpage for each project pitched. The pitch is usually in written form and offers a detailed description of the project. Creators can also include videos in their descriptions, and 86% of all projects have them although they are not obligatory (Mollick, 2014). Over the years, the video pitch has become widely recognized as one of the most important components of crowdfunding campaigns (Almerico, 2014). In our study, we therefore focus our analysis mainly on video pitches posted to garner resources via crowdfunding for indie digital games. Specifically, we focus our analysis on the salience and effect of both the logic of the aesthetic and/or the business logic.

Digital games are complex products whose creation takes a considerable amount of time and labor. In the indie-game settings, where development is undertaken by small teams of enthusiasts or in some cases by a single individual, game development may take years. One indie developer counted nearly thirty-nine hundred hours on the development of one game (Mirabello, 2014). Therefore, pushing the release date or not completing the game is quite common for indie-developers (Parker, 2017; Purchese, 2017). Consequently, potential crowd investors, called backers, are rightfully concerned about whether creative entrepreneurs are able to deliver on their promises. Similar to traditional investors, backers make decisions under conditions of uncertainty. Indeed, some backers think along the lines of traditional investors; for them, it is important "*that the creator sounds like they have a solid plan moving forward and what needs to be done to produce the product, especially if they are a first time creator. If you have a good idea but no plan, I'm not going to give you my money*" (Tompet Games, 2017, para. 13). Expectations of a more traditional business pitch are further reinforced by the crowdfunding culture that has established over the past years and recommendations in handbooks for creators providing guidance for a "successful" pitch structure. For instance, it is recommended that a creator introduces herself or the team, mentioning previous experience and projects, her motivation and passion for the project, the project schedule, and the budget breakdown (Kickstarter's Creator Handbook, 2018). These templates primarily address *pragmatic* concerns of potential backers: Whether or not the team has enough experience, has invested their own funds, and whether they have a sound plan for finishing the project under development.

On the other hand, "*no form of popular entertainment inspires as much passionate devotion (among other things) as does the video game*" (Vissers, 2018, para. 32). Potential backers are often gamers themselves, and some of them "*don't understand why some* [creators] *have flashy videos nothing to do with gameplay, designers talking about their passion, etc. all of which can be there but should not take precedent over important stuff* [the game idea]" (Tompet Games, 2017, para. 10).

Therefore, another way to persuade potential investors is to show them the game trailer, game pieces, concept art, or game mechanics and features. These elements are associated with the aesthetic logic and are likely to appeal to the emotions of potential backers in order to convince them first and foremost about the aesthetic value of the game and the game experience. In the game industry, this is often done by showcasing cinematic and gameplay trailers. While such trailers are used as marketing material, they are also a "*figurative vision*" of the game, or "*the idealized versions of a game, where every move is flawless, every camera angle is perfect, every shot is beautiful, and every bullet is extra-bullety*" (Livingston, 2015, para. 2). Thus, inherent in the aesthetic logic is the affective appeal to potential backers, addressing their emotions by creating excitement about the game idea and providing a glimpse of the game world, atmosphere, story, and gameplay.

Creators may also try to combine the two logics, that is, appealing to emotions while also addressing the pragmatic considerations of potential investors. Overall, creators of crowdfunding pitches have to make decisions about whether to emphasize the business logic by adopting a business-like template for their pitch, whether to draw on the aesthetic logic and craft a cinematic game trailer, or whether to try and combine these two logics.

Sample and Data Collection

This quantitative study uses multiple linear regression analysis to test our hypothesized ideas. Video pitches have been widely recognized as one of the most important components of crowdfunding campaigns (Almerico, 2014). In this paper, we examine the pitches of new digital games posted on the crowdfunding platform Kickstarter with the purpose of attracting backers to financially support a project. On Kickstarter, entrepreneurial individuals can seek funding for their creative ideas across several categories, including video games, with more than 10,000 game projects posted on the platform (Purchese, 2017).

We collected data for this project in 2017. The initial dataset consisted of 2086 projects, predominantly belonging to the Kickstarter category "video games," of which we randomly sampled 600 projects for our analysis. After removing nonrelevant projects such as fundraising for conferences, hackathons, and extra features for already existing games, we were left with 485 projects posted between 2009 and 2017 that specifically covered games by indie developers (amateurs and independent companies as opposed to large corporations). The final dataset comprised 321 successfully funded projects and 164 unsuccessful projects, those that did not receive enough attention from backers.

Table 7.2 Multiple logics and their manifestation in crowdfunding video pitches for new digital games

Logic multiplicity	Aesthetic logic	Business logic	Hybrid (blending of aesthetic and business logics)
Basis of attention in creation of a crowdfunding pitch	Appeal to emotions to create excitement about the game. Usually achieved through evoking aesthetic appeal to the game idea by providing a glimpse of the gaming world, its atmosphere, story, and gameplay	Appeal to pragmatic considerations of decision makers. Usually achieved through adopting a business-like pitching template, e.g., highlighting the reason for the funding request, the product, the timeline, the team	Attempt to combine the prescriptions of both logics to appeal to the emotions and pragmatic concerns of the evaluators
Goals of a pitch	Create excitement and enthusiasm about the game idea, and what the final product is going to look like	Address pragmatic concerns of potential investors, and convince them in the ability to deliver the final product	Both evoke an emotional response and address pragmatic considerations
Coding scheme	Video pitches excluding the creators and business-oriented concerns and only showcasing game-related information and footage (e.g., cinematic trailer or gameplay) are considered to prioritize the aesthetic logic	Pitches that follow a business-like pitching template, namely, pitches that mainly feature the creator(s)/team, not the game itself, are considered to be predominantly guided by the business logic. These are usually inspired by the Kickstarter template (Kickstarter's Creator Handbook, 2018). Here, creators discuss who they are, how far they have arrived at the process of creation, why they need the funding and so on	Pitches that incorporate both, a game trailer and a more traditional business-like pitch

Measures

We use multiple linear regression analysis to test our ideas. Backers' support is our dependent variable. In addition to our explanatory variables, we included a set of control variables. Below, we describe all variables in detail.

Backers' support—dependent variable. In crowdfunding, the attractiveness of a project is a multifaceted concept that can be investigated using various measures (Ahlers, Cumming, Günther, & Schweizer, 2015). In this study, to measure how attractive a posted project is to the crowd, we used the number of backers per crowdfunding project. This measure is commonly used to operationalize the amount of investor attention a project receives (Ahlers et al., 2015; Kuppuswamy & Bayus, 2018a, b). For the regression analysis, we applied a square root transformation as recommended for count data that are positively skewed and include zeroes and small values close to zero (Burns & Burns, 2008; McDonald, 2009).

Logic multiplicity—explanatory variables. To examine how multiple logics are dealt with in pitch creation and affect backers' support, we content-analyzed all sampled crowdfunding video pitches with regard to the predominant use of the aesthetic and/or business logic. We did so by developing a coding scheme capturing how the different logics (or a blend of the two) are materialized in the form of concrete elements in video pitches (Table 7.2).

Development stage—explanatory variables. Based on existing literature and frameworks, we differentiated between early and advanced stages of project development. In particular, we draw on Ramadan and Widyani (2013), who studied the game development life cycle, and a range of other frameworks suggested by various authors and gaming organizations (e.g., Blitz Game Studios GDLC, 2011; Chandler, 2009; Hendrick, 2009). Together, these frameworks suggest two "extreme" stages of game development, *early* and *advanced stage*. Most of the frameworks also suggest a middle stage; however, because we were interested in analyzing the interaction between the development stage and logic used, we opted to omit the middle ground between early and advanced and focused our analysis only on the extreme stages of project development. Table 7.3 presents the definition of the two development stages and illustrates our coding of the Kickstarter projects into these two categories.

To determine where in the idea development cycle a project was located at the moment of pitching, we carefully analyzed the information provided by the creators in video pitches. In addition, we used the information provided on projects' webpages. Specifically, we read through the project description, paying special attention to the sections "Why Kickstarter" and "Risks and challenges," which is where the creators tend to share information about how far along they are in the

Table 7.3 Development stages of digital games

Development stage	Definition	Examples indicating the development stage taken from Kickstarter project webpages and video transcripts (data source)
Early	Projects in the pitching phase or those in early development. These projects may have concept art and an overall idea of the game, possibly with some initial attempts to make an early mockup (an early, non-playable prototype)	"Writing, design and art have already begun." "We started to create this game four months ago. We have managed to create a 200-page dossier describing the game, hundreds of artworks, dozens of 3D models and several animation cells. The project, which we want to develop, is very ambitious." "We've started the project three months ago."
Advanced	Projects that have playable prototypes as well as those that are nearly completed and in need of funding to cover the costs of marketing or postproduction	"We decided to wait a little longer than most to share our game with you guys. Now we're almost done!" "The gameplay code is 100% complete and all in-game art and sound effects are also now 100% complete." "Yargis is already developed to the point where it is easily sellable."

Table 7.4 Control variables included in the study

Name	Description
Images	Number of images on the page
Staff picked	Whether the project was featured by Kickstarter's staff
Word count	Word count of campaign page
Goal	Funding goal (in USD)

process of game creation. We also searched for any links or references to "early pre-alpha," "playable demo," "pre-alpha," "alpha," "beta," and "prototype," as those keywords are typically used to refer to the development stage of a game. In addition, for cases for which it was especially hard to determine the stage of idea development, we also looked at the project updates because in those updates, creators commonly post milestones such as "alpha to download" or "beta is finally done." Following these coding schemes, one of the authors and a research assistant coded ca. 500 video pitches for these several elements.

Control variables. We included several control variables that were found to affect crowdfunding outcomes in previous studies (Cumming & Hornuf, 2018; Kuppuswamy & Bayus, 2018a; Mollick, 2014). Table 7.4 presents these variables in detail, all sourced from the various project campaign webpages.

Results

Since our main explanatory variables were coded into categories, we had to decompose these variables and the interaction effect between them into a set of dummy variables to include them in the regression model. We ran multiple linear regression with the help of IBM SPSS Statistics to analyze the data. Our final dataset consisted of 485 projects. Table 7.5 presents the descriptive statistics, including means, standard deviations, and correlations.

Converting categorical variables into dummy variables is often problematic because it may generate correlations between predictor variables. To understand whether multicollinearity truly exists and poses a serious

Table 7.5 Descriptive statistics: correlations, means, and standard deviations

	Variable	Mean	Std. Deviation	1	2	3	4	5	6	7	8	9
1	Backers†	18.72	24.048									
2	Word count	1130.25	914.081	0.584***								
3	Images	14.12	17.794	0.583***	0.7***							
4	Staff Picked	0.33	0.471	0.452***	0.215***	0.339***						
5	Goal	24,945.80	67,181.326	0.637***	0.393***	0.382***	0.223***					
6	Business	0.25	0.436	0.012	0.012	−0.091*	−0.069	−0.058				
7	Aesthetic	0.24	0.427	−0.019	0.013	0.047	0.005	−0.096*	−0.327***			
8	Hybrid	0.51	0.500	0.006	−0.021	0.039	0.056	0.132**	−0.591***	−0.569***		
9	Early	0.26	0.439	−0.027	−0.118**	−0.145***	−0.038	0.014	0.13**	−0.001	−0.112**	
10	Advanced	0.42	0.494	0.036	0.007	0.057	0.029	−0.014	−0.045	−0.008	0.046	−0.505***

$N = 485$; $^{*}p < .05$; $^{**}p < .01$; $^{***}p < .001$
†—square root transformed

problem for a study, it is suggested to examine the variance inflation factors (VIFs), which normally range from 0.1 to 10 (Chen & Rothschild, 2010; Landau & Everitt, 2004). In this study, none of the VIFs of the explanatory variables were higher than 1.8 or lower than 1.1, indicating that multicollinearity does not pose a problem for our analysis.

Table 7.6 presents the results of the multiple regression analysis using the number of backers (square root transformed) as our dependent variable. We ran four models. The first model comprises only the control variables. The second model investigates whether the hybrid

Table 7.6 Multiple regression analysis using the number of backers (square root transformed) as the dependent variable

Variable	Model 1: Controls	Model 2: Hybrid	Model 3: Business logic in early-stage projects	Model 4: Aesthetic logic in advanced-stage projects
Word count	0.253*** (0.001)	0.244*** (0.001)	0.242*** (0.001)	0.243*** (0.001)
Images	0.16*** (0.056)	0.164*** (0.055)	0.179*** (0.056)	0.177*** (0.056)
Staff picked	0.249*** (1.533)	0.251*** (1.527)	0.251*** (1.519)	0.251*** (1.52)
Goal	0.421*** (0)	0.431*** (0)	0.423*** (0)	0.421*** (0)
Hybrid		−0.066* (1.361)		
Business*Early			0.105** (2.764)	
Aesthetic*Advanced				0.061* (2.427)
Model R^2	0.622	0.626	0.637	0.636
Adjusted R^2	0.619	0.622	0.628	0.628
ΔR^2	–	0.004*	0.015**	0.014*
Model df	4	5	11	11
Residual df	480	479	473	473

Standard errors in parentheses (#.###). All models compared with Model 1
$N = 485$
Model 3: Early projects with hybrid and aesthetic logics as the reference category; Model 4: Advanced projects with hybrid and business logics as the reference category. Therefore, in both models, six dummy variables are included in the models that are not reported in this table
$*p < .05$; $**p < .01$; $***p < .001$

approach to pitch creation is superior in attracting backers over the alternatives (Hypothesis 1). The third and fourth models test the interaction effect between project development stages and institutional logics (Hypotheses 2a and 2b).

In all models, all four control variables were significant: Whether or not the staff featured the project on the platform, the goal, the number of words in project description, and the number of images. In line with previous studies, images can be effective communication tools (Koch & Siering, 2015; Xu Yang, Rao, Fu, Huang, & Bailey, 2014), alleviating information asymmetries that exist in online settings in general (Ba, Whinston, & Zhang, 2003; Mavlanova, Benbunan-Fich, & Koufaris, 2012) and in reward-based crowdfunding specifically (Courtney, Dutta, & Li, 2017). Similarly, the amount of information shared (represented by the number of words) potentially reduces the information asymmetry between backers and creative entrepreneurs.

Hypothesis 1 suggests that using a hybrid approach over other alternatives in pitch creation will increase the number of backers. While we do not find support for the hypothesis, model 2 nonetheless suggests interesting results. In contrast to our assumption, controlling for the other variables in the model, entrepreneurs' attempts to draw on and include various elements from multiple logics seem to negatively affect the number of backers that a project attracts ($B = -0.066$; $p < 0.05$).

Furthermore, the results of models 3 and 4 offer interesting insights. In line with our assumptions, our findings indicate that there is an interaction between the idea development stage and the way of handling multiple logics in attracting backers to support crowdfunding projects. Hypothesis 2a states that creative projects at an early stage will attract a higher number of backers if the business logic is used to pitch the project. We find support for this hypothesis ($B = 0.105$; $p < 0.01$). The projects at an early stage of development seem to benefit from employing the business logic in pitch construction. The presented effect is positive and significant. Hypothesis 2b states that creative projects at an advanced stage will attract a higher number of backers if the aesthetic logic is used to pitch the project. The regression analysis also provides support for this assumption ($B = 0.061$; $p < 0.05$).

Finally, as a robustness check, we ran regression analysis using the total amount of money a project received (square root transformed) as a dependent variable (Ahlers et al., 2015; Gorbatai & Nelson, 2015). The results partially support the results of the main analysis. The hybrid approach does not seem to have a significant impact on the amount of money raised ($B = -0.049$; $p < 0.06$). Similarly, employing the aesthetic logic in pitch creation for advanced projects has no effect on the amount of money raised. However, utilizing the business logic in pitch creation at an early phase of project development seems to positively affect the amount of money a project receives ($B = 0.106$; $p < 0.001$).

Discussion and Conclusion

Crowdfunding is becoming increasingly important in raising funds for organizations in the creative and cultural sector. In this study, we examined how creative entrepreneurs construct crowdfunding pitches under conditions of multiple institutional logics and how potential backers evaluate their attempts. In particular, we investigated which of the two logics, the aesthetic logic or business logic, or both logics in concert are most effective in mobilizing backers. We did so by studying indie-developers and their video pitching practices on the crowdfunding platform Kickstarter.

Contrary to our assumption, aspiring entrepreneurs' attempts to highlight both the pragmatic business concerns and aesthetic potential in a single pitch seem to hold little appeal for potential investors. One possible explanation is that a hybrid approach to pitch creation tends to lead to the creation of longer pitches, which risks boring the audience. As recent research demonstrates, individuals' attention span tends to decrease (Weinreich, Obendorf, Herder, & Mayer, 2008), with engagement declining significantly after the second minute of watching a video (Fishman, 2016). This is also reflected in the recommendations for Kickstarter videos—to keep them within two to three minutes (Dunlap, 2015 on Kickstarter Campus). Another potential explanation is that mixing the two logics does not lead to a true new logic and therefore, does not resonate with any existing or new audience, instead generating confusion and legitimacy discounting among potential investors (Zuckerman, 1999).

However, it is important to mention that while coding the videos, we encountered different configurations of what we call a hybrid approach to pitching. Some distinctions, for instance, lie in the order of content presentation and the degree of hybridity of the various elements associated with the distinct logics. Future studies could go deeper and study the degree of hybridity and its effects on crowdfunding success. Would well-blended, organically integrated components of different logics be more effective in attracting funders over other hybrid configurations?

Our findings also illuminate that the business logic for early-stage ideas and the aesthetic logic for advanced-stage ideas are most beneficial in pitch creation compared with the alternatives. Early-stage projects propose only an idea for a game rather than a complete prototype, meaning that there is a high level of uncertainty (Pindyck, 1993). In such situations, employing the business logic in pitching helps to mitigate investors' uncertainty, as it addresses the pragmatic concerns of potential investors and enables them to assess the entrepreneurs' skills, commitment, and existing resources, all factors that have been shown to positively affect the propensity of receiving funding (Chen et al., 2009; Pollack et al., 2012). This is an interesting finding given that prior and related studies found that the business logic was counterproductive in garnering resources from investors (Allison, McKenny, & Short, 2013; Jones et al., 2010). However, those studies did not differentiate between early and advanced stages of development. Future studies should take a similarly fine-grained approach to further investigate how various and potentially conflicting logics play out in pitching processes.

The appeal of the aesthetic logic at an advanced phase of product development likewise seems to be reasonable. As games are significantly more fleshed out at an advanced development stage, entrepreneurs are able to create trailers that are more aesthetically and affectively appealing, which makes them more attractive for potential investors and customers (Khalid & Helander, 2006). Moreover, an almost complete game may simultaneously serve as tangible evidence of creative entrepreneurs' professional skills and their ability to deliver the final product.

Taken together, the findings of our study advance insights at the intersection between the literature on entrepreneurship and institutional theory and hold important implications for the literature on creative industries and crowdfunding. First, our study resonates and further enriches prior research on business pitches for financial resource acquisition (Balachanda, 2013; Chen et al., 2009; Pollack et al., 2012). Thus far, scholars have paid only limited attention to the institutional underpinnings of business pitches and the interaction of multiple institutional logics with the actual development stage of a project. Our study advances existing insights by investigating how several logics in concert or alone have an impact on the social evaluation by crowdfunding investors at distinct stages of project development. Furthermore, most studies have been conducted in the context of traditional settings of entrepreneurs seeking resources via seed funds or venture capitalists. We thus contribute to the limited body of literature on entrepreneurial resource acquisition that illuminates the institutional antecedents in these processes (Jones et al., 2010; Lounsbury & Glynn, 2001). In addition, while previous studies have examined institutional logics within written business pitches and their effects on professional peers (Jones et al., 2010), we investigated these effects on the mass-market audience in the context of crowdfunding—a novel way of raising capital outside of traditional financial channels.

Second, studying creative entrepreneurship in the crowdfunding setting is intriguing because it makes it possible to investigate entrepreneurial efforts and institutional processes during the earliest stages of new venture formation. Although these emerging stages have been highlighted as particularly important (Aldrich, 1999; Lounsbury & Glynn, 2001), they have received only scant attention from entrepreneurship scholars, probably given the difficulties in data access. Our study thus offers insights into nascent entrepreneur-investor interactions before an actual enterprise is formed.

Third, we also contribute to the literature on the creative industries interested in the impact and use of digital technologies. The question of how the creative industries change and adopt in the digital era has stimulated increasing research interest in recent years (Bakhshi & Throsby, 2012; Mangematin, Sapsed, & Schüßler, 2014). The rise of digital technologies has fostered profound changes in the creative industries. However, digital technologies not only catalyze novel product and service innovations but also lead to new business models in creative sectors such as online book publishing, music and video streaming platforms, and film production (Benghozi & Salvador, 2016; Rüling & Duymedjian, 2014). They also offer novel forms of resource acquisition and new tools to interact with constituents and form a community. In digital games, the emerging crowdfunding phenomenon seems to be actively transforming the industry landscape by providing independent game developers access to funding opportunities, thus eliminating the need for intermediaries (Writer, 2016). In this way, crowdfunding may offer creative individuals a chance for artistic expression and creative independence.

Moreover, although this study examines pitching practices within the gaming industry, our findings likely represent the broader creative and cultural sector. Here, the industries share a high degree of commonality in terms of skills, production processes, underlying product ideas, and dynamics (Aarseth, 2006; Currid & Williams, 2010), with certain social disagreements between artistic considerations and economic concerns being a common and well-established phenomenon (Eikhof & Haunschild, 2007; Throsby, 2001; Tschang, 2007). Supporting artistic ideas online is becoming a staple of creative production, with categories related to art and culture being prominent on crowdfunding platforms such as Kickstarter and membership platforms such as Patreon. Our study illuminates how such disagreements may play out in online pitches and highlights their effect on crowdfunding outcomes.

At the industry level and in the long term, such transformations may lead to higher-level changes in organizational, social, and economic structures and activities—a topic that future studies need to address (Powell, 2017). Does crowdfunding create or motivate different kinds of producers, products, or producer-customer interactions? These are important research questions to examine in future research.

Acknowledgements The authors would like to thank the volume editors as well an anonymous reviewer for their helpful comments and suggestions. We also thank Ajla Nesimovic for her research assistance.

References

Aarseth, E. (2006). The culture and business of cross-media productions. *Popular Communication, 4*(3), 203–211.

Agrawal, A., Catalini, C., & Goldfarb, A. (2014). Some simple economics of crowdfunding. *Innovation Policy and the Economy, 14*(1), 63–97.

Ahlers, G. K., Cumming, D., Günther, C., & Schweizer, D. (2015). Signaling in equity crowdfunding. *Entrepreneurship Theory and Practice, 39*(4), 955–980.

Aldrich, H. E. (1999). *Organizations evolving*. London: Sage.

Aldrich, H. E., & Fiol, C. M. (1994). Fools rush in? The institutional context of industry creation. *Academy of Management Review, 19*(4), 645–670.

Allison, T. H., McKenny, A. F., & Short, J. C. (2013). The effect of entrepreneurial rhetoric on microlending investment: An examination of the warm-glow effect. *Journal of Business Venturing, 28*(6), 690–707.

Almerico, K. (2014). *6 tips to create a top-notch crowdfunding video*. Entrepreneur.

Alvarez, J. L., Mazza, C., Pedersen, J. S., & Svejenova, S. (2005). Shielding idiosyncrasy from isomorphic pressures: Towards optimal distinctiveness in European filmmaking. *Organization, 12*(6), 863–888.

Ba, S., Whinston, A. B., & Zhang, H. (2003). Building trust in online auction markets through an economic incentive mechanism. *Decision Support Systems, 35*(3), 273–286.

Bakhshi, H., & Throsby, D. (2012). New technologies in cultural institutions: Theory, evidence and policy implications. *International Journal of Cultural Policy, 18*(2), 205–222.

Balachandra, L. (2011). *Pitching trustworthiness: Cues for trust in early-stage investment decision-making*. Newton: Carroll School of Management.

Balachandra, L., Briggs, A. R., Eddleston, K., & Brush, C. (2013). Pitch like a man: Gender stereotypes and entrepreneur pitch success. *Frontiers of Entrepreneurship Research, 33*(8), 2.

Barnett, C. (2013). *Top 10 crowdfunding sites for fundraising*. New York: Forbes.

Baron, R. A., & Markman, G. D. (2003). Beyond social capital: How social skills can enhance entrepreneurs' success. *Academy of Management Perspectives, 14*(1), 106–116.

Battilana, J., Sengul, M., Pache, A. C., & Model, J. (2015). Harnessing productive tensions in hybrid organizations: The case of work integration social enterprises. *Academy of Management Journal, 58*(6), 1658–1685.
Benghozi, P. J., & Salvador, E. (2016). How and where the R&D takes place in creative industries? Digital investment strategies of the book publishing sector. *Technology Analysis & Strategic Management, 28*(5), 568–582.
Blitz Games Studios, "Project Lifecycle". (2011). Available at http://www.blitzgamesstudios.com/blitz_academy/game_dev/ project_lifecycle.
Brooks, A. W., Huang, L., Kearney, S. W., & Murray, F. E. (2014). Investors prefer entrepreneurial ventures pitched by attractive men. *Proceedings of the National Academy of Sciences, 111*(12), 4427–4431.
Brush, C. G., Greene, P. G., & Hart, M. M. (2001). From initial idea to unique advantage: The entrepreneurial challenge of constructing a resource base. *Academy of Management Perspectives, 15*(1), 64–78.
Burns, R. P., & Burns, R. (2008). *Business research methods and statistics using SPSS*. Thousand Oaks, CA: Sage.
Chandler, H. M. (2009). *The game production handbook*. Ontario, Canada: Jones & Bartlett Publishers.
Chen, C. F., & Rothschild, R. (2010). An application of hedonic pricing analysis to the case of hotel rooms in Taipei. *Tourism Economics, 16*(3), 685–694.
Chen, X. P., Yao, X., & Kotha, S. (2009). Entrepreneur passion and preparedness in business plan presentations: A persuasion analysis of venture capitalists' funding decisions. *Academy of Management Journal, 52*(1), 199–214.
Clark, C. (2008). The impact of entrepreneurs' oral pitch presentation skills on business angels' initial screening investment decisions. *Venture Capital, 10*(3), 257–279.
Courtney, C., Dutta, S., & Li, Y. (2017). Resolving information asymmetry: Signaling, endorsement, and crowdfunding success. *Entrepreneurship Theory and Practice, 41*(2), 265–290.
Cumming, D., & Hornuf, L. (Eds.). (2018). *The Economics of crowdfunding: Startups, portals and investor behavior*. London, UK: Palgrave Macmillan.
Currid, E., & Williams, S. (2010). Two cities, five industries: Similarities and differences within and between cultural industries in New York and Los Angeles. *Journal of Planning Education and Research, 29*(3), 322–335.
Dailey, L., & Mumford, M. D. (2006). Evaluative aspects of creative thought: Errors in appraising the implications of new ideas. *Creativity Research Journal, 18*(3), 385–390.

Dalpiaz, E., Rindova, V., & Ravasi, D. (2016). Combining logics to transform organizational agency: Blending industry and art at Alessi. *Administrative Science Quarterly, 61*(3), 347–392.

Doblinger, C., Soppe, B., & Huber, S. (2019). Converging logics. Coopetitive ties and innovation in the early clean transportation industry. *Proceedings of the 2019 Academy of Management Meeting.*

Eikhof, D. R., & Haunschild, A. (2006). Lifestyle meets market: Bohemian entrepreneurs in creative industries. *Creativity and Innovation Management, 15*(3), 234–241.

Eikhof, D. R., & Haunschild, A. (2007). For art's sake! Artistic and economic logics in creative production. *Journal of Organizational Behavior, 28*(5), 523–538.

Elsbach, K. D., & Kramer, R. M. (2003). Assessing creativity in Hollywood pitch meetings: Evidence for a dual-process model of creativity judgements. *Academy of Management Journal, 46*(3), 283–301.

Erikson, T., & Sørheim, R. (2005). 'Technology angels' and other informal investors. *Technovation, 25*(5), 489–496.

Fishman, E. (2016). *How long should your next video be?* WISTIA.

Flew, T. (2012). *The creative industries. Culture and policy*. London, UK: Sage.

Frey, B. S., & Eichenberger, R. (1995). On the rate of return in the art market: Survey and evaluation. *European Economic Review, 39*(3–4), 528–537.

Friedland, R., & Alford, R. R. (1991). Bringing society back in: Symbols, practices and institutional contradictions. In W. W. Powell & P. J. DiMaggio (Eds.), *The new institutionalism in organizational analysis* (pp. 232–267). Chicago: University of Chicago Press.

Galbraith, C. S., McKinney, B. C., DeNoble, A. F., & Ehrlich, S. B. (2014). The impact of presentation form, entrepreneurial passion, and perceived preparedness on obtaining grant funding. *Journal of Business and Technical Communication, 28*(2), 222–248.

Glynn, M. A. (2000). When cymbals become symbols: Conflict over organizational identity within a symphony orchestra. *Organization Science, 11*(3), 285–298.

Glynn, M. A., & Lounsbury, M. (2005). From the critics' corner: Logic blending, discursive change and authenticity in a cultural production system. *Journal of Management Studies, 42*(5), 1031–1055.

Goodrick, E., & Reay, T. (2011). Constellations of institutional logics: Changes in the professional work of pharmacists. *Sage, 38*(3), 372–416.

Gorbatai, A., & Nelson, L. (2015). *The narrative advantage: Gender and the language of crowdfunding* (Research Papers). Haas School of Business, University of California, Berkeley.

Greenwood, R., Raynard, M., Kodeih, F., Micelotta, E. R., & Lounsbury, M. (2011). Institutional complexity and organizational responses. *Academy of Management Annals, 5*(1), 317–371.

Hendrick, A. (2009). *Project management for game development.*

Henry, C. (Ed.). (2007). *Entrepreneurship in the creative industries: An international perspective*. Cheltenham, UK: Edward Elgar Publishing.

Jones, C., & Livne-Tarandach, R. (2008). Designing a frame: Rhetorical strategies of architects. *Journal of Organizational Behavior: The International Journal of Industrial, Occupational and Organizational Psychology and Behavior, 29*(8), 1075–1099.

Jones, C., Livne-Tarandach, R., & Balachandra, L. (2010). Rhetoric that wins clients: Entrepreneurial firms use of institutional logics when competing for resources. In D. S. Wesley & J. D. Robert (Eds.), *Institutions and entrepreneurship* (pp. 183–218). Bingley, UK: Emerald Group Publishing Limited.

Kerr, A. (2006). *The business and culture of digital games: Gamework and gameplay*. Thousand Oaks, CA: Sage.

Kerr, C. (2017). *10,000 game projects have been funded through Kickstarter.* Gamasutra.

Khalid, H. M., & Helander, M. G. (2006). Customer emotional needs in product design. *Concurrent Engineering, 14*(3), 197–206.

Kickstarter Creator Handbook. (2018). Available at https://www.kickstarter.com/help/handbook/.

Koch, J. A., & Siering, M. (2015). Crowdfunding success factors: The characteristics of successfully funded projects on crowdfunding platforms. In *Proceedings of the 23rd European Conference on Information Systems (ECIS 2015),* Münster, Germany.

Kuppuswamy, V., & Bayus, B. L. (2018a). A review of crowdfunding research and findings. In P. N. Golder & M. Debanjan (Eds.), *Handbook of research on new product development* (pp. 361–374). Cheltenham: Edward Elgar Publishing.

Kuppuswamy, V., & Bayus, B. L. (2018b). Crowdfunding creative ideas: The dynamics of project backers. In D. Cumming & L. Hornuf (Eds.), *The economics of crowdfunding* (pp. 151–182). Cham: Palgrave Macmillan.

Landau, S., & Everitt, B. S. (2004). *A handbook of statistical analyses using SPSS*. Boca Raton, FL: Chapman & Hall.

Livingston, C. (2015). *Are cinematic trailers worth getting excited about?* PCGamer. Available at https://www.pcgamer.com/face-off-are-cinematic-trailers-worth-getting-excited-about/#comment-jump.

Lounsbury, M., & Glynn, M. A. (2001). Cultural entrepreneurship: Stories, legitimacy, and the acquisition of resources. *Strategic Management Journal, 22*(6–7), 545–564.

Luo, H. (2014). When to sell your idea: Theory and evidence from the movie industry. *Management Science, 60*(12), 3067–3086.

Maiolini, R., Cappa, F., Leone, M. I., & Pinelli, M. (2018). The impact of narrative style and entrepreneur's experience in crowdfunding campaigns. In *Third Entrepreneurial Finance Conference Proceedings 2018*. Milano, Italy.

Mangematin, V., Sapsed, J., & Schüßler, E. (2014). *Disassembly and reassembly: An introduction to the special issue on digital technology and creative industries, 83,* 1–9.

Mason, C., & Stark, M. (2004). What do investors look for in a business plan? A comparison of the investment criteria of bankers, venture capitalists and business angels. *International Small Business Journal, 22*(3), 227–248.

Massolution. (2015). *The crowdfunding industry report* (Complete Report).

Mavlanova, T., Benbunan-Fich, R., & Koufaris, M. (2012). Signaling theory and information asymmetry in online commerce. *Information & Management, 49*(5), 240–247.

McDonald, J. H. (2009). *Handbook of biological statistics*, 2 (pp. 173–181). Baltimore, MD: Sparky House Publishing.

McKenny, A. F., Allison, T. H., Ketchen, D. J., Jr., Short, J. C., & Ireland, R. D. (2017). How should crowdfunding research evolve? A survey of the entrepreneurship theory and practice editorial board. *Entrepreneurship Theory and Practice, 41*(2), 291–304.

Mirabello, J. (2014). *How long does it take to make an Indie game?* Gamasutra.

Mollick, E. (2014). The dynamics of crowdfunding: An exploratory study. *Journal of Business Venturing, 29*(1), 1–16.

O'Connor, E. (2002). Storied business: Typology, intertextuality, and traffic in entrepreneurial narrative. *The Journal of Business Communication (1973), 39*(1), 36–54.

Oliver, C. (1991). Strategic responses to institutional processes. *Academy of Management Review, 16*(1), 145–179.

Pache, A. C., & Santos, F. (2010). When worlds collide: The internal dynamics of organizational responses to conflicting institutional demands. *Academy of Management Review, 35*(3), 455–476.

Pache, A. C., & Santos, F. (2013). Inside the hybrid organization: Selective coupling as a response to competing institutional logics. *Academy of Management Journal, 56*(4), 972–1001.

Parker, L. (2017). Video game raised $148 million from fans. Now it's raising concerns. *The New York Times*.

Pershina, R., & Soppe, B. (2017). Let the games begin: Institutional complexity and the design of new products. In M. A. Höllerer, T. Daudigeos, & D. Jancsary (Eds.), *Multimodality, meaning, and institutions* (pp. 219–254). Bingley: Emerald Publishing Limited.

Pietraszkiewicz, A., Soppe, B., & Formanowicz, M. (2017). Go pro bono: Prosocial language as a success factor in crowdfunding. *Social Psychology, 48*(5), 265–278.

Pindyck, R. S. (1993). Investments of uncertain cost. *Journal of Financial Economics, 34*(1), 53–76.

Pollack, J. M., Rutherford, M. W., & Nagy, B. G. (2012). Preparedness and cognitive legitimacy as antecedents of new venture funding in televised business pitches. *Entrepreneurship Theory and Practice, 36*(5), 915–939.

Powell, W. W. (2017). A sociologist looks at crowds: Innovation or invention? *Strategic Organization, 15*(2), 289–297.

Purchese. (2017). *Is Kickstarter for video games dead? An investigation.* Eurogamer.

Ramadan, R., & Widyani, Y. (2013, September). *Game development life cycle guidelines.* In Advanced Computer Science and Information Systems (ICACSIS), 2013 International Conference on (pp. 95–100). IEEE.

Rao, H., Monin, P., & Durand, R. (2005). Border crossing: Bricolage and the erosion of categorical boundaries in French gastronomy. *American Sociological Review, 70*(6), 968–991.

Reay, T., & Hinings, C. R. (2009). Managing the rivalry of competing institutional logics. *Organization Studies, 30*(6), 629–652.

Ross, T. (2011). *What really worries game designers: Game design driven by psychological theory and behavioral quantification.* Gamasutra.

Rüling, C. C., & Duymedjian, R. (2014). Digital bricolage: Resources and coordination in the production of digital visual effects. *Technological Forecasting and Social Change, 83*, 98–110.

Smets, M., Jarzabkowski, P., Burke, G. T., & Spee, P. (2015). Reinsurance trading in Lloyd's of London: Balancing conflicting-yet-complementary logics in practice. *Academy of Management Journal, 58*(3), 932–970.

Svejenova, S., Slavich, B., & AbdelGawad, S. G. (2015). *Creative entrepreneurs. The Oxford handbook of creative industries* (pp. 184–199). Oxford, UK: Oxford University Press.

Takahashi, D. (2017). *Data-driven versus intuition-driven game design*. Venturebeat.

Thornton, P. H. (2004). *Markets from culture: Institutional logics and organizational decisions in higher education publishing*. Stanford: Stanford University Press.

Thornton, P. H., Jones, C., & Kury, K. (2005). Institutional logics and institutional change in organizations: Transformation in accounting, architecture, and publishing. In *Transformation in cultural industries* (pp. 125–170). Bingley: Emerald Group Publishing Limited.

Thornton, P. H., & Ocasio, W. (1999). Institutional logics and the historical contingency of power in organizations: Executive succession in the higher education publishing industry, 1958–1990. *American Journal of Sociology, 105*(3), 801–843.

Thornton, P. H., & Ocasio, W. (2008). Institutional logics. *The Sage Handbook of Organizational Institutionalism, 840*, 99–128.

Throsby, D. (2001). *Economics and culture*. Cambridge: Cambridge University Press.

Tompet Games. (2017). *What 27 superbackers think is the most important element on your Kickstarter page*. Available at https://tompetgames.wordpress.com/2017/10/09/what-27-superbackers-think-is-the-most-important-element-on-your-kickstarter-page/.

Tschang, F. T. (2007). Balancing the tensions between rationalization and creativity in the video games industry. *Organization Science, 18*(6), 989–1005.

Vissers, J. (2018). *8 facts you should know before crowdfunding a video game on Fig*. Meverick. Available at https://www.merchantmaverick.com/8-facts-you-should-know-before-crowdfunding-a-video-game-on-fig/.

Weinreich, H., Obendorf, H., Herder, E., & Mayer, M. (2008). Not quite the average: An empirical study of Web use. *ACM Transactions on the Web (TWEB), 2*(1), 5.

Writer, S. (2016). *How crowdfunding changed gaming*. Atomic.

Xu, A., Yang, X., Rao, H., Fu, W. T., Huang, S. W., & Bailey, B. P. (2014, April). Show me the money!: An analysis of project updates during crowdfunding campaigns. In *Proceedings of the SIGCHI conference on human factors in computing systems* (pp. 591–600). ACM.

Zimmerman, M. A., & Zeitz, G. J. (2002). Beyond survival: Achieving new venture growth by building legitimacy. *Academy of Management Review, 27*(3), 414–443.

Zuckerman, E. W. (1999). The categorical imperative: Securities analysts and the illegitimacy discount. *American Journal of Sociology, 104*(5), 1398–1438.

8

Museums and Technology for Value Creation

Mauro Romanelli

Introduction

Museums as cultural organisations are using technology to involve the audience as users to contribute to cultural heritage knowledge. As organisations that use the Internet, social media, virtual and interactive technologies, museums should contribute to value co-creation as a source for knowledge sharing and creation, as well as learning and education within cultural ecosystems. Museums as educational institutions, information-based, knowledge-driven and learning-oriented organisations (Bagdadly, 1997; Freedman, 2000; Hein, 1998; Hooper-Greenhill, 2007; MacDonald & Alsford, 1991; Marty, 2007a) are embracing various technologies to develop user engagement and support the participation of the audience in cultural activities (Bearman & Gebra, 2008; Simon, 2010) promoting social innovation by following an audience-centred orientation (Consiglio, Cicellin, Scuotto, & Ricchezza, 2017) in order

M. Romanelli (✉)
Department of Business and Economics,
University of Naples Parthenope, Naples, Italy
e-mail: mauro.romanelli@uniparthenope.it

J. Strandgaard Pedersen et al. (eds.), *Technology and Creativity*,
https://doi.org/10.1007/978-3-030-17566-5_8

to develop value co-creation processes (Antón, Camarero, & Garrido, 2018). Museums as memory and cultural institutions collect, preserve, research and display cultural heritage connecting the past with the present and future and promoting social value and action (Burton & Scott, 2007; Hein, 2005). As audience-driven, production-centred, intensive-information and knowledge-oriented organisations (Bonacini, 2012; Freedman, 2000; Gilmore & Rentschler, 2002; Marty, 2007b), museums evolve coherently with technological developments as communities that contribute to creating value and constructing service experience within cultural ecosystems, involving the audience as active participants in the defining of cultural heritage contents and strengthening the relationships between technology, the public and the museum as an organisation that creates value by human resources (Ind & Coates, 2013; Minkiewicz, Evans, & Bridson, 2014; Prahalad & Ramaswamy, 2013; Vargo & Lusch, 2008). Museums contribute to sustaining value co-creation processes using technologies to develop interactive and dialogic communication and legitimise information and knowledge management (Antón et al., 2018; Capriotti & Kuklinski, 2012; Freedman, 2000; MacDonald & Alsford, 1991). As agents of social innovation (Castells, 2001), museums are open to cultural participation of users to generate and share their own museum content (Bonacini, 2012; Russo, 2011; Russo, Watkins, Kelly, & Chan, 2008; Simon, 2010).

Investigating research regarding the relationships between the use of technologies, user participation and involvement and museum staff, the idea of a museum as an organisation and value creation remains an unexplored area of study despite the increasing attention of scholars to the introduction of technologies within the cultural heritage field. This study helps to identify the trajectories that museums are following in order to create value in involving the audience as users in cultural heritage and developing the museum as a community-oriented means of value creation. This study aims to provide an interpretive view to identify how museums are changing by using the web, digital, interactive and virtual technologies and environments to create value involving the audience in defining cultural heritage contents. Studying the role of technologies within museums contributes to understanding how museums are changing to enable value co-creation in the cultural heritage field. Museums contribute to developing and sharing knowledge and information about heritage within cultural ecosystems (Borin & Donato, 2015; Davies, Paton, & O'Sullivan, 2013). They are also embracing the Internet and interactive technologies in order to promote value co-creation, driving service innovation by opening to the participation of the audience in order to generate new knowledge to their audience and encourage new cultural experiences. Technologies help museums to serve the educational mandate, sustain learning experience and preserve cultural heritage by adapting to the changing world and involving potential visitors to take part in the production and value creation regarding cultural heritage (Anderson, 1999; Bautista, 2014; Hein, 1998; Hooper-Greenhill, 2007). Museums embracing technology cede authority, enabling staff and users to develop both cultural experiences and interactive-collaborative processes that rely on knowledge transfer and information sharing within the museum as a community (Crooke, 2006; Kelly, 2010; Schweibenz, 2011; Watson, 2007). Museums should pay attention to the social dimension of computer-based technologies and applications that support cognitive processes (Antinucci, 2007) and exert an influence on behaviour, experience and the integration of exhibits and visitors (Economou & Pujol, 2008).

This study aims only to provide an interpretive and qualitative framework. The research relies on considering the literature related to the advent and introduction of the Internet, social media and virtual-interactive technologies and environments within museums that are opening up to an increasing level of user involvement and participation in the definition of cultural heritage content. The selected contributions are summarised and interpreted (Denyer & Tranfield, 2006) in a narrative synthesis as a flexible approach to studies addressing a different aspect of the same phenomenon. A narrative approach helps provide a description of data in order to develop and present new perspectives on emerging issues and to advance theoretical models (Dixon-Woods, Agarwal, Young, Jones, & Sutton, 2004). Referred journal articles were selected from *Google Scholar* as the main web source and database.

The chapter is organised in the following way. After Introduction, in section "Museums as Information and Knowledge-Based, Education- and Learning-Oriented Organisations" museums are presented as information- and knowledge-based, education- and learning-oriented organisations. In section "Driving Change Within Museums as Communities by Technologies", it is elucidated how technologies contribute to change within museums as communities. In section "Museums Contribute to Value Co-creation by Technologies", we look at how technologies drive museums towards value co-creation and involving users in cultural heritage content. Section "How Technologies Enable Value Co-creation Within Museums" outlines how technologies enable museums to promote value co-creation by revitalising user involvement and participation (from communication to sustaining learning and education), by rethinking virtual museums from managing collections to creating and sharing information and knowledge, rediscovering the role of museum information professionals as mediators between museum knowledge source and the needs of users as active co-producers of knowledge and a new source for value. Finally, conclusions are outlined.

Museums as Information and Knowledge-Based, Education- and Learning-Oriented Organisations

As institutions centred on the citizen, museums have a social role within contemporary world (Knell, 2019). As memory institutions and information-oriented organisations, as well as custodians of cultural heritage assets and values and storehouses of knowledge (Bagdadly, 1997; Freedman, 2000; Marty, 2007a), museums should "serve society by helping provide the knowledge its members need to survive and progress" (MacDonald & Alsford, 1991: 305). They contribute to sustaining the development of society; museums acquire, conserve, research, communicate and exhibit for the purposes of study, education and enjoyment, material evidence of people and their environment (*Icom*, 2004); they promote understanding and interpreting of the nature of objects, things and artefacts (Pearce, 2003); museums support interacting with the public, meeting various and different visitor experience expectations (Sheng & Chen, 2012), providing information, education and recreation, promoting learning and shaping knowledge (Hooper-Greenhill, 1992, 2007).

As institutions that preserve values, identity and memory within a community, museums contribute to creating social value for the public by incorporating heritage as resources inherited from the past, history, continuity, values, beliefs, knowledge and traditions (Burton & Scott, 2007; Kurin, 2004). Museums as memory institutions are sites for critical reflection on the past (Hooper-Greenhill, 1992) and promote knowledge, guaranteeing the best conditions for public use and the fruition of cultural heritage as a concept that is changing over time (Council of Europe, 2005; Vecco, 2010) and evolving from considering monuments, objects and preservation to paying attention to people and functions, as well as sustainable use and development (Loulanski, 2006). "Museums are part of the fabric of societies and communities, and their value is both acknowledged and enhanced by seeking and strengthening relations, exchanges and activities within these nested ecosystems" (Sabiescu & Charatzopoulou, 2018: 330). The museum of the future should promote innovation, and strengthening the individual experience within a museum creates a new public sphere of knowledge where the visitor can admire the innovation of the artist and learn to become an innovative actor (Weibel, 2018).

As information-intensive organisations and bridges between information and knowledge (Freedman, 2000; MacDonald & Alsford, 1991; Marty, 2007a), museums contribute to developing, creating and sharing knowledge and information about heritage within cultural ecosystems (Davies et al., 2013; Borin & Donato, 2015). As organisations "concerned with generation, the perpetuation, the organisation and the dissemination of information" (MacDonald & Alsford, 1991: 306), museums should "help their audiences exploit effectively the information resources in their self-directed quest for knowledge" (MacDonald & Alsford, 1991: 306) because "the role of museums, in the future, that of the knowledge municipality, lies in legitimizing information and information processes and in being an advocate for knowledge as the province of the people" (Freedman, 2000: 303). They should use the information as what can be communicated to people and knowledge as the result of the interaction within community (Orna & Pettitt, 2010) and to create understanding (MacDonald & Alsford, 1991). Museums focusing on the internal communities as museum professionals or on the external audience as visitors select different concepts of knowledge and understanding with meanings being constantly rediscovered or fixed. Museums maintaining a single narrative and interpretation focus on *visitors* only to *attract them* for accessibility and enjoyment, spreading knowledge. When the truth is dependent on context, museums open up to multiple and flexible interpretations of knowledge and understanding. The meanings are constantly rediscovered. The community outside as stakeholders *(forum)* encourages visitors in creating meaning from the collections actively contributing to civic society as a shared depository (Davies et al., 2013).

As knowledge-based organisations (Bagdadly, 1997; Freedman, 2000), museums provide authentic knowledge to their audience (Russo & Watkins, 2007). They tend to manage and interpret collections, collect and provide information as organisations that use, disseminate and share knowledge and modify work practices and structures coherently with changing social, economic and political contexts and issues (Hooper-Greenhill, 1992; Leon, 2013). As institutions that communicate and interact with the public through exhibitions (Hooper-Greenhill, 1995), museums need to engage the public in the cultural value creation as participatory communities that promote social capital and identity, cohesion and exchange, public awareness and economic benefits (Burton & Scott, 2007; Murzyn-Kupisz & Dzialek, 2013; Scott, 2003, 2010). Museums as knowledge municipalities legitimise the processes of capture, management and dissemination of information and knowledge (Freedman, 2000) about cultural heritage as a source that gives citizenship and civic virtue content (Duncan, 2003), relying on understanding the values and beliefs of people to promote cultural diversity, creativity and continuity in the public sphere (Kurin, 2004). As sustainable institutions that achieve multiple goals, serving the interests of different kinds of public members, museums should develop and fulfil a cultural mission by driving local economic and cultural growth and improving the quality of life (d'Harnoncourt, DiMaggio, Perry, & Wood, 1991; Pop & Borza, 2014). As organisations open to the public, museums are always educational institutions that preserve culture, promote social action (Hein, 2005), enable visitors to interact with object learning and facilitate learning experience as a social process of meaning construction, beliefs and values (Lord, 2007; Macfarlan, 2001). Museums as learning environments shape the knowledge and influence learning, enabling learners as proactive actors to engage in their experience, culture and emotions (Hein, 2006; Hooper-Greenhill, 2007), constructing meanings in the mind by interacting with objects, environment and users (Hein, 1999).

Driving Change Within Museums as Communities by Technologies

As interpersonal communicators (Hooper-Greenhill, 1995), museums should strategically promote interaction between museum staff, objects, artefacts and the public, engaging with a working audience and active participants in an interactive process (Balogun, Best, & Lê, 2015; Romanelli, 2017) within a community where museums and users share the same interests and goals (Rounds, 2012), and the audience is an active agent that influences how museums act and represent what a museum examines (Karp, 1992). Museums represent the community and reinvent themselves as a centre that supports community development and redefines the relationship between the museum and the public towards a shared authority (Burton & Scott, 2007; Duclos-Orsello, 2013) as an effective and legitimised institution in information provision and communication (MacDonald & Alsford, 1991; Schweibenz, 1998, 2011) that creates public value through promoting knowledge and awareness about cultural heritage (Holden, 2006).

Museums contribute to building inclusive and cohesive communities and promoting community development, collaboration and identity (Crooke, 2006). "Museums reflect the concerns of the society in which they are located, and their relationship with the communities they serve is renegotiated and reinvented as their purposes develop and change" (Watson, 2007: 13). They are becoming spaces of cultural innovation and cultural connectors that support identities, meanings and values within society (Castells, 2001), promoting social innovation by following an audience-centred orientation (Consiglio et al., 2017). Rediscovering museums as communities implies redesigning their identity as social spaces living in contemporary society (Crooke, 2006). Rethinking a museum as a community helps reinforce its purposes more than interests involved in the museum (Watson, 2007) and helps it to empower the public (Freedman, 2000) and serve cultural and social functions because "no single museum has a monopoly on truth nor can present a complete picture of the human condition: no more should we imagine that all heritage can be encompassed by museums" (MacDonald & Alsford, 1991: 309). "Museums and heritage have been used to express community and to look at the role of objects in symbolizing community and expressing senses of belonging" (Crooke, 2006: 174).

As responsive, effective and trustable institutions in information society, museums use technologies in order to improve information management and provision (MacDonald & Alsford, 1991; Schweibenz, 2011) "making their information sources accessible to the public", "utilising all information and communication technologies now available" (MacDonald & Alsford, 1991: 310). Technology enables museums as institutions to become mass communication oriented (Hooper-Greenhill, 1995) to better exert a civilising influence and adhere to an educative mission within society (Keene, 1997). In the information era, museums develop and enhance cultural innovation, sustaining the participation of audiences in cultural heritage in order to develop better quality of life within communities (Castells, 2001) by promoting social and public value (Burton & Scott, 2007). Technologies enable the museum to abandon the exclusive role of a key intermediary of knowledge about collections and promote a shared authority on cultural heritage, democratising knowledge and adapting to changing and contemporary society (Bautista, 2014; Duclos-Orsello, 2013; Knell, 2019; Schweibenz, 2011). As organisations embracing social media and interactive technologies, museums are social platforms and ecosystems (Brown & Mairesse, 2018) that offer a "space for conversation, a forum for civic engagement and debate, and opportunity for a variety of encounters among audiences and the museum"

(Proctor, 2010: 36). They should pay attention to the collection of objects for storing and managing information creating and sharing new knowledge rather than using it in terms of communication and dissemination of knowledge. As a community that relies on trust-based active participation of users, museums shape knowledge using technology to develop two-way communication to empower the public as a key actor to promote cultural value creation and enhance the experience of visitors as co-creators of public value and producers of information and knowledge working in collaboration with museum staff as a community (Kelly, 2010; Schweibenz, 1998, 2011; Scott, 2010). As organisations that are undergoing the transition from Web to Web 2.0 and embracing virtual-interactive and digital technologies, museums are evolving from being consumption-centred, custodial-oriented and collection-driven institutions designed for preservation to becoming production-centred/audience-driven organisations that sustain active participation of users in cultural content creation, fostering museum staff–visitor and user interactions and creating a visitor-friendly environment that relies on dynamic information, passion and emotion, dialogic interaction, connected and collective expertise, bidirectional and participatory communication and collaboration, as well as cultural contents sharing (Bonacini, 2012; Capriotti & Kuklinski, 2012; Gilmore & Rentschler, 2002; Schweibenz, 2011). Technologies are socially shaped (Williams & Edge, 1996) in order to drive meaningful communication within museums (Antinucci, 1998). "Digital technology presents great opportunities for cultural heritage communities to reach a broader audience in new ways" (Tang, 2005: 51). Digital technologies and digital objects help museums as meeting places and contact zones to communicate and interact with audiences, to promote meanings and dialogue and encourage audiences to become active participants involved with cultural heritage (Pallud & Straub, 2014; Pruulman-Vengerfeldt & Aljas, 2011; Srinivasan, Becvar, Boast, & Enote, 2010). In embracing advanced virtual technologies following a constructivist view, museums exploit their educational potential, delivering results to a global audience and supporting public awareness and entertainment by involving the audience as active participants (Addison, 2000; Roussou, 2002, 2008).

Museums Contribute to Value Co-creation by Technologies

Value co-creation relies on sustaining the interaction between consumers and firms involved in joint creation of value that is unique to the individual (Prahalad & Ramaswamy, 2013). Service systems are considered as value co-creation configurations of people, technology, value propositions that connect internal and external service systems, and shared information (Maglio & Spohrer, 2008). Museums contribute to value co-creation using technologies to support the participation of audiences and encourage user involvement and sustained learning and education by providing interactions and communication between the user and museum information professionals as user-centred mediators (Marty, 2011; Marty, Sayre, & Fantoni, 2011). In particular, technologies as operant resources help museums to develop service innovation and improve economic, financial and social performances (Camarero, Garrido, & Vicente, 2011), involving the customer to act as a co-creator of value, recipient of service provision and value and a proactive user to design accessible, effective and productive services and processes (Caridà, Colurcio, & Melia, 2014; Magnusson, Matthing, & Kristensson, 2003). Value creation is interactive and networked. The value is always subjective, experiential, contextual and determined by the beneficiary. Technologies are driving museums to embrace a service-centred paradigm, promote actor-driven service innovation and value co-creation following customer-oriented and relational service-centred views to emphasise the intangible aspects of the museum experience (Alcaraz, Hume, & Mort, 2009; Antón et al., 2018; Padilla-Meléndez & del Àguila-Obra, 2013; Vargo & Lusch, 2008; Vargo, Maglio, & Akaka, 2008). Museums contribute to co-creating the experience of the consumer and the value as a derived outcome, promoting active participation and physical interaction, enabling cognitive and emotional immersion, and tailoring the experience with the museum staff and technologies (Minkiewicz et al., 2014). The Internet and other social and collaborative technologies are leading museums to co-create value, building participative processes and meanings with people

(Ind & Coates, 2013; Padilla-Meléndez & del Àguila-Obra, 2013). Technologies enable museums to sustain user-led innovation for knowledge sharing and creation (Russo et al., 2008), engaging audiences in the co-creation of cultural interactive experiences and content (Russo, 2011), reshaping the process of learning (Russo & Watkins, 2007), employing the input of the public as a central contribution (Arnold & Geser, 2007) and developing new applications for user-generated content and the creation of web-based communication in cultural heritage (Silberman, 2007). Museums use technologies that make the collections more accessible to the public and promote innovations that support learning and educational orientation, mediating between market orientation and social performance (Camarero & Garrido, 2008; Garrido & Camarero, 2010). Museums promote value co-creation and support service experience interactions with audience to actively encourage user involvement and participation, enhancing the learning experience (Hazan, 2007) and enabling the creation of an emotional space, leading the visitor to re-understanding, re-interacting and re-reading the objects (Bearman & Gebra, 2008; Schweibenz, 2011; Witcomb, 2007). Virtual technology and digital applications enable museums to involve the users in the co-creation of digital cultural heritage (Marty et al., 2011; Russo et al., 2008), building co-creative environments for value co-creation and sharing (Russo & Watkins, 2007) developing a many-to-many model of communication that enables the interpretation of collections from a visitor perspective (Russo et al., 2007).

How Technologies Enable Value Co-creation Within Museums

Technologies enable museums to offer new opportunities for public fruition and the definition of cultural contents of heritage, information and knowledge management, sharing and creation. Technologies help museums as knowledge- and information-oriented organisations to store and manage information sources to create, communicate, share and disseminate knowledge involving the audience as proactive users and co-producers of value in cultural heritage (Schweibenz, 2011). Technologies enable museums to sustain value co-creation by following some directions: rediscovering the user involvement and participation ranging from communication to sustaining education and learning; rethinking virtual museums along a *continuum* from managing collections to creating and sharing knowledge and information; rediscovering the role of museum information professionals as user-centred mediators that interact with museum information resources and meet the changing needs of users.

Rediscovering the User Involvement and Participation: From Communication to Sustaining Learning and Education

Technologies help people view the museum collections (Bearman & Gebra, 2008) and provide information on web databases (Schweibenz, 2011), making museums audience-oriented and social institutions that enable the users to actively participate in cultural content definition (Bearman & Trant, 2008). "The Internet is a great opportunity which the museums should use to broaden its audience" (Schweibenz, 1998: 194). As participatory institutions that support user engagement (Bonacini, 2012; Simon, 2010), museums are using social media and moving from a one-to-many communication in which curatorial expertise is broadcast to the community via a two-way participatory communication system (Russo et al., 2008). Museums are strategically embracing the Internet and selecting a social media strategy to engage the audience in order to develop a loyalty relationship over time (Padilla-Meléndez & del Àguila-Obra, 2013; McGrath, 2018).

Museum websites and web interfaces act as information sources and a communication channel should help reinforce a strategic link between the website and the physical place (Wilson, 2011), opening new ways of dealing with multiple users, sustaining the generation of story-based environments and driving record searches about the collection database (Dyson & Moran, 2000). Thereby, museums should provide more efficient e-services and searching tools for content- and theme-based facilities (Lazarinis, 2011). They are still privileging a one-way channel (Capriotti & Kuklinski, 2012) that involves top-down communication and limited user involvement and dialogic engagement (Bonacini, 2012; Fletcher & Lee, 2012).

As a trusted partner that provides reliable information in participatory communication on the web, museums "should use social media to create a positive online museum experience for virtual visitors" (Schweibenz, 2011: 11) where museum staff and users develop a dialogue, interact, communicate and learn (Kelly, 2010; Schweibenz, 2011). They should drive the visitor as an active participant that contributes to creating knowledge (Mancini & Carreras, 2010) and generating and sharing their own museum-centred content (Simon, 2007). Museums are embracing digital and interactive information technology to involving participants, developing a multi-directional collaboration with the public (Capriotti & Kuklinski, 2012; Simon, 2010). Web 2.0 facilitates interactive information and knowledge management and sharing and feedback, as well as collaboration and user-centred design, unlike Web 1.0, which was used as a tool mainly focused on information provision (Bonacini, 2012). Web 2.0 is open to decentralisation of knowledge and democratises cultural production, taking into account the perspectives of the different users that interact between them (Russo & Watkins, 2007). In embracing social media, museums act as a trusted network that engages online participants to distribute community knowledge, becoming a custodian of cultural content (Russo et al., 2007). In using social networking services, museums develop *awareness* to increase the diversity of the audience, *comprehension* to enhance visitor understanding and knowledge about collections to strengthen the relationship between museums and visitors, promoting *engagement* in order to connect visitors and museum staff and reinforce the relationship between the visitor and museum (Chung, Marcketti, & Fiore, 2014).

Museums are providing an increasing amount of opportunities for accessible and flexible education and learning, developing new interactive technologies (Lòpez, Margapoti, Maragliano, & Bove, 2010) and building virtual environments as independent of physical spaces that enable the user to have new experiences while interacting with virtual humans and accessing to information created during the interaction (Machidon, Duguleana, & Carrozzino, 2018; Schroeder, 2008). Technologies and multimedia applications help the museum to reinvent the educational and cultural role in the society (Hein, 2005; MacDonald & Alsford, 1991) and redefine learning processes and spaces (Miller, 2010). Technologies contribute to enabling the creation of learning and emotional spaces and leading to a re-reading of those displayed objects (Witcomb, 2007), improving the quality of museum experiences and learning (Lehn & Heath, 2005) and valuing the message in terms of technical, aesthetic and pedagogical implications in the presentation and interpretation of objects (Economou, 1998). Visual objects should help reinforce and experience effective communication, investigation and learning (Du Terroil, 1975). Interactive, advanced and virtual technologies drive museums to sustain the learning and educational process, supporting individual psychological and cultural growth and sustaining both leisure, recreation, entertainment and education as complementary aspects while driving the audience to actively participate in and determine their own experience (Addis, 2005; Falk, Moussouri, & Coulson, 1998; Roussou, 2002). Virtual heritage helps to provide formative educational experiences and disseminate knowledge through electronic manipulations of time and space (Roussou, 2002; Stone & Ojika, 2000), enabling the user to interact with virtual humans (Machidon et al., 2018) and providing virtual environments that contribute to increasing educational purposes, as well as the learning and motivation of participants that interact with digital objects and personalise learning activities (Carrozzino & Bergamasco, 2010; Ott & Pozzi, 2011). Technologies enable museums to provide context-aware ubiquitous environments that help learning processes and self-learning activities (Chen & Chen, 2018; Chen & Huang, 2012; Chiou, Tseng, Hwang, & Heller, 2010).

Rethinking Virtual Museums: From Managing Collection to Creating and Sharing Information and Knowledge

New technologies that are computer-based and rely on informatics lead museums to add a digital dimension and form to traditional and physical dimensions reconciling and combining authority and participation for the definition of contents about cultural heritage by building a virtual museum (Tsichritzis & Gibbs, 1991) as a place without the barriers of space and time, as hypothesised by Malraux (1965) in *Le Museè Imaginaire*. This type of museum is an interactive and virtual space that allows each artefact to be displayed, and people can operate and play with artefacts for providing information and exhibiting cultural objects in digital formats (Schweibenz, 1998, 2011). Virtual museum refers to a museum that "will deal with virtual artefacts, in a virtual setting accessible from telecommunication network in a participatory manner. Such museum is a service not a location" (Tsichritzis & Gibbs, 1991: 18). Virtual museum exhibitions provide a great amount of information that helps virtual visitors to understand museum information sources (Styliani, Fotis, Kostas, & Petros, 2009). In particular, the features of the virtual museum are well defined and described by Schweibenz (2004): "it can offer real objects to its visitors, as the traditional museum does. But it can extend the ideas and concepts of collections into the digital space and in this way reveal the essential nature of the museum. At the same time the virtual museum will reach out to virtual visitors who might never be able to visit a certain museum in person". In a virtual museum, digital media aids in the exhibition, education and research functions, leading users to play an active role by changing views or objects by interactive interfaces. The exhibition is displayed in multiple platforms on users' demand, the representation occurs by digital movies and data. The virtual museum without real place or space "is a logically related collection of digital objects composed in a variety of media, and, because of its capacity to provide connectedness and various points of access, lends itself to transcending traditional methods of communicating and interacting with the visitors being flexible toward their needs and interests; it has no real place or space, its objects and the related information can be disseminated all over the world" (Schweibenz, 1998: 191). The strength and authenticity of the virtual museum is focused on being information Internet-centred and communicative projection: its objects and the related information are disseminated everywhere (Antinucci, 2007; Schweibenz, 2011). New technologies help virtual museums to manage and deliver information in any form and at any time (Qarabolaq, Inallou, Hafezi, & Tabaei 2013). Three categories of virtual museums are identified: the *brochure* museum aiming at informing future visitors containing administrative and general information about the museum; the *content* museum, which acts as a database containing detailed information about the museum collections, with the content presented in an object-oriented way making information available about the museum collections; the *learning* museum, establishing a personal relationship between the virtual visitor and museum, with a website offering different points of access to the virtual visitors, presenting the information in a way that is context-oriented, educationally enhanced and linked to additional information. This invites the visitor to learn more about a subject and visit again (Styliani et al., 2009). Designing a virtual museum helps foster cultural participation, and engagement promotes inclusion and diversity through experiences engendered for the visitors and users (Niccolucci, 2007; Robles-Ortega, Feito, Jiménez, & Segura, 2012). Virtual museums should be designed in order to strengthen user-constructed experiences based on content, structure, functionality and interaction (Deshpande, Geber, & Timpson, 2007).

Rediscovering the Role of Museums as User-Centred Mediators

Technologies enable museums to function as modern knowledge-oriented and intensive-information organisations that legitimise information and knowledge processes using information sources to create new knowledge about cultural heritage (Freedman, 2000; Marty, 2011). "A museum offers a unique environment from which to study the way in which knowledge is accumulated, analysed, and distributed by information professionals" (Marty, 1999: 1083). In any information society, museums should integrate technology and human resources in order to set information policies, manage information resources and promote changes in work and the roles of museum informational professionals in order to generate new knowledge for their audience (Marty, 2007a). In particular, the advent of new and advanced technologies and museum informatics implies that museum information professionals should adapt to changing capabilities and act as user-centred mediators in order to provide successful interactions between museum and users, understanding what visitors are looking for on websites, making information resources available and meeting the changing information needs and expectations of museum information resource users (Marty, 2006a, 2008). Technologies contribute to enhancing museum professionals as information professionals that develop new methods of information organising and access to the collections, integrating new technologies in the exhibits using virtual environments to personally tailor the experience for each individual visitor and user (Marty, 2006a, 2007b, 2011). Museums are knowledge enablers that integrate knowledge, content acquisition and organisation to develop applications in academic research, exhibition and education for users (Hsu, Ke, & Yang, 2006). Web 2.0 technologies support knowledge sharing and collaborative learning through social interaction (Barak, Orit, Zvia, & Dory, 2009). Information technology helps improve information and knowledge management within museums, encouraging collaboration among museum professionals and museum users (Marty, 2011). New technologies help museum staff experts and motivated individuals or interested communities to reconstruct and reinterpret knowledge and information about collections (Verboom & Arora, 2013). The Internet is enabling museums as information utilities (MacDonald & Alsford, 1991) and service-oriented information organisations (Marty, 2006b) to actively use information in terms of generation, perpetuation, organisation and dissemination to generate new knowledge to their audience. The information is embedded in both the organisational memory and its collections and the documented information resources (Huvila, 2013). Museum educators play a proactive role in guiding virtual experiences for learning enabling museums to respond to visitor needs, providing multiple and different experiences (Roussou, 2004). Web 2.0 technologies enable museum professionals to connect with the public involving general people in the museum environment (Duff, Carter, Howarth, Ross, & Dallas, 2010). Museums as repositories of knowledge and information utilities sustain social and financial performances, and they should improve the organisational processes by strengthening the work and skills of museum professionals as curators and educators, meeting the needs of visitors and acting as user-centred mediators. The Internet and interactive and virtual technologies drive museums as information-based organisations (Marty, 2006a, 2007a) to enable museum professionals to concentrate their efforts on using information technology to meet the needs of visitors through new forms of interactivity, working to improve the museum experience for users by focusing on digitisation technologies, information policy and collaboration initiatives (Marty, 2011). Museum educators and staff facilitate co-creation beyond the traditional view of holding and disseminating knowledge, enhancing the museum's educational potential in their work. Museum professionals can use a variety of new technologies in order to support the changing needs and expectations of online visitors (Marty et al., 2011). New technologies help museum professionals to bridge information and technologies to serve as user-centred mediators, enabling users to interact positively with museum information resources and behave as advocates that represent and meet the changing needs of users, creating personal collections as active participants in the co-construction of digital knowledge and cultural heritage (Marty, 2006b, 2007b, 2011).

Conclusions

As organisations that embrace technology, museums have become communities that promote dialogue, develop meanings and rediscover knowledge and information sources and capabilities for value creation about cultural heritage. Museums contribute to designing a community within cultural heritage and ecosystems, promoting value co-creation, service and social innovation using the Internet, embracing social media and developing interactive and virtual technologies and environments in order to support participatory engagement and involve the users as co-producers of knowledge in cultural heritage content. Museums empower museum information professionals as user-centred mediators, developing core competencies in managing museum information and knowledge sources, as well as interacting, communicating and collaborating with users as active co-producers of knowledge and value in regard to cultural heritage. As communities that develop a shared authority on cultural heritage, museums are embracing technologies and encouraging the participation of users in defining cultural contents on collections. Today, museums as communities utilise the Internet, as well as virtual and interactive technologies to promote and reinforce interaction between objects, information and users, but they also encourage and accept new information from visitors to the community.

As shown in Fig. 8.1, museums using information technology and moving from traditional web technologies to building virtual-interactive technologies and environments support the user involvement and participation proceeding towards a shared authority on the definition of cultural contents about heritage in relation to the changing user role, which is evolving from merely being consumers to becoming co-producers of knowledge about cultural heritage. In developing the potential of information technology to promote new cultural experiences and involve users as co-producers and co-creators of new knowledge, museums contribute to expanding the *value co-creation area* transitioning from being communication-oriented institutions to becoming completely participatory. Museums evolve from maintaining authority on cultural heritage to involving the audience and communities to defining cultural contents and sustaining a shared authority on cultural heritage. As organisations dealing with information as a key source, museums should engage the users as co-producers and active participants and promote technology-driven innovation to develop processes and communication that encourage user participation, rediscovering the participation

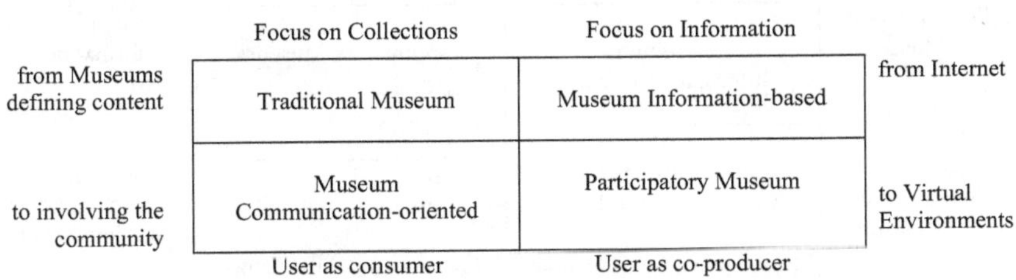

Fig. 8.1 Changing museums encouraging participation by technologies

about cultural contents definition as a source for value co-creation within museums as communities.

The contribution of this study is to elucidate how museums identify different pathways for value co-creation. Museums as audience- or collection-driven organisations use technologies to develop information provision sources or support communication and interaction, fostering user involvement and participation in cultural heritage by relying on museum human resources as information museum professionals and developing the potential provided by new technologies that drive museums to be participatory and social-oriented, learning-based and educational communities.

As collection-based institutions, museums contribute to promoting value co-creation and service innovation by embracing virtual and interactive technologies paying attention to the role of human resources and organisation redesign for developing and improving communication and interaction by involving the audience in knowledge sharing and creation, as shown in Fig. 8.2.

Museums as repositories of knowledge and information-intensive organisations should always be improving their organisational processes and enhancing human resources, sustaining active user participation in defining cultural contents and promoting knowledge and value co-creation. As audience-driven organisations, museums develop the potential of new technologies in order to support communication and interaction. Museums as collection-based and technology-driven organisations distribute information on cultural artefacts, providing

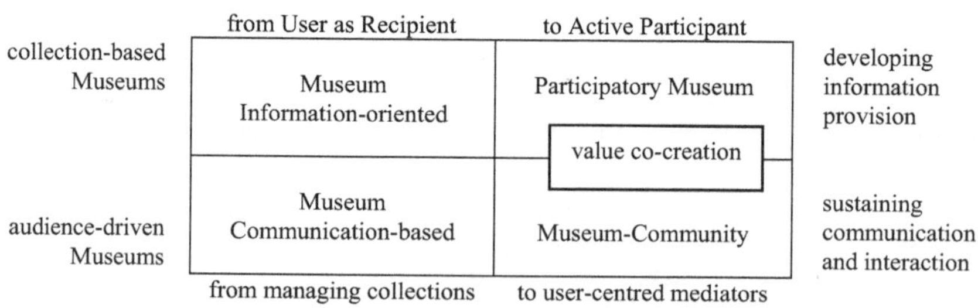

Fig. 8.2 Creating value within museums: a framework of analysis

information about collections to the user as mere recipients. As meeting places and social platforms for knowledge sharing and innovation, museums sustain value co-creation by embracing new technologies to involve the audience, engaging the user to participate in developing informative and social spaces for creating knowledge and managing information.

Museums should become cultural and social institutions that contribute to value co-creation developing the potential offered by virtual environments and interactive technology in order to promote human-centred design and vision, new service innovations and business models. Technologies contribute to enabling user involvement, active participation, co-production and personalisation of individual experiences, and they help information museum professionals to develop information and knowledge sources to interact with users leading the museum as an organisation to become a community within social and cultural ecosystems and society. Museums as communities support interactive, virtual and advanced technologies, relying on human resources, museum capabilities and user knowledge in order to develop information and knowledge management strategies, seeking solutions for participatory engagement and involving the users in managing information and knowledge about collections of digital materials, as well as to create value in the field of cultural heritage.

Future research perspectives imply to investigate how museums are facing the challenge of change and innovation driven and supported by technology in order to create new knowledge, social and public value by involving the users that interact with museum information professionals to develop the museum as a community that proceeds to generate knowledge, create value and ensure the wealth of communities within society.

References

Addis, M. (2005). New technologies and cultural consumption—Edutainment is born! *European Journal of Marketing, 39*(7–8), 729–736.

Addison, A. (2000). Emerging trends in virtual heritage. *IEEE Multimedia, 7*(2), 22–25.

Alcaraz, C., Hume, M., & Mort, G. S. (2009). Creating sustainable practice in a museum context: Adopting service-centricity in non-profit museums. *Australasian Marketing Journal (AMJ), 17*(4), 219–225.

Anderson, M. L. (1999). Museums of the future: The impact of technology on museum practices. *Daedalus-Boston-Mass, 128*, 129–162.

Antinucci, F. (1998). Musei e nuove tecnologie: dov'è il problema? *Sistemi intelligenti, 10*(2), 281–306.

Antinucci, F. (2007). The Virtual museum. *Archeologia e Calcolatori, Supplemento, 1*, 79–86.

Antón, C., Camarero, C., & Garrido, M.-J. (2018). Exploring the experience value of museum visitors as a co-creation process. *Current Issues in Tourism, 21*(12), 1406–1425.

Arnold, D. B., & Geser, G. (2007). *Research agenda for the applications of ict to cultural heritage*. Budapest: Archeolingua.

Bagdadly, S. (1997). *Il museo come azienda. Management e organizzazione al servizio della cultura*. Milano: Etas.

Balogun, J., Best, K., & Lê, J. (2015). Selling the objects of strategy: How frontline workers realize strategy through their daily work. *Organization Studies, 36*(10), 1285–1313.

Barak, M., Orit, H., Zvia, K., & Dory, Y. J. (2009). MOSAICA: A Web-2.0 based system for the preservation and presentation of cultural heritage. *Computers & Education, 53*(3), 841–852.

Bautista, S. S. (2014). *Museums in the digital age: Changing meanings of place, community, and culture*. Lanham: AltaMira Press.

Bearman, D., & Gebra, K. (2008). Transforming cultural heritage institutions through new media. *Museum Management and Curatorship, 23*(4), 385–399.

Bearman, D., & Trant, J. (2008). Technologies, like museums, are social. In *Proceedings of the International Conference on Museums and the Web (MW08)* (pp. 3–8).

Bonacini, E. (2012). Il museo partecipativo sul web: forme di partecipazione dell'utente alla produzione culturale e alla creazione di valore culturale. *Il capitale culturale. Studies on the Value of Cultural Heritage, 5*, 93–125.

Borin, E., & Donato, F. (2015). Unlocking the potential of IC in Italian cultural ecosystems. *Journal of Intellectual Capital, 16*(2), 285–304.

Brown, K., & Mairesse, F. (2018). The definition of the museum through its social role. *Curator: The Museum Journal, 61*(4), 525–539.

Burton, C., & Scott, C. (2007). Museums: Challenges for the 21st century. In R. Sandell & R. R. Janes (Eds.), *Museum management and marketing* (pp. 49–66). London: Routledge.

Camarero, C., & Garrido, M. J. (2008). The role of technological and organizational innovation in the relation between market orientation and performance in cultural organizations. *European Journal of Innovation Management, 11*(3), 413–434.

Camarero, C., Garrido, M. J., & Vicente, E. (2011). How cultural organizations' size and funding influence innovation and performance: The case of museums. *Journal of Cultural Economics, 35*(4), 247–266.

Capriotti, P., & Kuklinski, H. P. (2012). Assessing dialogic communication through the internet in Spanish museums. *Public Relations Review, 38*(4), 619–626.

Caridà, A., Colurcio, M., & Melia, M. (2014). Rethinking and improving the health care service through interactive web technologies. In E. Baglieri & U. Karmakar (Eds.), *Managing consumer services: Factory or theater?* (pp. 191–210). Cham: Springer.

Carrozzino, M., & Bergamasco, M. (2010). Beyond virtual museums: Experiencing immersive virtual reality in real museums. *Journal of Cultural Heritage, 11*(4), 452–458.

Castells, M. (2001). Museums in the information era: Cultural connectors of time and space. *ICOM News*, Special Issue, pp. 1–4.

Chen, C. C., & Huang, T. C. (2012). Learning in a u-Museum: Developing a context-aware ubiquitous learning environment. *Computers & Education, 59*(3), 873–883.

Chiou, C. K., Tseng, J. C., Hwang, G. J., & Heller, S. (2010). An adaptive navigation support system for conducting context-aware ubiquitous learning in museums. *Computers & Education, 55*(2), 834–845.

Chung, T. L., Marcketti, S., & Fiore, A. M. (2014). Use of social networking services for marketing art museums. *Museum Management and Curatorship, 29*(2), 188–205.

Consiglio, S., Cicellin, M., Scuotto, A., & Ricchezza, D. (2017). L'approccio audience-centric dei musei: un processo di innovazione sociale. *Prospettiveinorganizzazione, 8*.

Council of Europe. (2005). *Framework convention on the value of cultural heritage for society*. Faro, 27 October 2005.

Crooke, E. (2006). Museums and community. In S. Macdonald (Ed.), *A companion to museum studies* (pp. 170–185). Oxford: Blackwell.

d'Harnoncourt, A., DiMaggio, P. J., Perry M., & Wood, J. N. (1991). The museum and the public. In M. Feldstein (Ed.), *The economics of art museums* (pp. 35–60). Chicago: The University of Chicago Press.

Davies, S. M., Paton, R., & O'Sullivan, T. J. (2013). The museum values framework: A framework for understanding organisational culture in museums. *Museum Management and Curatorship, 28*(4), 345–361.

Denyer, D., & Tranfield, D. (2006). Using qualitative research synthesis to build an actionable knowledge base. *Management Decision, 24,* 213–227.

Deshpande, S., Geber, K., & Timpson, C. (2007). Engaged dialogism in virtual space: An exploration of research strategies for virtual museums. In F. Cameron & S. Kenderline (Eds.), *Theorizing digital cultural heritage: A critical discourse* (pp. 261–279). Cambridge: MIT Press.

Dixon-Woods, M., Agarwal, S., Young, B., Jones, D., & Sutton, A. (2004). *Integrative approaches to qualitative and quantitative evidence.* London: Health Development Agency.

Du Terroil, A. (1975). *Museum education: Recent trends in learning environments.*

Duclos-Orsello, E. (2013). Shared authority: The key to museum education as social change. *Journal of Museum Education, 38*(2), 121–128.

Duff, W. M., Carter, J., Howarth, L., Ross, S., & Dallas, C. (2010). The museum environment in transition: The impact of technology on museum work. In C. Cirinnà & M. Lunghi (Eds.), *Cultural heritage on line. Empowering users: An active role for user communities* (pp. 1000–1005). Firenze: Firenze University Press,

Duncan, C. (2003). Art museums and the ritual of citizenship. In S. M. Pearce (Ed.), *Interpreting objects and collections* (pp. 291–298). London: Routledge.

Dyson, M. C., & Moran, K. (2000). Informing the design of web interfaces to museum collections. *Museum Management and Curatorship, 18*(4), 391–406.

Economou, M. (1998). The evaluation of museum multimedia applications: Lessons from research. *Museum Management and Curatorship, 17*(2), 173–187.

Economou, M., & Pujol, L. (2008). Educational tool or expensive toy? Evaluating VR evaluation and its relevance for virtual heritage. In Y. Kalay, T. Kvan, & J. Afflek (Eds.), *New heritage: New media and cultural heritage* (pp. 242–260). London and New York: Routledge-Taylor and Francis Group.

Falk, J. H., Moussouri, T., & Coulson, D. (1998). The effect of visitors' agendas on museum learning. *Curator: The Museum Journal, 41*(2), 107–120.

Fletcher, A., & Lee, M. J. (2012). Current social media uses and evaluations in American museums. *Museums Management and Curatorship, 27*(5), 505–521.

Freedman, G. (2000). The changing nature of museums. *Curator: The Museum Journal, 43*(4), 295–306.

Garrido, M. J., & Camarero, C. (2010). Assessing the impact of organizational learning and innovation on performance in cultural organizations. *International Journal of Nonprofit and Voluntary Sector Marketing, 15,* 215–232.

Gilmore, A., & Rentschler, R. (2002). Changes in museum management: A custodial or marketing emphasis. *Journal of management development, 21*(10), 745–760.

Hazan, S. (2007). A crisis of authority: New lamps for old. In F. Cameron & S. Kenderline (Eds.), *Theorizing digital cultural heritage: A critical discourse* (pp. 133–147). Cambridge: The MIT Press.

Hein, G. E. (1998). *Learning in museum.* London: Routledge.

Hein, G. E. (1999). The constructivist museum. In E. Hooper-Greenhill (Ed.), *The educational role of the museum* (pp. 73–79). London and New York: Routledge.

Hein, G. E. (2005). The role of museums in society: Education and social action. *Curator: The Museum Journal, 48*(4), 357–363.

Hein, G. E. (2006). Museum education. In S. Macdonald (ed.), *A companion to museum studies* (pp. 340–352). Oxford: Blackwell.

Holden, J. (2006). *Cultural value and the crisis of legitimacy: Why culture need a democratic mandate.* London: Demos.

Hooper-Greenhill, E. (1992). *Museums and the shaping of knowledge.* London: Routledge.

Hooper-Greenhill, E. (1995). Museums and communication: An introductory essay. In E. Hooper-Greenhill (Ed.), *Museum, media, message* (pp. 1–12). London: Routledge.

Hooper-Greenhill, E. (2007). Museums: learning and culture. In E. Hooper-Greenhill (Ed.), *Museum and education: Purpose, pedagogy, performance* (pp. 1–14). London: Routledge.

Hsu, T.-H., Ke, H.-R., & Yang, W.-P. (2006). Unified knowledge-based content management for digital archives in museums. *The Electronic Library, 24*(1), 38–50.

Huvila, I. (2013). How a museum knows? Structures, work roles, and infrastructure of information work. *Journal of the American Society for Information Science and Technology (JASIST), 64*(7), 1375–1387.

ICOM News, No. 3, 2004. http://icom.museum/pdf/E_news2004/p3_2004-3.pdf.

Ind, N., & Coates, N. (2013). The meanings of co-creation. *European Business Review, 25*(1), 86–95.

Karp, I. (1992). Introduction: Museums and communities: The politics of public culture. In I. Karp & C. Mullen Kreamer (Ed.), *Museums and communities* (pp. 1–17). Washington and London: Smithsonian Institution Press.

Keene, S. (1997). Becoming digital. *Museum Management and Curatorship, 15*(3), 299–314.

Kelly, L. (2010). How Web 2.0 is changing the nature of museum work. *Curator: The Museum Journal, 53*(4), 405–410.

Knell, S. (2019). *The contemporary museum*. London: Routledge.

Kurin, R. (2004). Museums and intangible heritage: Culture dead or alive. *Icom News, 57*(4), 7–9.

Lazarinis, F. (2011). Exploring the effectiveness of information searching tools on Greek museum websites. *Museum Management and Curatorship, 26*(4), 391–408.

Lehn, D., & Heath, C. (2005). Accounting for new technology in museum exhibitions. *International Journal of Arts Management, 7*(3), 11–21.

Leon R. D. (2013). From the sustainable organization to sustainable knowledge based organization. *Economic Insights—Trends and Challenges, 2*(2), 63–73.

Lòpez, X., Margapoti, I., Maragliano, R., & Bove, G. (2010). The presence of Web 2.0 tools on museum websites: A comparative study between England, France, Spain, Italy and the USA. *Museum Management and Curatorship, 25*(2), 235–249.

Lord, B. (2007). *The manual of museum learning*. Rowman: Altamira.

Loulanski, T. (2006). Revising the concept for cultural heritage: The argument for a functional approach. *International Journal of Cultural Property, 13*(2), 207–233.

MacDonald, G. F., & Alsford, S. (1991). The museum as information utility. *Museum Management and Curatorship, 10*(3), 305–311.

Macfarlan, S. J. (2001). A consideration of museum education collections: Theory and application. *Curator: The Museum Journal, 44*(2), 166–178.

Machidon, O. M., Duguleana, M., & Carrozzino, M. (2018). Virtual humans in cultural heritage ICT applications: A review. *Journal of Cultural Heritage, 33*, 249–260.

Maglio, P. P., & Spohrer, J. (2008). Fundamentals of service science. *Journal of the Academy of Marketing Science, 36*(1), 18–20.

Magnusson, P. R., Matthing, J., & Kristensson, P. (2003). Managing user involvement in service innovation: Experiments with innovating end users. *Journal of Service Research, 6*(2), 111–124.

Malraux, A. (1965). *Le Musée imaginaire 1947*. Paris: Gallimard.

Mancini, F., & Carreras, C. (2010). Techno-society at the service of memory institutions: Web 2.0 in museums. *Catalan Journal of Communication & Cultural Studies, 2*(1), 59–76.

Marty, P. F. (1999). Museum informatics and collaborative technologies: The emerging socio-technological dimension of information science in museum environments. *Journal of the American Society for Information Science, 50*(2), 1083–1091.

Marty, P. F. (2006a). Finding the skills for tomorrow: Information literacy and museum information professionals. *Museum Management and Curatorship, 21*(4), 317–335.

Marty, P. F. (2006b). Meeting user needs in the modern museum: Profiles of the new museum information professional. *Library & Information Science Research, 28*(1), 128–144.

Marty, P. F. (2007a). The changing nature of information work in museums. *Journal of the American Society for Information Science and Technology, 58*(1), 97–107.

Marty, P. F. (2007b). Museum professionals and the relevance of LIS expertise. *Library & Information Science Research, 29*(2), 252–276.

Marty, P. F. (2008). Museum websites and museum visitors: Digital museum resources and their use. *Museum Management and Curatorship, 23*(1), 81–99.

Marty, P. F. (2011). My lost museum: User expectations and motivations for creating personal digital collections on museum websites. *Library & Information Science Research, 33*(3), 211–219.

Marty, P. F., Sayre, S., & Fantoni, S. F. (2011). Personal digital collections: Involving users in the co-creation of digital cultural heritage. In G. Styliaras, D. Koukopoulos, & F. Lazarinis (Eds.), *Handbook of research on technologies and cultural heritage: Applications and environments* (pp. 286–304). Hershey: IGI Global.

McGrath, K. (2018). *The role of social media in small museums in Michigan.*

Miller, J. D. (2010). Adult science learning in the internet era. *Curator: The Museum Journal, 53*(2), 191–208.

Minkiewicz, J., Evans, J., & Bridson, K. (2014). How do consumers co-create their experiences? An exploration in the heritage sector. *Journal of Marketing Management, 30*(1–2), 30–59.

Murzyn-Kupisz, M., & Dzialek, J. (2013). Cultural heritage in building and enhancing social capital. *Journal of Cultural Heritage Management and Sustainable Development, 3*(1), 35–54.

Niccolucci, F. (2007). Virtual museums and archaeology: An international perspective. *Archeologia e Calcolatori, 1,* 15–30.

Orna, E., & Pettitt, C. (2010). What is information in the museum context?. In R. Parry (Ed.), *Museums in a digital age* (pp. 28–38). London: Routledge.

Ott, M., & Pozzi, F. (2011). Towards a new era for cultural heritage education: Discussing the role of ICT. *Computers in Human Behavior, 27*(4), 1365–1371.

Padilla-Melèndez, A., & del Àguila-Obra, A. R. (2013). Web and social media usage by museums: Online value creation. *International Journal of Information Management, 33*(5), 892–898.

Pallud, J., & Straub, D. W. (2014). Effective website design for experience-influenced environments: The case of high culture museums. *Information & Management, 51*(3), 359–373.

Pearce, S. M. (2003). Introduction. In S. M. Pearce (Ed.), *Interpreting objects and collections* (pp. 1–16). London: Routledge.

Pop, I. L., & Borza, A. (2014). Increasing the sustainability of museums through international strategy. *Economia. Seria Management, 17*(2), 248–264.

Prahalad, C. K., & Ramaswamy, V. (2013). *The future of competition: Co-creating unique value with customers*. Boston: Harvard Business Press.

Proctor, N. (2010). Digital: Museum as platform, curator as champion, in the age of social media. *Curator: The Museum Journal, 53*(1), 35–43.

Pruulmann-Vengerfeldt, P., & Aljas, A. (2011). Digital cultural heritage—Challenging museums, archives and users. *Journal of Ethnology and Folkloristics, 3*(1), 109–127.

Qarabolaq, Z. F., Inallou, M. S., Hafezi, H. A., & Tabaei, A. N. M. (2013). The role of PREMIS preservation metadata in information management in virtual museums. *Procedia—Social and Behavioral Sciences, 73,* 396–402.

Robles-Ortega, M. D., Feito, F. R., Jiménez, J. J., & Segura, R. J. (2012). Web technologies applied to virtual heritage: An example of an Iberian Art Museum. *Journal of Cultural Heritage, 13*(3), 326–331.

Romanelli, M. (2017). Le strategie dei musei si realizzano attraverso le persone. *Prospettiveinorganizzazione, 8*.

Rounds, J. (2012). The museum and its relationships as a loosely coupled system. *Curator: The Museum Journal, 55*(4), 413–434.

Roussou, M. (2002). Virtual heritage: From the research lab to the broad public. *Bar International Series, 1075,* 93–100.

Roussou, M. (2004). Learning by doing and learning through play: An exploration of interactivity in virtual environments for children. *ACM Computers in Entertainment, 2*(1), 1–23.

Roussou, M. (2008). The components of engagement in virtual heritage environments. *Proceedings of New Heritage: Beyond Verisimilitude—Conference on Cultural Heritage and New Media* (pp. 265–283), Hong Kong.

Russo, A. (2011). Transformation in cultural communication: social media, cultural exchange, and creative connections. *Curator: The Museum Journal, 54*(3), 327–346.

Russo, A., & Watkins, J. (2007). Digital cultural communication: Audience and remediation. In F. Cameron & S. Kenderline (Eds.), *Theorizing digital cultural heritage. A critical discourse* (pp. 149–164). Cambridge: MIT Press.

Russo, A., Watkins, J., Kelly, L., & Chan, S. (2007). Social media and cultural interactive experiences in museums. *Nordisk Museologi, 1,* 19–29.

Russo, A., Watkins, J., Kelly, L., & Chan, S. (2008). Participatory communication with social media. *Curator: The Museum Journal, 51*(1), 21–31.

Sabiescu, A., & Charatzopoulou, K. (2018). The museum as ecosystem and museums in learning ecosystems. In A. Vermeeren, L. Calvi, & A. Sabiescu (Eds.), *Experience design: Crowds, ecosystems and novel technologies* (pp. 325–345). Cham: Springer.

Schroeder, R. (2008). Defining virtual worlds and virtual environments. *Journal for Virtual Worlds Research, 1*(1), 1–3.

Schweibenz, W. (1998). The "virtual museum": New perspectives for museums to present objects and information using the internet as a knowledge base and communication system. *Proceedings des 6. Internationalen Symposiums für Informationswissenschaft* (pp. 185–200), Prag, 3–7 November.

Schweibenz, W. (2004). Virtual museums. The development of virtual museums. *Icom News Magazine*, No. 3.

Schweibenz, W. (2011). Museums and Web 2.0: Some thoughts about authority, communication, participation and trust. In G. Styliaras, D. Koukopoulos, & F. Lazarinis (Eds.), *Handbook of research on technologies and cultural heritage: Applications and environments* (pp. 1–15). Hershey: IGI Global.

Scott, C. (2003). Museums and impact. *Curator: The Museum Journal, 46*(3), 293–310.

Scott, C. (2010). Museums, the public, and public value. *Journal of Museum Education, 35*(1), 33–42.

Sheng, C. W., & Chen, M. C. (2012). A study of experience expectations of museum visitors. *Tourism Management, 33*(1), 53–60.

Silberman, N. (2007). Cultural heritage and the information technologies. In F. Niccolucci (Ed.), *Digital applications for tangible cultural heritage: Report on the state of the union policies, practices and developments in Europe* (Vol. 2, pp. 95–104). Budapest: Epoch.

Simon, N. (2007). Discourse in the blogosphere: What museums can learn from Web 2.0? *Museums & Social Issue, 2*(2), 257–274.
Simon, N. (2010). *The participatory museum*. Santa Cruz: Museum 2.0.
Srinivasan, R., Becvar, K. M., Boast, R., & Enote, J. (2010). Diverse knowledges and contact zone within the digital museum. *Science, Technology and Human Values, 35*(5), 735–768.
Stone, R., & Ojika, T. (2000). Virtual heritage: What next? *IEEE Multimedia, 7*(2), 73–74.
Styliani, S., Fotis, L., Kostas, K., & Petros, P. (2009). Virtual museums, a survey and some issues for consideration. *Journal of cultural Heritage, 10*(4), 520–528.
Tang, M. C. (2005). Representational practices in digital museums: A case study of the national digital museum project of Taiwan. *The International Information & Library Review, 37*(1), 51–60.
Tsichritzis, D., & Gibbs, S. J. (1991). Virtual museums and virtual realities. *Ichim* (pp. 17–25).
Vargo, S. L., & Lusch, R. F. (2008). Service-dominant logic: Continuing the evolution. *Journal of the Academy of Marketing Science, 36*(1), 1–10.
Vargo, S. L., Maglio, P. P., & Akaka, M. A. (2008). On value and value co-creation: A service systems and service logic perspective. *European Management Journal, 26*(3), 145–152.
Vecco, M. (2010). A definition of cultural heritage: From the tangible to intangible. *Journal of Cultural Heritage, 11*(3), 321–324.
Verboom, J., & Arora, P. (2013). Museum 2.0: A study into the culture of expertise within museum blogosphere. *First Monday, 18*(8), 1–12.
Watson, S. (2007). Museums and their communities. In S. Watson (Ed.), *Museums and their communities* (pp. 1–23). London: Routledge.
Weibel, P. (2018). Manifesto for a new museum. In G. Bast, E. G., Carayannis, & D. F. J., Cambpbell (Eds.), *The future of museums* (pp. 49–52). Cham: Springer.
Williams, R., & Edge, D. (1996). The social shaping of technology. *Research Policy, 25*(6), 865–899.
Wilson, R. J. (2011). Digital heritage behind the scenes of the museum website. *Museum Management and Curatorship, 26*(4), 373–389.
Witcomb, A. (2007). The materiality of virtual technologies: A new approach to thinking about the impact of multimedia in museums. In F. Cameron & S. Kenderline (Eds.), *Theorizing digital cultural heritage: A critical discourse* (pp. 35–48). Cambridge: MIT Press.

9

Reassembling Cultural Journalism in the Digital Age

Ursula Plesner

Introduction: The Digitalization of Journalism

As digital infrastructures develop and spread, the media production industry changes drastically. Changes include a broadening of journalistic voices and formats, as seen in the spread of citizen journalism, blogging, and alternative media outlets (Gulyás & Hammer, 2013). We can also observe a precarization of journalism (Bögenhold & Fachinger, 2013) in the sense that established media offer fewer stable and well-paid jobs and move toward the use of more freelancing. This is due to increased competition from free media content and due to established media's declining income. Implications of technological and the ensuing societal changes can be observed in various types of organizations and occupations. For instance, the media production industry trends heavily influence public service media institutions. It is well described how they are challenged by digitalization, changing audience habits, political-economic pressures,

U. Plesner (✉)
Copenhagen Business School, Frederiksberg, Denmark
e-mail: up.ioa@cbs.dk

J. Strandgaard Pedersen et al. (eds.), *Technology and Creativity*,
https://doi.org/10.1007/978-3-030-17566-5_9

and commercial competition (Gulyás & Hammer, 2013; Steenfadt, Glowacki, Nikoltchev, Cabrera Blasquez, & Kus, 2011). The new opportunities for distribution as well as the new competitive environment have implications for journalism as it is understood and practiced both outside and within established media organizations.

If we zoom in on the changing practices of those occupied in the media industry, it is evident that the large majority of journalists have become accustomed to produce online content, creating short stories for web pages, and using social media to create awareness of their work or as a distribution channel for their stories. This is also the case within established media organizations (traditional newspapers, television corporations, and so on), but here, digitalization is more than producing digitized content—it is also about negotiating new organizational structures and occupational categories and thus understanding the role and tasks of journalists differently. An organizational approach to digitalization allows us to reflect on how negotiations about new roles, tasks, and values impact how journalism is understood and practiced (Picard, 2015; Rottwilm, 2014). It allows us to reflect upon how societal and technological trends result in changes in everyday practices, which in turn result in changing occupations.

The present chapter offers an analysis of professional struggles around digitalization in a public service broadcaster, showing how new technologies and tasks become elements in cultural journalism in new ways. It poses the question how actors renegotiate or 'reassemble' cultural journalism in the digital age and proposes that changes in roles, tasks, and values are slowly changing journalism as an occupation—not in any simple manner but allowing for a multitude of approaches to the digitalization of journalism. I draw on Latour's (2005) term 'reassemble,' which has been coined to indicate that any social phenomenon is the result of ongoing work to assemble human and non-human elements. Here, it is used to suggest that an occupation is not a stable thing, but the result of ongoing negotiations both among people and in relation to technologies.

In this chapter, I will share observations from fieldwork in a large, well-established public broadcasting cooperation, focusing on changes brought about by digitalization. One particular observation illustrates why this organization is an interesting case, because it captures how some of its journalists rephrased the news criteria that form the basis of their work as a reaction to the changing competitive environment. During a strategy presentation in the culture division, the editor-in-chief presented a set of new news criteria. Traditional news criteria would not mention an age range or a particular medium, but these criteria did. The first one said: 'Is it relevant for younger users? Show them why your content means something for precisely them.' The second said: 'Is it understandable for younger users? New users should be able to start here.' And the third asked: 'Is the content attractive for younger users? We compete with the entire internet, not just the news media.' Together, the criteria expressed both a concern with the increasing competition for attention on the Internet and a concern with how cultural journalism can be produced in accordance with a new set of values. As we will see in the analysis below, the new focus on age and consumers is contested among journalists in the public service broadcaster, but nevertheless, such articulations indicate how editors and journalists have begun to take into account the changing media landscape in ways that intervene in their everyday professional judgment and choices. This observation is in line with journalism studies showing that news output—also from traditional outlets—seems to be based on different criteria in the age of the Internet (Harcup & O'Neill, 2001). As the chapter will show, this development has come about through more than a decade of struggles between traditional flow TV journalists and 'the digitals,' as journalists working primarily with the web call themselves. The latter is a growing occupational group, whose members have spent a lot of resources defining their tasks, adjusting to technological developments, and justifying their raison d'être. They have both struggled to prove their worth in relation to the organization's top management and in relation to their colleagues who produce flow TV. In turn, they have begun to attract more resources and their products increasingly supplement or replace traditional flow TV formats, so traditional TV journalists experience a shift in power balance. The changes are interesting from an organizational point of view because they are not radical breaks brought about by new technologies, but processes of re-negotiating organizational and occupational practices as technologies emerge, converge, or slowly go out of fashion.

The purpose of the present chapter is to examine how actors renegotiate or 'reassemble' cultural journalism as an occupation in the digital age through an analytical focus on their engagement with changing technologies and tasks in everyday work. The culture division of the Danish Broadcasting Corporation was chosen as site of observation because here, a profound organizational restructuring has taken place in an attempt to adapt to new media consumption patterns and the increased competition created by digitalization. As part of the restructuring, a new strategy ('a Digital Great Leap Forward') was written, a new organizational entity ('Digital Culture News') was established, and 'the digitals' were assembled physically and began to attract larger budgets. The chapter engages with the literature on professions and perspectives on technology in organizations to create an analytical sensibility toward the interconnectedness of digitalization and changes in the journalistic occupation. Here, the journalistic occupation is understood as a phenomenon, which needs to be 'assembled' from both technical and organizational elements. Further below, it will be clarified how *professional* struggles are part of *occupational* changes—professions and occupations are not synonyms, but related.

The analysis falls in two main sections, 'technologies' and 'tasks.' Each examines the mundane technologies and mundane everyday tasks that emerge with digitalization and discuss the professional struggles involved. Within each theme, the analysis highlights how actors (journalists, editors, managers) describe changes in cultural journalism and how they contribute to defining or redefining their occupation. The chapter concludes with reflections on the micro-level elements, which go into reassembling cultural journalism in the digital age. It proposes that these micro-level elements are indicative of changes related to digitalization common to occupations across the creative industries.

Professions and Technologies

The literature on *professions* and perspectives on *technology in organizations* inspire this chapter's exploration of occupational changes and digital technologies' role in these changes. The two bodies of literature provide different analytical sensibilities in the context of digital journalism. This section first turns to the literature on professions, highlighting its interest in occupational groups' attempts to 'professionalize.' With inspiration from the literature on technology in organizations, the section proceeds to propose that technology is not only a macro-factor influencing change but can be understood as specific entities that make a difference for 'social' phenomena such as professions. With this approach to technology, occupations can be conceptualized as assemblages of humans and non-humans and the reorientation and reorganization of work as 'reassembling' cultural journalism.

It has been debated whether journalism is a profession at all or if it is simply a craft, an activity, or an ideology (Deuze, 2005). It is common to see professions as dependent on 'formal education, licensing, codes of ethics, relationships of trust between professional and client, a public service imperative over commercial interest, social status, and so forth' (Lewis, 2012: 839). But professions can also be seen as constructions—or outcomes of actors' ongoing attempts to define themselves as a profession through references to specialized knowledge and special skills. So even if journalism is not a profession in the strict sense above, it is possible to examine as an occupation engaged in ongoing work to 'professionalize' (ibid.).

Professional Struggles

Hereby, it becomes relevant to mobilize the literature on professions, drawing inspiration from its ongoing concern with professional struggles to maintain legitimacy and police jurisdictions (Abbott, 1988; Bechky, 2003; Bucher, Chreim, Langley, & Reay, 2016) and on changes in and challenges to professions (Noordegraaf, 2015; Reay, Golden-Biddle, & Germann, 2006). Although journalists lack the claim to exclusivity that for instance doctors or lawyers uphold, they engage in some of the same dynamics of boundary drawing, establishment of expert positions, and attempts to protect the perceived 'core' of their occupation. A review of the literature on 'the ideology of journalism' proposes that this core is built upon well-established values of public service, objectivity, autonomy, immediacy, and ethics (Deuze, 2005). With regard to the second value, objectivity, Abbott argued that although journalism is 'a permeable occupation,' it has in fact succeeded in establishing itself as a legitimate provider of objective facts about the world (Lewis, 2012) by continuously invoking the occupational core value of objectivity. As we will see below, one particularly important struggle in relation to the digitalization of cultural journalism has to do with the values attached to objectivity and subjectivity, respectively.

In line with the above, it has been proposed that occupational dynamics and professional dynamics are partly overlapping (Anteby, Chan, & DiBenigno, 2016) even if occupations and professions are not quite. When journalism scholars talk about journalism as an occupational ideology, they talk about how journalists collectively and continuously contribute to defining, redefining, or reproducing what 'real' journalism is (Deuze, 2005). These articulatory practices can be understood as professional struggles, and they can become rather fierce, not least because they are connected to resources. In the case of the public broadcaster, the struggles about the definition of real cultural journalism are at the same time a question of values and a question of the allocation of resources.

Organizational Professionalism

In addition to internal organizational struggles among journalists, journalism as an occupation more broadly seems to be under the same type of attack as professionals in health care, law, etc. The latter experience a weakening of autonomous spaces and professional values in light of pressures such as increased budgetary control, managerial supervision, and organizational reforms (Noordegraaf, 2015). Noordegraaf argues that the changing societal context of professional work gives rise to other types of professionalism than the 'pure' form, emphasizing an emerging imperative of taking the organization into account as a professional. Noordegraaf's concept of 'organizational professionalism' means that a concern for the quality of professional work must go hand in hand with an understanding of what the organization has to deliver, given the societal context. The luxury of operating in a protected space without consideration of the societal context seems untenable. As already indicated, interpretations of the technological and societal context make a real difference for how culture journalists in the public broadcaster go about their daily tasks, and reorganizations of work are made with reference to external demands and the survival of the organization in a competitive environment.

Technological Agency in Professional Practices

In investigating how occupations change through the establishment of new practices, it is useful to pay attention to technological agency in professional practices. It is an established view that changes in work practices are often technology-driven, but such claims tend to be based on macroanalyses (Reay et al., 2006), as when we make references to 'digital transformations' as an abstract societal phenomenon. By contrast, it is possible to zoom in on how particular technologies make a difference in everyday work.

Reay and colleagues propose to examine the micro-processes of change in professions (ibid.). In their case, focus is on the role of *human* agency in changing professions, but in the case of digitalization and changes in the journalistic occupation, it makes sense to include *technological* agency in a framework analyzing occupational changes. With an interest in professional struggles and in the micro-processes of changing occupations, the analysis below addresses changes in journalism as an occupation as they take place in everyday work, with a dual focus on technology and on the choices and actions of individuals.

The ambition of taking into account both human and technological agencies and their interplay is inspired by Science and Technology Studies (STS) (Latour, 2005), which have provided a technology-sensitive vocabulary used in theorizations of how technology, work, and organization mutually shape each other (Grint & Woolgar, 1997). An STS-inspired approach to cultural journalism in the digital age is useful because it emphasizes that the implementation of digital technologies does not necessarily lead to specific outcomes—outcomes depend on the organizational context, users, and technologies. STS thus directs attention to situated practices and encourages detailed empirical studies of work at the everyday level. From this perspective, technology is not a macro-phenomenon, but specific entities potentially influencing practice. A concept such as affordances (Hutchby, 2001) allows us to zoom in on the interplay between technological properties and human perception, in the sense that it captures the fusing of a technology's potentials and users' interpretation of these potentials. An STS perspective encourages us to maintain a dual focus on technological agency and on human agency in the study of everyday work. The title of the chapter, reassembling cultural journalism, refers to the concept of assemblages, which is widely used in STS (along with near synonyms such as actor-networks, networks, and others). It refers to the idea that 'the social' is not an overarching explanatory factor in relation to practice, but that social phenomena are continuously created and recreated in relations between human and non-human entities (Latour, 2005). In relation to the discussions above, this entails that 'ideology,' 'societal context,' and other macro-concepts are not used as explanations of changing practices—rather, an analysis of occupational changes will describe those changes through a focus on how, for instance, technologies, people, strategies, and a number of other—heterogeneous—elements are linked and form new occupational realities. This can be seen as a process of 'reassembling' the occupation.

The Case: A Media Production Organization

The analysis builds on a qualitative case study of digitalization in a public broadcasting corporation carried out at a time where the transformation from more traditional cultural journalism to more digitized journalistic practices is ongoing. The organization was founded by the state in 1925 as a public service corporation and today about 94% of the Danish population uses one or more of its products every week. To give an idea about its size, it employs about 3000 people on different types of contracts, and in 2017, it produced about 43,800 hours of television and 105,300 hours of radio. In 2017, it had 1,706,000 weekly users of its homepage.[1] The organization has a matrix structure where specialized sections deliver content to a number of channels and digital platforms. Its history is obviously heavily marked by technological developments and by expectations by politicians and taxpayers to produce relevant content via relevant media channels. It is an interesting site for studying changes related to digitalization because the organization has a number of long-term employees and a very established tradition of producing radio and television. Since it is not born digital, ongoing debates take place about what digitalization means to the industry, the organization, and the employees.

The empirical material analyzed in this chapter is a continuation of a larger study of digitalization in the broadcasting corporation (see Plesner and Raviola [2016] for a study of changes in the organization's news work). The culture division was chosen as topic of analysis for this chapter because it has recently embarked on reorganizing journalistic work and defining what digital cultural journalism is supposed to be. Because a new strategy, a new organizational structure, and a new set of daily practices have been intensely discussed within the division, this organizational context offers rich illustrations of different interpretations of 'digital cultural journalism.' Actors' accounts give indications of how the traditional way of doing cultural journalism is challenged by a new occupational group, 'the digitals'—i.e., employees who have acquired a certain digital literacy and work with production of cultural journalism on new digital platforms.

Approach: Accounts of Digitalization

The analysis is based on empirical material consisting of strategy documents, a strategy power point presentation, observation notes from meetings in the newly established 'Digital Culture News' section, and 10 unstructured interviews with top managers, middle managers, and journalists. The interviews lasted around 45–60 minutes and revolved around changing priorities and practices in the production of cultural journalism. They took place in various corners of the work spaces and were rather informal. The interviewees were promised anonymity, and the quotes used below were sent to them for approval. This is all the more important because the topic of professional struggles in the organization could be seen as sensitive. All interviews were recorded and transcribed in full length.

The empirical material does not allow for a realist account of what cultural journalism is or how the occupation changes, but for an analysis of how actors 'reassemble cultural journalism' through ways of talking, ways of accounting for their work, ways of using technologies, and ways of relating to the public. Their accounts are full of factual statements—on budgets, numbers of clicks, and historical developments—but the analysis below is not a history of digitalization based on such facts. Rather, it assumes that the uses of such facts are part of the construction of the occupation. Due to this focus, observations of actual technology use or interactions around technology have not been included in the analysis. Instead, it is analyzed how particular technological affordances emerge through the fusing of the technological potentials and users' interpretation of these potentials. As indicated above, the empirical site is a large, complex organization, and although digitalization does not leave any corner of the organization untouched, it does not mean the same across the organization. The interpretations and struggles in focus in this chapter are marked by voices of employees who are hired to be a type of frontrunners regarding digitalization, so in the following analysis, critique of new practices and standards are often reported and indirect. A few people interviewed are more skeptical of how digitalization changes the organization and its products. Given that there is a strong and sustained management push regarding the digitalization agenda, it was a deliberate choice to give voice to employees who work actively with realizing the strategy. It was also a deliberate strategy to include accounts from and reports of more skeptical employees to show where the tensions are.

Following from the above-described interest in micro-processes of change in the journalistic occupation and from the theoretical interest in assemblages as a lens to see these changes through, the analytical strategy was to interrogate how technologies (or the interpretation of technologies), and changing daily practices led to redefinitions of—and struggles about—journalism as an occupation. All the interview material was organized in Nvivo according to the following codes: technology, tasks, change, professional roles, and professional relations. On the basis of this, syntheses were made and illustrative quotes pulled into the analysis.

The analysis is structured around two themes, namely technologies and tasks. The themes are inspired by the above-described STS approach to organization and work. From such an approach, mundane technologies and mundane everyday tasks are entry points into describing social phenomena—such as in this case 'changes in an occupation.' Within each theme, the analysis highlights how actors describe 'change' and how the occupation is defined or redefined. This allows for an account of how actors reassemble their occupation through their engagement with changing technologies and tasks.

Technologies and Tasks in Digital Cultural Journalism

Digital cultural journalism could be studied in many sites and from many angles, for instance, with a focus on its products, consumption, or new business models. But here, it is studied as a negotiated phenomenon within an organization, the Danish Broadcasting Corporation, where actors strive to define—or struggle about—what it may be. It is studied at a time where digitalization has been on the organization's agenda for some time but still gives rise to reorganizations and redefinitions of tasks, core values, and professional roles and identities. There seems to be a realization that journalism can no longer be a protected space governed by classical values, but has to take into consideration some kind of threat from a macro-phenomenon like digitalization, coming from outside of the organization. In August 2015, the top management of the culture division decided to embark on a strategy project (the 'Digital Great Leap Forward'). Apart from obtaining a broader audience reach through new platforms and formats, a goal was that '85% of all employees in the culture division should have a digital mindset by end 2017.'[2] Action plans were also created to ensure that the strategy was implemented. One was:

> We do not develop any concept without including the digital element from the beginning. Therefore, a digital employee has to be part of all concept development phases.[3]

Another element in the strategy was the establishment of a new editorial section, Digital Culture News. The person responsible for the strategy and the manager of the newly established section both had long employment histories in the broadcasting corporation where they had been among the first to begin producing content to the web page. In the early days, very little priority was given to the web, and it had relatively little traffic. It mostly contained news stories based on flow TV programs, and it was hard to convince employees to produce interesting content.[4] Since the web played a minor role in the organization, and since no resources were allocated to digital journalism, there was very little prestige and interest in this domain from the point of view of flow journalists. This started to change with new managers who began to allocate resources to the production of content for web and streaming[5] and with new strategies putting 'Social first.'[6] But it is not a settled issue what digital cultural journalism is or ought to be. It evolves through everyday adjustments to new technologies and in ongoing negotiations about the practice and purpose of cultural journalism. We will turn to these now.

Technologies in Cultural Journalism

The central technological change in the broadcasting corporation is the increased accessibility and speed of the Internet, which means that broadcasting channels of distribution (television and radio) become less important and digital platforms more important. The affordances of the Internet that make online and on-demand viewing and listening prevalent create new work conditions for journalists. They were previously trained to design formats and flows based on the premise that viewers would turn on the television or radio and stay in front of it, more or less. Now, on-demand formats such as streaming or podcasts need to be different from flow TV or flow radio. Such changes have extensive impact on both the daily work and the understanding of the task that the journalists have. For instance, cultural journalism previously included quizzes, studio programs with popular hosts and their guests, and long non-fiction programs. In some sections, these formats are no longer in use, because they do not work well as streaming content.[7] As an interviewee in the youth culture section explains, when users are accustomed to streaming and searching for entertainment on Facebook, journalists need to adjust to produce short, snappy content for Facebook to attract viewers. And then they must ensure that the programs deliver enough quality and have enough human interest to be worth streaming. As indicated in the quote below, adjustments are framed as a 'requirement' following from the technological development, and journalists talk about new dogma in their redefinitions of what cultural journalism is:

> We work with developing content that's appropriate for streaming, because it's different from broadcast. It requires another dramaturgy. We are aware of that and we have a 'streaming first' dogma for some of our programs. (interview with strategy consultant)

In the Digital Culture News section, there is another new dogma, namely the 'social first' dogma. 'Social first' is completely a technology-driven ambition, because it originates from the fact that users have increased the time they spend on platforms like Facebook, which means that content has to be tailored to such platforms.[8] It is not given which social media platforms are relevant, as this may change with either new consumption patterns or regulation, but several managers use the metaphor of the highway when they explain the importance of Facebook: This is where the traffic is. As it was expressed in the strategy slides, 'All video needs to be designed for Facebook first. All articles need to be shareable on Facebook. Create clickable content.'

The affordances of Facebook have created new user practices, and journalists are asked to format their product accordingly. The new demands to journalists are based on analyses of how Facebook works and what role it plays in potential users' lives. As a strategy consultant explains:

> ...on Facebook, what works is a complete story with its own dramaturgy and an emotional pay-off somehow. Something that makes you want to react, like writing a comment, liking, sharing, you know. Because if you don't, the posts die, they disappear in Facebook's algorithm. That demands a new mindset and it demands that you think about that target group on Facebook and imagine how they sit in the subway or sit on a toilet – that's where many people sit with their phones, right?

When the young viewers (whom the broadcasting corporation want to attract) scroll down their Facebook feed, the story goes that they scroll more than a mile every day, so it is vital to attract attention very efficiently. Managers and journalists across the culture division use the expression 'WTF television.'[9] They explain that it is necessary to make people think 'What The Fuck' when they come across a headline, a still photo or a short video. In the words of a young journalist, this expression has been all over his notebook, reminding him to make 'WTF-stories.'

Journalists' interpretation of technological platforms thus leads to the introduction of a new term to guide their work—a term that has little to do with the traditional core values of journalism. An editor-in-chief explains how the centrality of Facebook as a new distribution technology places public service on the same level as uncensored, user-generated, or sponsored content and creates a new type of competition for attention:

> ...you have a split second to catch people's attention [...] You're at war with the whole f*** internet, the latest posts from Kim Kardashian, ads, Trump's tweets [...] and people need to choose you out of pleasure, not duty. That is a game changer from the flow world to the digital world. Back then you could assume that people would watch the news because they felt a duty to be updated, but duty is dead on the internet. (interview with editor-in-chief)

The intense competition means that it is increasingly important to get users to choose cultural journalism rather than other kinds of entertainment—to get them to click on the stories that are shared on social media. The fact that clicks can be measured in real time is another technological development that influences cultural journalism. It has led to an increased focus on data and on monitoring what is working with the potential users and what is not:

> You have had to depend on your gut feeling for the past 500 years because you did not know how the newspaper would sell. But gut feeling will not survive digital platforms because we don't need it, we just need to collect the data we have in real time. (interview with editor)

Several journalists tell about their awareness of clicks. One loves the confirmation of interest that the technology allows for and looks at numbers a lot:

> I have a test out there called 'which TV-detective are you'. It was online yesterday at 7.30 and I just had to see how many people had taken it. I have never made a test before, and in no time 10.000 people had accessed it. It was crazy – my girlfriend became all annoyed because I was updating all the time. (interview with journalist)

Others link the number of clicks to public service, stating that is not public service if there is no public using what you have made. As a journalist puts it, 'a click is a pretty clear indicator, it is a starting point, we are not getting anywhere without a click.' He nuances the statement by noting that it is actually more interesting to get people to really engage with the content. Another journalist similarly links importance and reach by saying that he has a clear sense that what they do in the division benefits a lot of people. Here, it appears that the public service criterion (Deuze, 2005) is being tweaked in the direction of *serving a large, measurable public* rather than creating content that has an intrinsic public service value.

As we see, on a micro-, everyday level, technologies become coupled with new practices, values, and understandings of cultural journalism.

Technologies and Professional Struggles

Both managers and journalists working with digital cultural journalism often refer to how new media consumption patterns create a new competitive environment for journalism. It is debated how quality journalism can thrive when competition for attention and clickability becomes an issue. Some journalists believe that the most eager social media people are responsible for a decline in subject knowledge and professionalism in the coverage of culture because they are concerned with a particular target group with particular habits. Colleagues in the organization thus criticize digital culture journalists for running after high numbers of clicks. Conversely, in the eyes of a digital editor, the problem of 'click baits' is routinely raised without any understanding about what the issue of clicks is. She tells about how she listened to a panel debate about clickbaits and

> it struck me that I have never heard a debate about clickbait where someone who understands digital journalism participated. There are so many myths and so many prejudices, and no understanding of why it is crucial to construct the right headlines in a digital context. (interview with editor)

These professional struggles have to do with the public service ideal. To draw it up a bit sharply, 'the digitals' have the tendency to interpret public service as reaching and engaging a large number of people. One manager calls it 'irrelevant' to talk to 500 people only. When the numbers reach 500,000, it becomes relevant to spend resources on a story. Other journalists insist more on important content as seen from the organization's point of view. But there are also instances where perspectives meet. An editor insists that cultural journalism needs to adapt to the things that people have become used to on social media: the short attention span, the videos, and the storytelling mode. As she says, 'not to become shallow, but to succeed in communicating important stuff about society.' This can be interpreted as organizational professionalism (Noordegraaf, 2015)—the recognition that technological advances and new competition pose new challenges that require a redefined conception of public service.

For managers, it is an issue to address these professional struggles. One project leader explains how it is important for him to legitimize working with the social media dynamics in mind. Another articulates organizational professionalism by integrating concerns about numbers with concerns about content:

> I believe my social people can learn a great deal from my journalists and my journalists can learn a great deal from my social people. With my social people I see a tendency to say f*** this does not perform. It's too heavy, let's post something lighter. But we have an obligation to make an effort also with the heavy and difficult stuff. (interview with editor-in-chief)

In the process of reassembling cultural journalism, the new distribution channels and the interpretation of how it is necessary to interact with them produces new understandings about what culture journalists need to do (in particular, reaching out to users and monitoring the success of their stories) and how public service is to be understood (as being about a large public or important content). The technological affordances of the Internet and social media give rise to professional struggles because the interpretations of the technologies vary. The professional struggles revolve around new definitions of the core of journalism and the meaning of public service. These struggles are not only verbal, they also have more practical consequences for the types of tasks that journalists engage in. This is the topic of the following.

Tasks in Cultural Journalism

If we turn to the tasks that journalists do in their daily work, this gives indications of a changing occupation on the micro-level discussed above. Technologies bring about different daily work practices for journalists when they need to create shorter stories that are suitable for the web and mobile devices. Journalists need to monitor clicks and rethink still pictures on the web according to the clicks. And they need to reach out to users via social media. The affordances of, for instance, Facebook are constructed as legitimate logics to base daily journalistic work on. In the strategy presentation of the Digital Culture News manager, this is expressed in the following way:

> Before you write your article or produce your video, always ask yourself: How should the user react to the content on Facebook? Remember, there is no 'indifference reaction' on Facebook. And: Why should the user share this content?

The illustration on this slide was five Facebook emojis. The manager's point was that a given story should be crafted to result in one of these reactions.[10] This is just one example of the 'digital first' thinking, which top management wants to see implemented across the organization, and an example of how journalists contribute to redefining what cultural journalism is about. It also illustrates the point that journalism increasingly needs to consider its use of emotions to create engagement (Beckett & Deuze, 2016) and that the core value of objectivity does not appear to be a reference point that guides everyday work. In the competition for attention on digital platforms, users' emotions may carry more weight in decision-making than the traditional values of journalism.

Working with New Formats and Elements

One implication for journalists' everyday work is that some formats hardly exist anymore. Employees who were used to produce quizzes or other in-house formats need to get out of the house and do their own video footage. In some sections, journalists who were used to extended periods of producing long documentaries now need to spend more time delivering Facebook content and cannot just work on their storylines and visual material for a particular program.

As part of the ongoing redefinition of what digital journalism is, 'the digitals' are not only distancing themselves from flow TV and radio, but also from dated ways of doing *digital* journalism. When journalism began to go online, content would be TV formats such as trailers or it would be images or snippets taken from a TV program. But it is measurable that users only click on stories that seem to have an immediate payoff, and stories of what to expect from a TV program later on have little value for users who do not watch flow TV.[11] A manager explains how, in the early days of digitalization, net-journalism was about writing short articles. It has been a long process to make people realize that today, the combination of sound, image, video, graphics, text, interaction, and so on gives possibilities for creating much richer stories. Along these lines, several journalists tell about their dynamic work with large toolboxes:

> …now that you have a toolbox that changes all the time […] you need to utilize every format as well as you can, both to keep yourself updated and to make a varied product […] We often try to come up with new standard formats, but then you need to transform them because of new developments, first we had the tablet, then the mobile phone, then a larger mobile phone. (interview with journalist)

There is pressure from some managers to make journalists work more on headlines, still photos, and short videos produced specifically for Facebook. They have realized that social media cannot be used in the same way as a web page or a TV channel. A manager explains that in his section, they play with the idea of creating such a cool title that anyone would want to watch the program behind it and *then* make the program, instead of the other way around. And resources are spent on producing mind-blowing still photos that users simply *have* to click on. All these experiments with formats can be seen as attempts to figure out—continuously, as new technologies emerge—what can be done with the new technologies and what works in the new competitive environment.

Working with Reception and Distribution

The tasks of working with new formats go hand in hand with monitoring the effects of each choice. A lot of work goes into monitoring clicks, changing headlines and photos, and moving stories around on the web page, so they get more traffic. An editor sees this as a window to understand what users are interested in and adjust products accordingly. For her, editing a web page is a fun job because it gives real-time insight into what people like and into how tweaking things make people more interested. The same monitoring of clicks inspires journalists to twist stories. A journalist tells how,

> You can fool people by, say, before you would call him Beethoven and people would run away screaming, but if you call him Ludwig and tell that he is deaf – if it has any relevance of course, there is a limit because I cannot write anything in the headline that has no connection to the story – […] then people get surprised that this was about Beethoven – they did not expect that – they thought they were going to read something about some Ludwig, and that was not untrue, and it was a good story. (interview with journalist)

Several journalists train sneaking important content into their stories under an enticing headline. The quoted journalist talks about relating to users in entirely new ways by becoming better at making users interested in the things they ought to be interested in from a public service perspective. Such articulations among the journalists demonstrate how the competitive environment makes them step out of the 'protected space' (Noordegraaf, 2015) of public broadcasting journalism and produce user-oriented content on an entirely different level.

A lot of new tasks are about engagement. For example, users are invited to ask questions or provide content to specific programs or stories. This again leads to other new tasks, such as editing and relating to a lot of input. Additionally, managers insist that journalists need to take responsibility for the distribution of their products—they can no longer just hand in a tape to a distribution section:

> your job is not done before you have hit the users and before you have engaged them, so you also need to consider how to optimize your article for search engines so someone finds it on Google, you need to consider how it appears on the frontpage of dr.dk, in our news app, it needs to hit some people on Facebook, it needs to be able to create engagement on Facebook, the engagement it creates needs to be used in future work. (interview with editor-in-chief)

The tasks related to creating clickable content are not just imposed by section managers, but also by decisions made in the organization about what to pay for. The culture division is a section in a matrix structure in the sense that it delivers content to different channels only when it is ordered and paid for. A section manager tells how the top managers of the different channels have a strategy of only ordering content that will be clicked upon and content that works on streaming. The task of caring for reception and distribution thus seems to be a significant part of journalistic work in the digital age.

Tasks and Professional Struggles

The new tasks discussed above demand particular competencies. Among 'the digitals,' it is seen as lack of understanding and recognition that job advertisements call for digital editors who can write, edit, produce videos, code, etc. As an editor explains, this is like wanting a surgeon, a nurse, and an ambulance driver in the same person. According to several journalists, it is a struggle to redefine the tasks of digital journalism as being professionally demanding and worthy of respect. A journalist tells how 'it was always a struggle with the people producing [a particular program], they gave me a 50-page manuscript and did not see that when I shortened it, I actually did them a favor.' An editor tells about how colleagues would e-mail long texts to a digital employee who was supposed to layout it, find archival material for it, insert fact boxes, find suitable photos, add links, and so on.

Seen from the point of view of 'the digitals,' it is not until recently they have begun to build a kind of professionalism and professional self-esteem in relation to digital journalism. There is a lot of professional boundary drawing in their accounts of their position in the organization. Several journalists believe it has been a common understanding that anyone could do their job—that if there was a gap in the schedule, an intern could take the editor's role. And they tell about how a tendency has been to send underperforming employees to the digital area, to avoid promoting 'the digitals' to leading positions. They are critical of having mostly managers who have no experiences with digital journalism. When generalists and junior employees cover important stuff, '...you get that downgrading of the digital area. Instead of the digital being the strategically most important, it becomes the professionally dubious' (interview with editor).

We can thus observe an ongoing struggle in the organization between managers and journalists who are trained in the flow TV or radio tradition, who value the classical formats, and managers and journalists who have worked with the digitalization of news and social media for the past decade. 'The digitals' have been a marginal group both in newspaper production and in television production,[12] but have begun to attract attention and resources from management. While the majority still works on traditional flow TV and radio programs, some TV journalists are being retrained, some leave, and new occupational groups such as social media managers begin to grow in size and importance.[13] It is an ongoing negotiation how much retraining is needed to take care of the new tasks; everybody should potentially have 'a digital mindset,' but since flow television and radio still exist, there is also a need for journalists who are good at the traditional formats. Just like there is a need for bringing their skills into new formats. For instance, according to a manager, streaming formats require journalists with a solid background in television journalism, because they are good at creating narratives.

The professional struggles surrounding the tasks and organization of digital journalism are ongoing, but there are indications that the definitions of digital journalism could be changing in a direction where the contours of a common core (Deuze, 2005) emerge. One employee tells how the growing focus on streaming helps flow employees define digital journalism in a more productive way. According to this employee, the first wave of digitalization was all about social media and

> it became very polarized, we had someone over here who are very good at content and then we had someone over here producing for social media, stories of maximum 1:30, aimed at someone under twenty-nine and produced in 5 minutes.

By contrast, the employee identifies a second wave of digitalization where

> digitalization is no longer just social media, but a matter of streaming [...] In that case the polarization is less significant because producing for streaming is easy to learn for people with a flow background. They can easily take the professionalism they have obtained with regards to content into a streaming reality. In that way, it is easier to build a bridge from the past to the future.

In this account, the organization might still be threatened by competition, but the professionalism of the single employee is not. As such, digitalization makes sense in another way than when employees got the impression that journalism was becoming a question of producing something entertaining for social media in no time.

A new understanding of the imperatives installed by social media is also emerging in the Digital Culture News section. The manager has begun to articulate that 'click and reach' is not the only marker of success. Instead, engagement, user loyalty, and the time spent on each story are more important.[14] According to the manager, digital journalists should focus on fewer stories of higher quality. Where flow TV needs to fill a whole day on a given channel, it holds a potential for quality improvement that digital content can be provided in another tempo. Such developments might become important to the quality discussion taking place among traditional journalists and 'the digitals.' Assemblages—such as in this case a journalistic occupation—are always stronger if they attract more people and elements. The instances where digitalization is articulated as a matter of producing quality content for streaming or fewer web items of higher quality are interesting because they seem to attract both flow TV journalists and the digitals—opening up for a more collaborative reassembling of their occupation.

Concluding Remarks

The analysis shows how technological developments, managerial strategies, and the redefinition of daily tasks challenge the professionalism of journalists in a culture division of a public broadcaster. Some fundamental guidelines for news work (the news values) are redefined to fit the logics of social media use, organizational restructuring has given new privileges to 'the digitals,' and the affordances of online platforms create new demands to the journalistic output. In light of these developments, journalists 'reassemble' what cultural journalism is about by using new technologies, working with new formats, redefining tasks, reorganizing work, and redefining core values—in particular the public service value. By accounting for specific changes in everyday work, the analysis offered insights into technology-driven micro-processes of change. It indicated how affordances of the Internet challenges the established practices of traditional TV journalism, for instance when the 'like' and 'share' functionalities on Facebook are constructed as crucial if stories are to live and when these functionalities get to influence professional work.

Some of the changes in journalism are visible in the increasing prominence of new occupational roles (such as 'the digitals' and specifically social media managers) as journalism becomes increasingly digitized. This parallels the emergence of new occupational categorizations in news journalism such as 'the web people' (Huang & Heider, 2007) or 'the media manager' (Aguilar-Gutierrez & Lopez-De-Solis, 2010) and the reconfiguration of their profession experienced by news journalists (Plesner & Raviola, 2016). The incorporation of new technologies into news production routines has been shown to privilege laborers with technological skills, thus altering hierarchies and producing new tensions (Robinson, 2011). A similar tendency can be observed in cultural journalism, where a more central position and more resources are assigned to the people who formerly operated on the edge of the organization as 'webmasters' or the like. They can no longer be dismissed as technology nerds with a peripheral position but become partners in the conversations across the organization about redefinitions of public service and quality journalism in the digital age. In the reorganization of digital cultural journalism, numerous references are made to technological imperatives, users' expectations, and the competition that the organization faces. As such, many journalists articulate a form of organizational professionalism that reaches beyond the traditional—and maybe 'purer'—craft of journalism.

These insights about the negotiations of tasks, quality, and the status of the digitals contribute to the literature on changes in the journalistic profession in light of digitalization (Deuze, 2005; Gade & Raviola, 2009; Pavlik, 2000, 2013), showing that digitalization is more than producing 'digitized content'—it is also about understanding the role and tasks of journalists differently and about negotiating new organizational structures and occupational categories. The analysis highlights the complex work done to reassemble cultural journalism in the digital age. By doing so, it offers empirical insights into the everyday struggles making up what media and journalism studies have described as key tensions in the digital media era and in the context of the creative industries (Lewis, 2012). It has been suggested that this tension deserves more scrutiny 'for it has become an increasingly contested space for media workers who specialize in creating, filtering, and distributing information, and for whom professional identity, authority, and expertise are linked to their central role in directing [mass] media production and circulation processes' (Lewis, 2012). The analysis pointed to how professional values and tensions become organizational concerns and to how the emergence of organizational professionalism among journalists can alleviate the technology-driven tensions described in the media and journalism literature.

The analysis also indicated how dynamic the assemblages are. New technological possibilities and new definitions of digitalization continue to offer new elements to the assemblage of cultural journalism as an occupation. It follows that the journalistic occupation and professional struggles continue to change and perhaps that the relatively polarized positions depicted in this chapter will be replaced by new understandings of both technologies and tasks, as indicated toward the end of the analysis.

The chapter contributes to the literature on changing professions with its STS informed approach. This approach allows us to examine the interplay between technology and work practices on an everyday level and to pay attention to both technological agency and human agency in the development of the profession. With this perspective, we leave the macro-accounts of technology-driven changes in the profession (Reay et al., 2006), but at the same time, explore how professional and jurisdictional struggles are not purely human phenomena—technological affordances can be examined as elements in the assemblages that change the profession. Opening up the technological dimension makes it possible to discern different ways of engaging with technologies and hence different ways of reassembling cultural journalism in the digital age.

I have analyzed changing practices related to digitalization in a small corner of the media production industry. Other creative industries concerned with the generation or exploitation of knowledge and information face similar competition for attention and have similar technological infrastructures and hence possibilities for rethinking their tasks and work practices. It is a common condition across creative industries that digitalization comes with processes of reassembling occupations and professions, but it is an open question how, as such processes depend on specific technologies and their interpretations.

Notes

1. https://www.dr.dk/om-dr/fakta-om-dr/dr-i-korte-traek, accessed 5 December 2018.
2. Strategy document, p. 1.
3. Strategy document, p. 4.
4. Interviews with strategy consultant and editor-in-chief of Digital Culture News.
5. Interview with manager of the central media unit responsible for ordering content, interview with editor-in-chief of Digital Culture News.
6. Strategy slides.
7. Interview with editor-in-chief of the Youth Culture section.
8. Interviews with strategy consultant and editor-in-chief of Digital Culture News.
9. Interviews with editor-in-chief of the Digital Culture News, the editor-in-chief of the Youth Culture section, two journalists, and observations from strategy meeting.
10. Strategy slides.
11. Interviews with managers.

12. Interviews with journalists.
13. Interviews with strategy consultant, editor-in-chief of the Digital Culture News, and the editor-in-chief of the Youth Culture section.
14. Strategy slides and interview with editor-in-chief of the Digital Culture News and two journalists.

References

Abbott, A. D. (1988). *The system of professions: An essay on the division of expert labor*. Chicago: University of Chicago Press.

Aguilar-Gutierrez, M., & Lopez-De-Solis, I. (2010). New workflows in a digital newsroom: The case of TVE's informative services. *El profesional de la información, 19*(4), 395–403.

Anteby, M., Chan, C. K., & DiBenigno, J. (2016). Three lenses on occupations and professions in organizations: Becoming, doing, and relating. *Academy of Management Annals, 10*(1).

Bechky, B. A. (2003). Sharing meaning across occupational communities: The transformation of understanding on a production floor. *Organization Science, 14*(3), 312–330.

Beckett, C., & Deuze, M. (2016). On the role of emotion in the future of journalism. *Social Media + Society, 2*(3).

Bögenhold, D., & Fachinger, U. (2013). Self-employment, journalism and hybridization: The decline of a profession. *Global Business & Economics Anthology, 2*, 122–131.

Bucher, S. V., Chreim, S., Langley, A., & Reay, T. (2016). Contestation about collaboration: Discursive boundary work among professions. *Organization Studies, 37*(4), 497–522.

Deuze, M. (2005). What is journalism? Professional identity and ideology of journalists reconsidered. *Journalism, 6*(4), 442–464.

Gade, P., & Raviola, E. (2009). Integration of news and news of integration: A structural perspective on news media changes. *Journal of Media Business Studies, 6*(1), 87–111.

Grint, K., & Woolgar, S. (1997). *The machine at work: Technology, work and organisation*. Cambridge: Polity.

Gulyás, Á., & Hammer, F. (2013). *Public service media in the digital age: International perspectives*. Newcastle upon Tyne: Cambridge Scholars Publishing.

Harcup, T., & O'Neill, D. (2001). What is news? Galtung and Ruge revisited. *Journalism Studies, 2*(2), 261–280.

Huang, J. S., & Heider, D. (2007). Media convergence: A case study of a cable news station. *International Journal on Media Management, 9*(3), 105–115.

Hutchby, I. (2001). Technologies, texts and affordances. *Sociology, 35*(2), 441–456.

Latour, B. (2005). *Reassembling the social: An introduction to actor-network-theory* [Clarendon lectures in management studies]. Oxford: Oxford University Press.

Lewis, S. C. (2012). The tension between professional control and open participation. *Information, Communication & Society, 15*(6), 836–866.

Noordegraaf, M. (2015). Hybrid professionalism and beyond: (New) forms of public professionalism in changing organizational and societal contexts. *Journal of Professions and Organization, 2*(2), 187–206.

Pavlik, J. (2000). The impact of technology on journalism. *Journalism Studies, 1*(2), 229–237.

Pavlik, J. V. (2013). Innovation and the future of journalism. *Digital Journalism, 1*(2), 181–193.

Picard, R. (2015). *Journalists' perceptions of the future of journalistic work.* Oxford.

Plesner, U., & Raviola, E. (2016). Digital technologies and a changing profession. *Journal of Organizational Change Management, 29*(7), 1044–1065.

Reay, T., Golden-Biddle, K., & Germann, K. (2006). Legitimizing a new role: Small wins and microprocesses of change. *The Academy of Management Journal.*

Robinson, S. (2011). Convergence crises: News work and news space in the digitally transforming newsroom. *Journal of Communication, 61*(6), 1122–1141.

Rottwilm, P. (2014). *The future of journalistic work: Its changing nature and implications.* Oxford: Reuters Institute for the Study of Journalism.

Steenfadt, O., Glowacki, B. B., Nikoltchev, S., Cabrera Blasquez, F. J., & Kus, M. (2011). *Future or funeral? A guide to public service media regulation in Europe*. Warsaw: Open Society Foundations.

10

Digital Transformation and Business Model Innovation in the Film Industry: The Case of Movieday.it

Adriano Solidoro and Gianluigi Viscusi

Introduction

Up till a decade ago the business model for movie exhibition was easy to perceive: theatrical release in combination with television sales and home cinema releases (video and DVD). Now, many questions have arisen in response to the growing popularity of online Video on Demand (with numerous platforms competing for consumers including Netflix, Amazon Instant Video, and iTunes) and new technologies such as broadband Internet and connected devices that play movies (including Internet-connected TVs, tablets and mobile phones).

A. Solidoro (✉)
Università Di Milano-Bicocca, Milan, Italy
e-mail: adriano.solidoro@unimb.it

G. Viscusi
École Polytechnique Fédérale de Lausanne (EPFL),
Lausanne, Switzerland

J. Strandgaard Pedersen et al. (eds.), *Technology and Creativity*,
https://doi.org/10.1007/978-3-030-17566-5_10

As already happened in other industries impacted by the consequences of digital transformation (Matt, Hess, & Benlian, 2015), also in the film industries digital enabled business trends are transforming the value chain from supply-led to demand-led, therefore, altering the exclusivity of existing suppliers and gatekeepers. This is visible especially in the independent movie[1] distribution value chain, which is being affected by a changing relationship with a new type of consumer, an "active audience" in terms of consumption behaviours, but also on the arena of social networks, which help to more deeply engage their customers and support the needs of their communities. These communication tools, which facilitate collaboration and enable user-generated contributions on the web, have given birth to participatory culture (see Jenkins, Ito, & Boyd, 2016) and encouraged greater consumer engagement in all stages of the filmmaking process. To some extent, distribution has always been social due to its affiliation with marketing, which aims to develop relationships with consumers. However, social media have brought distribution to the level of a social "phenomenon" because they have opened it up to public participation, enabling consumers to add value to projects in unprecedented ways; major online distribution platforms, like *Netflix* and *YouTube*, demonstrate this trend by offering their users a set of social features (i.e. rating, commenting, sharing, tagging, etc.).

It might be argued—therefore—that film distribution is turning into a demand-led market, instead of a supply-led one. Thus, film distributors can now create new release models to better respond to consumer demand, leaving behind the restrictions of traditional distribution systems and changing the relationship between the elements of the film value chain. This is going to change the traditional production function, co-creating values across borders and re-defining the role of intermediaries (agents, distributors), gatekeepers (cinemas) and experts (critics, influencers) as effects of digitalization on the film industry.

Therefore, cinema industry's players are currently struggling to understand how to survive (and thrive) in a reorganizing "market space" (Rayport & Sviokla, 1995) that is more and more multilayered and changeable. Since cinemas do not offer an exclusive access to movies anymore, it becomes even more important to present a various and distinctive cinema programme, in order to give added value to the customer. Consequently, cinemas are more and more becoming a supply-led market where exhibitors are the gatekeepers for curating entry into the theatrical retail environment, as well as for creating opportunities for theatrical exhibits as unique events. The rise of technologies such as 3D, high frame rates, IMAX systems, and Dolby Atmos sound, and experiment with new theatre designs to further improve immersion and comfort represent a clear goal of creating event experiences to increase audience numbers (Gubbins, 2012, 2014).

Also, the independent distributors have looked to exploit the power of "movie as an event", but in different ways (and at minimal additional cost). Attempts are made for providing additional value to the theatrical experience. Some examples are:

- Live participative premières (and to distribute this event by streaming the introductions and Q&A's simultaneously to a connected network of several cinemas and with the audience invited to take part in the interview by sending questions through Facebook and Twitter).
- Hybrid events, which combine audience participation and theme-based activities before the screening of movies (conferences or more ludic events such as masquerade with dressed up audience).
- "Cinema on demand", or "user driven cinema exhibition" based on critical mass ticketing facilitated by crowd sourcing platforms (such as screenly.io in Spain, tugg.com and gathr.us in USA, ourscreen.com in UK and Movieday.it in Italy), where consumers turn to social media for their decision-making and for programming.

Taking these issues into account, in the studied substantive area of the digital transformation of the film industry by new ventures we aim to provide a theoretical understanding of the key issues and concepts guided by the following questions:

- *What are the key issues of business model innovation in the digital transformation of film industry?*
- *What characterizes the role of intermediaries, gatekeepers and experts?*
- *How to reconfigure the conceptual framework of movie content distribution through movie theatres?*
- *How to reconfigure the concept of the movie theatre as traditional projection space and as an institutional site?*

To answer these questions, we are going to consider also the institutional work of new ventures as "purposive action of individuals and organizations aimed at creating, maintaining and disrupting institutions" (Lawrence, Leca, & Zilber, 2013; Lawrence & Suddaby, 2006: 215). To this end, this chapter investigates the case of *Movieday.it* (http://www.movieday.it) an Italian start-up founded in 2014 and awarded with many national prizes for innovation. About 230 Italian cinemas are partnering and since the opening over 350 screenings have been held (many sold-outs). *Movieday.it* challenges the conventional top-down programming of movie events with a bottom-up programming that comes after the bookings. Programming is therefore based on personal purpose or even community purpose. In this way, customers share the power of the gatekeeper position with the industry. No more "Push" but "Pull" mode. We may even call it "cinema on demand", or "user driven cinema events", where consumers turn to social media for their decision-making and for programming. As we are going to see in what follows, new ventures, as the considered case of *Movieday.it*, innovate the business models[2] of the film industry by changing its architecture through an action on either the content, structure or governance of the activities performed by the different actors having a role in the production, promotion, access and the showing of movies.

Intermediaries, Gatekeepers and Experts

The above-mentioned crowd sourcing web platforms for theatrical movie events (such as *Movieday.it*, in Italy, *screenly.io* in Spain, *tugg.com* and *gathr.us* in the USA, ourscreen.com in the UK) acts as new intermediaries in the film industry for their capacity to bring together crowd sourcing potential with theatrical distribution. As for gatekeepers, with "cinema on demand", or "user driven cinema exhibition" based on critical mass ticketing which is channelled through independent online user-groups, customers share the power of the gatekeeper position with the industry.

Finally, the considered platforms (Movieday.it is the empirical case we'll analyse), stimulating the cultural diversity of the audience by expanding the choice of movies, weaken the role of traditional movie experts (critics, directors, producers, etc.), inspiring new conversations around cinema and facilitating audience interaction and the sharing and curating of informative content, not necessarily supported by the traditional establishment (newspaper columns, dedicated television shows, academia recognitions, festivals juries, etc.).

In summary, for filmmakers, engaging with audiences early on in the filmmaking process, even before the movie is produced, can allow them to measure interest and help them understand how their movies can best be released into the marketplace. Audience involvement in the early stages of a project also allows producers to gain feedback and new ideas that may, ultimately, impact the content in the final movie. Furthermore, audiences can be called upon to aid in the launch and promotion of a movie. By offering personal endorsements via social networking services, audiences can significantly enhance a movie's visibility and also actively participate in the crowd funding of the production.

The Case Study

In this chapter, we discuss an embedded single case study (Hewson, 2008; Scholz & Tietje, 2002), whose rationale is to represent an exploratory case study (Yin, 2009). The study is the result of a qualitative research based on an interpretive stance to field study (Klein & Myers, 1999; Walsham, 1993), adopting the approach for analysis and theory development proposed by Gioia, Corley, and Hamilton (2013).

The subject of investigation is Movieday is an Italian start-up created in 2014 that has developed a homonymous web platform which value proposition is creating a direct connection amongst film owners, cinemas and the audience. Movieday web platform enables users to create an event (a movie show), just choosing a movie (from a selection of over 1000 independent, new, classic and original movies that Movieday has pre-contracted), a cinema (amongst the 230 cinema partners). If the screening reaches a minimum threshold of reservations, the projection is confirmed.

Movieday key activities are focused on the development of the platform and the incentive for the use of its products and services by the three customer profiles: audience, movie owners and partner cinemas.

The Audience

The audience is at the centre of Movieday's system. In addition to being reached by the Movieday film campaigns in a targeted way to participate to the screenings of interest, a single viewer can organize screening events for his own recreational, cultural or associational purposes, through the Theater On Demand service, enriching projections with meetings and side discussions. This is currently Movieday core business service that allows both movie owners and common viewers to organize online events in cinemas throughout Italy. The organizer of the event takes care of a geo-localized event promotion and communication to other local moviegoers, communities and media, thanks to a set of tools and assistance from Movieday (Facebook groups and events are amongst the most used tools).

If, by the week before the projection date, a sufficient number of pre-sales to cover the economic demand for cinema and film is reached, the event is confirmed. Tickets are purchased online on the platform and in the hall on the day of the event for those who could not buy online, if there are still places available. The platform orders the shipment of the film to the cinema via digital delivery or via courier. After the projection, the platform calculates and distributes the odds attributed to the movie owner (40%) and the cinema (40%), and retains its 20% share.

But Theater On Demand is not the only service for moviegoers. Movieday platform promotes and distributes movies not only into the cinemas but also in any other channels (TV, VOD, Schools, etc.) and allows costumers to rent films for screenings even in spaces other than cinemas: schools, libraries and associations (this service is referred as Community Screenings).

The potential value for the audience can be described as follow: freedom of choice of films to be seen at the cinema; aggregation of communities around various topics of interest; unique experience of cultural enjoyment and much richer than a "simple" vision in the hall; co-participation for the programming of cinemas in local community.

The screenings of the films promoted on Movieday record an average of 120 moviegoers, the highest ever, according to data issued by Cinetel (2017). This might be related to the fact that Movieday aggregates communities and brings them to the cinema gathered by the theme of a film that represents them, crafting an experience based on sharing and engagement.

Movieday encourages the online purchase of tickets; the audience is profiled and reaches easily the film that raises its interests. In fact, on Movieday, the audience is invited to organize projections, both in partner cinemas and in other venues, or to participate in screenings organized by other users.

Faced with this kind of "connected" user, accustomed to getting online content and turning its own passions in an online aggregator and conversation engine, the current movie offer is inadequate and slow, not much "smart". In fact, the total lack of the moviegoers profiling represents the major issue, given the very low rate of online tickets purchase, which, for further paradox, are also sold at a higher price. Not by chance in the USA, services such as MoviePass (https://www.moviepass.com/), a monthly subscription card to watch anything, and booking via Facebook have been launched.

Movie Owners

Movieday web platform products and services are not only offered to moviegoers, but also to different categories of movie owners. Italian distribution companies (i.e. Disney Italian, Medusa, Tucjer, etc.) have made their film libraries available for projections directly organized by the fans of all connected cinemas. Twenty-five distribution companies have made available over one thousand movies on Movieday (in 2018). Moreover, two Italian distribution platforms (Wanted and Cinema) have already launched films via Movieday carrying out special events and the engagement of fan base communities.

For movie owners, the value proposition of the platform is the development of trustworthy relationship amongst producers, distributors and cinemas, therefore, creating a brand new and more solid value chain amongst the players involved. The platform has been designed as a smart tool which leverages on data analysis to link contents through the direct demand of moviegoers, in attempting to provide a perfect balance between offer and demand, as well as registering high-quality and scalable sales information. Thanks to an in-depth analysis of the data generated, Movieday—provides movie owners with insightful advices on crafting the best launch strategy for a screening campaign and its exploitation on other channels. Movie owners have the assistance of a Movieday Film Campaign Manager, a professional figure capable of designing and implementing the most advanced movie promotion campaigns through the platform. Activating communities, creating synergies, engaging partners and finally multiplying the participation of the people involved.

Movieday platform also provides to independent films a direct channel to theatre venues, getting rid of any intermediaries. Owners of new, unreleased Italian films that can turn their fans into viewers and promoters of screenings in all partner cinemas and access other sales channels (TV, VOD, Home Video) both in Italy and abroad. To date (end of 2017), over twenty films are under contract on the Movieday platform; the acquisition of foreign titles has begun in June 2017, whereas two foreign movies have already signed distribution contacts via Movieday (data Movieday).

80% of Movieday audience is generated by new, non-distributed and distributed movie projections, through innovative marketing campaigns involving communities of fans. The remaining 20% (data Movieday) is generated by projections organized directly by common moviegoers for personal, cultural and recreational (birthday parties, associative activities, etc.) purposes.

As for the independent movie distributed, it is worth mentioning the case of *Unlearning*, the documentary on the subjects of downshifting and sharing economy based on the story of an Italian family (the film director, his wife and six-year-old daughter) from Genoa, leaving their city for six months, travelling across Italy, surviving through exchange and barter. *Unlearning* was screened simultaneously in 35 cities throughout Italy. Against a cost of production of €1500, *Unlearning* has produced 101 screenings, almost all sold out, bringing over 12,000 people to theatres for a total box office of 70,000 euro (data Movieday). After each screening, a special guest moderated the debate on the theme of the film. *Unlearning* has been awarded of several prizes (Cinemambiente 2015; Marcellino de Baggis 2015; Terra di Tutti Film Festival 2015; Versus Festival 2015) and it was a success not only in terms of box office, but also from the point of view of sharing, of the physical and emotional participation of the fan base community, pro-actively involved by the film campaigner and by the film director himself even long before the film was released (mainly via Facebook).

Roughly 1100 new films are produced in Italy each year, 10,000 in Europe and around 50,000 in the world, but only 500 films are distributed in Italian movie venues and only 200 are sold on other channels (data Cinetel, 2017). This suggests that there is a long tail of unexpressed market potential, since 98% of the films are non-distributed—remaining unsold to markets—although there is an existing audience interested in the content willing to screen and purchase it, whereas the remaining 2% gets a poor distribution because of an old and downsized distribution chain. Specifically, the theatrical distribution system is outdated because of the lack of tracking and profiling of the audience purchasing a ticket. Considering around €100 million of tickets purchases in cinemas each year, we don't have any history or data of the customers. Thus, it is worth mentioning that 180 out of 1180 new movies produced in Italy in 2017 (data Cinetel, 2017). Have been distributed through *Movieday.it*, a number not usually managed by the incumbent distributors operating in the Italian market.

Moreover, through a dedicated marketplace, movie owners can sell projection licences, fixed rental rates, associations, schools, companies, hospitals and other groups of interested people who require the screening of the film in spaces other than cinema venues.

Movieday has also created MD Logistik, a software and a department entirely dedicated to the creation, management and delivery of physical and broadband film copies that can be marketed on a large scale and not just for Movieday screenings.

Partner Cinemas

In Movieday business model, cinemas remain the best "device" of fruition, as the physical experience of the shared viewing and reunited community can only be lived at the cinema.

At the end of Movieday has signed deals with over 230 movie theatres, nearly 20% of the total venues in Italy, which are now connected to the platform (data Cinetel, 2017).

There are over 1140 cinemas in Italy for a total of 3300 screens, showing a very low occupancy rate. Indeed, cinemas are amongst one of the most underemployed businesses, since they remain closed most of the time (in the mornings, in the afternoon, in the summer). When they are open, they show a very low average occupancy rate. An outdated distribution system, obliging cinemas to programme their movies independently from their potential success; the lack of adequate marketing strategies, the lack of a renewed experience of content fruition; and the lack of connection between cinemas and the audience are the main reasons leading to this issue in the distribution business.

Movieday value proposition to cinemas is a technological platform that makes them liaise directly with the audience and with films' owners, allowing anyone to organize screenings in few clicks. Cinemas have access to a management panel available on Movieday where they set up and manage their availability, economic demands, events created in their rooms, their receipts, their film deliveries and the online pre-sale system that resets business risk because screenings are confirmed only if a minimum number of pre-sales is reached (lowering to zero the commercial risk the movie theatre should sustain).

The Business Environment

The trends Movieday is fully embracing for its growth are the following: "prosumerization", analysed within the field of film promotion; the steady increase of online transaction for purchases, in Italy and in the world; the sharing and on-demand economy (i.e. online technologies allow people to use products and services for which they are in mutual need of each other, without purchasing from established companies).

Movie.it web platform is not only one of its kind, in the USA, Tugg.com and Gathr.us are the forerunner platforms. The best performing and most evolved is Tugg, founded in 2012, which is the principal reference model for Movieday, connecting over 85% of US cinemas and setting up roughly 100,000 screenings in 5 years, Tugg has kicked off its international expansion in other English-speaking countries.

Other similar platforms were launched in the Europe: Screen.ly in Spain and Ourscreen.com in UK. The latest launch, in 2016, of a new platform with global ambitions, is Demand.film, founded by one ex-partner at Tugg, already operating in the UK, Ireland, Australia, New Zealand and Germany.

The Future

Movieday has concluded a first phase of investments that allowed its entry into the market and the consolidation of the service. Further development can only be enabled by important investments that will mainly concern the technological evolution of the platform and the systems for tracking and profiling audiences and films with a large data-set, applying also AI-Artificial Intelligence to build a predictive distribution model (the service under construction is called I-TDS Intelligent Theatrical Distribution System). Under further development are also the diffusion of MD Logistik; the construction of an international techno-commercial network for the acquisition and distribution of films on all channels; and the production of original Movieday content.

Core Processes of Digital Start-Ups in the Film Industry

In this section, we present a conceptual description emerging from the analysis of the case of *Movieday.it*, where the emerging core categories are in this case two basic social processes (Glaser, 1978). Specifically, we have identified first a basic social structural process (BSSP) of *marketizing movies* that can be associated to an institutional work (Lawrence & Suddaby, 2006) eventually leading to a de-institutionalization (Oliver, 1992) of the film industry and culture. The second core category is the basic social psychological process (BSPP) of *becoming platform*, using it to sustain identity and normative networks construction (Lawrence & Suddaby, 2006) as well as validate the institutional work.

Thus, the conceptual description can be considered as the basis for a provisional theory on *becoming platform in the substantive area of digital start-ups active in the film industry and its being accomplished by marketizing movies.* As said, the proposed theory should provide an early understanding of the key issues at stake in the digital transformation of the film industry by new ventures and their business models; this should also provide a framework for replying to the research questions mentioned in the introduction to this chapter. In what follows, we discuss the two core categories resulting from the coding of the collected data.

Marketizing Movies

Considering the BSSP of *marketizing movies*, it refers to the framing and the translation of all the movie-related activities and objects (including the parameter for movie production and evaluation) in terms of market principles, specifically through the functional simplification and abstraction (Kallinikos, 2006, 2012) of their specific characteristics into the ones of digital artefacts. Furthermore, we have identified four stages for the BSSP: *strategizing, connecting to the platform first, crowdsourcing* and *exhibiting.*

The first stage is connected to the constant need of defining new value propositions and *evolving business models* for the new competitive markets continually emerging due to technological innovation, changes in audiences' preference, etc. The second stage concerns the need for *connecting to the platform first*, this means (i) for movie directors, to digitize their movies for distribution and (ii) for the owners of cinema halls, to embed the platform in their systems, thus creating a virtually direct connection with movie directors, movie owners and the audience. This stage is thus about questioning the connection of platform, cinemas, audience and directors from an infrastructure perspective (Star & Ruhleder, 1996). The third stage presents crowdsourcing as the main way to talk to the audience first and move from a "push" to a "pull" perspective, where the public becomes the programmer, using social media as communication and selection tools, and the critic is not anymore the influencer for the movie apart from the ones explicitly targeting an "essai" audience.

The fourth stage deals with a specific characteristic of the case under study, that is *exhibiting* the movie rather than simply showing it on screen, thus moving it from the status of being the key and main subject of the film industry to be merely one amongst of other objects making up events that are guided by customer experience and experiential marketing perspectives and aims.

Becoming Platform

Considering the BSPP of *becoming platform*, it concerns four stages.

The first stage is *framing the difference* of *Movieday.it* with regard to the traditional stakeholders in the film industry, especially emphasizing the change implied by their being a digital platform that is not simply an alternative distribution channel. The difference is then explained by the informants pointing out their being frustrated because of the current state of film industry, in relation to the limits and constraints posed by regulations as well as to a set of issues referring to political, functional and social pressures, eventually worth considering as the antecedents for de-institutionalization (Oliver, 1992). Yet, a major difference with traditional stakeholders is also explained by mentioning technical and managerial capabilities (which are very innovative for the film industry, although state-of-the-art for other industries).

The second stage is *filling education gap* in terms of providing the necessary digital skills and capabilities to cinema halls, producers, distributors and especially directors. This stage aims at making all the different stakeholders acquainted with the use of the digital platform as well as with use of data and analytics for a better design of the product (the movie itself) and the configuration of movie halls as "event places".

The previous stage is strictly connected to the stage three, which is *flattening and balancing*. This stage is about the need of dealing, on the one hand, with the flattening of the movie and cinema hall characteristics to the general attributes of digital artefacts and marketing requirements, while, on the other hand, preserving the aesthetic and cultural peculiarities of documentaries and independent movies, thus keeping intact the variety of the film catalogue on the platform.

This last point can be appreciated by considering the fourth stage *experiencing the cinema hall* and the different stances around this provided by the interviewees, actually representing different perspectives in relation to two different types of cinema halls owners: general purpose and essai halls owners. The first group is more crowd-oriented, the second community oriented. The first is focused on revenues, the second on values other than the economic value and sustainability.

Discussion

Movieday.it platform offers "cinema on demand", or "user driven cinema exhibition". The audience can choose a movie (amongst a large, pre-selected assortment of available titles) to be screened and has the option of booking a time slot at a cinema screening room if a critical amount of sold tickets is reached, the movie exhibit will be held. Thus, the business model considers two of the above-mentioned key design elements characterizing the activity system of an organization: *content* (in this case, for example, the focus on the choice and booking of movies) and *structure* (in this case, the mode and sequence in which the activities of choosing, promoting, booking and showing a movie are connected).

As for this latter, the case suggests that the film industry may partly share the power of the gatekeeper position with their customers: "Push" changes into "Pull"; the audience becomes the programmer, using social media as a communication tool. In this way, the conventional top-down programming is changed into bottom-up bookings with a personal purpose or even community-based cinema programming. On-demand screenings are promising, this because the audience is engaged and enabled to choose a movie and organize an event while, at the same time, theatre owners are able to contract a low-risk screening (if a sufficiently large audience turnout is not guaranteed, the worst-case scenario is a cost-free cancellation).

The success of the events organized via *Movieday.it* platform suggests that watching a movie in a social space still has considerable potential for attracting new audiences. This seems to confirm Gubbins (2014: 51) statement, that in an age of ubiquitous media and an interactive, "always-on" mobile culture, the value of unique experiences increases. The case of *Movieday.it* also suggests that the assumption that the theatrical market will be completely undermined by multi-platform release is inconsistent.

The case shows how the business model of "cinema on demand" may help cinema owners to present an assorted and distinctive cinema programme, in order to give added value to the customer. The challenge is to attract people with different preferences and expectations (people from different cultural backgrounds or with different cultural consumption habits) presenting a plurality of content. For this, it is necessary to develop a visionary strategy in order to widen the existing network of customers and to engage audiences that are not yet currently attending screenings in a cinema. This means to have a more dynamic and flexible programming (especially for Multiplex) and/or to create opportunities for the theatrical exhibit as a unique event, therefore, to have a balanced mix of active and passive programming (which partly turns the supply chain into a demand chain).

Movieday.it creates also a new path for institutional communication—between independent movies and (especially documentaries) and cinema theatres—and social interaction—with audiences (the stages of "talk to the audience first" and "exhibiting" of the above mentioned "marketizing movies" process). On-demand cinema platforms enable filmmakers, independent distributors and movie fans to crowd fund and plan community-driven screenings of specialized movies and event cinema, bringing further diversity, events and community dynamics to the big screen.

Thanks to the crowd sourcing ticketing, *Movieday.it* gives to independent filmmakers the opportunity of having direct access to the theatrical exhibitions, this implying the removal of the traditional sales agent, or distributor, who traditionally funds and executes all marketing activities (the stage of "connecting to the platform first" of the above mentioned "marketizing movies" process). Niche audiences, marketed directly, have significant value if they can be reached less expensively. Communities offer the potential for fan bases and, on occasion, significant commercial core audiences. This is a potential narrowing of the movie value chain, whereby the producer is brought much closer to the audience (and hence the revenue streams are being recouped) that is of significant interest.

One of the consequences of digitization is that the borderline between informal movie distribution and screening and established exhibitions is blurred (the stage of "flattening and balancing" of the above mentioned "becoming platform" process). For a cinema owner it could be profitable, or otherwise interesting, to reach out to the status of a "movie club", because it is appealing to a devoted audience who is passionate about cinema. For example, thanks to *Movieday.it* platform, independent distributors have the chance to organize live participative premières and special screenings with onstage interviews with the movies' directors and producers, or theme-based conference before the screening of the movie.

Movieday.it platform, therefore, brings up new ideas, showing new market possibilities, and enable market actors to reshape market activity and thus creating new revenue streams. By engaging with the potential audience earlier and to a greater degree, through social media and online content, independent producers create greater demand and thus increase revenues. Furthermore, in order to claim a larger share of revenues (or simply reach sustainability), filmmakers pro-actively pursue dis-intermediation by bypassing some segments of the traditional movie value chain.

It's also as a consequence of these emerging practices that traditional distribution business processes of feature movies around the world are changing (and therefore the film industry's overall structures). Digitalization is enabling—or forcing—independent filmmakers to apply a DIY (do-it-yourself) distribution strategy, especially when the production funding requirements are not linked to a specific distribution plan. Since Kickstarter pioneered online crowdfunding[3] in 2009, this form of financing has entered the mainstream as a way to co-fund ideas, projects and start-ups, and movie production is not an exception (see, e.g., Junction jct.com—platform specialized in equity financing of movies).

In the case of the above-mentioned documentary *Unlearning* (see Case Study), marketing played a much more important role from the beginning of the feature filmmaking process, its influence continuing right through to the movie's release. As shown in Fig. 10.1, this process embraces multi-directional ways of marketing and interacting with audiences in order to minimize both commercial and institutional risks. The communication channels are multi-directional since information is produced by both producer and director, as well as by audiences. Some marketing process and interactions with audiences were activated prior to the funding decision, so conception is tested even before funding.

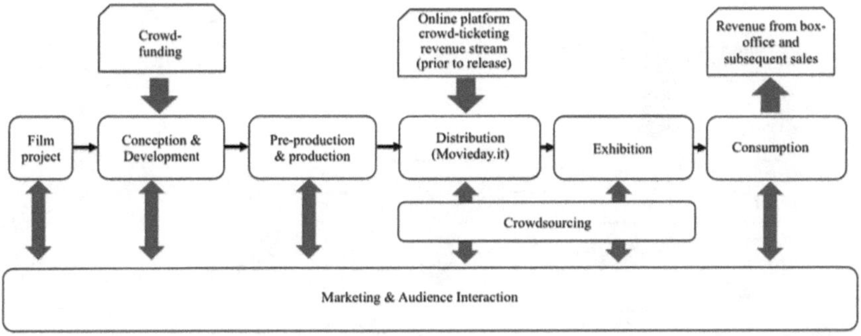

Fig. 10.1 Demand-led feature movie value chain (Hexagon shaped boxes represent revenue streams, while value chain activities are shown in the rounded rectangles)

Furthermore, from the point of view of a funder/investor, monetary streams are generated "up-front" to enable project implementation. Some revenue streams may also emanate from the box office, but this post-release source plays a secondary role, because contrary to the conventional movie business model the project is crowd funded and therefore the producers do not need to recoup their initial investment.

As shown in Fig. 10.2, on the one hand, financial streams in the typical movie value chain are mainly used up-front (conception, development, pre-production and production of the movie); on the other hand, revenue streams are generated at the end of the value chain mainly by box office and subsequent sales. The marketing strategies are usually used at the distribution and exhibition stages and the communication channels are unidirectional because information is produced by distribution and marketing experts and sent to—and consumed by—audiences.

The case study also suggests that there is potential for alternative release strategies that have to be carefully considered. *Movieday.it* release approach is considered more relevant for independent feature movies because their box office visibility is generally lower and their theatrical runs shorter. By embracing such demand-led change, cinemas are able giving audiences access to a wider range of movies, including those that may otherwise have been underplayed, as well as having a vehicle with which to test new business models.

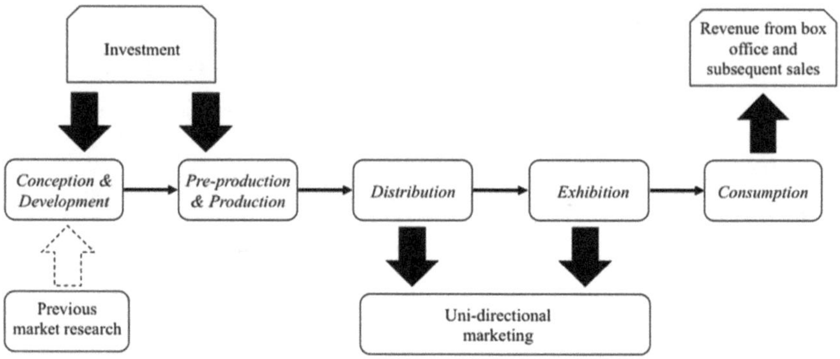

Fig. 10.2 "Traditional" feature movie value chain (Hexagon shaped boxes represent revenue streams, while value chain activities are shown in the rounded rectangles)

Moreover, release windows in the traditional movie value chain may become an irrelevant barrier between content and audience. In order to manage uncertainty and be able to reformulate the movie value chain for the digital age, recognizing and interpreting new evaluative frameworks are becoming integral. The case study suggests that new approaches to marketing and packaging movie products can be successful when they are aligned with consumer demands (the stage of "evolving business models" in the process of "marketizing movies"). Producers and distributors have often treated their exchanges as a zero-sum game, one party's gains correspond to the other party's losses. But this misalignment is an impediment to a more successful integrated industry and precludes consumers from having access to a wider range of movies. Therefore, independent movie producers need to achieve a "hybrid" model, which is to say a model that demands to understand and master tools for selling and marketing, but simultaneously requests to be able to design and be active on digital and social media channels that are becoming more and more necessary for winning an audience.

In this scenario, *Movieday.it* platform can function to link the innovation with a new business model and, simultaneously, as the creator of communication channels between agents and actors located in quite different parts of the traditional value chain (the stage of "filling education gap" in the process of "becoming platform"). Furthermore, some of the actors target of *Movieday.it* are "low-end or new-market footholds" (Christensen, Raynor, & McDonald, 2015: 5), consequently not considered by actual incumbents in the film industry. This is in line with the perspective on disruptive innovation originated by the work of Christensen (1997; Christensen et al., 2015) where the business model that the technology enables is considered the source of the disruptive impact (see also DaSilva & Trkman, 2014; Vorbach, Wipfler, & Schimpf, 2017). Yet, it is worth considering that at the state of the art a distinction has been made by Markides (2006: 19) between disruptive technological innovation, disruptive business model innovation and disruptive product innovation, each having different conditions of emergence, effects on competitions, and consequently reactions by the market incumbents. In this case study, we cannot talk about a complete "disruptive impact" to the traditional business model, but somewhat, it would be more exact to say that a new business model can counterpart though not replace conventional businesses. Nevertheless, the case study suggests adjustments to the value chain that, before the "digital transformation", few could have predicted.

However, it is also worth noting that the attitude of the digital start-up in the case study (focused on marketing, on enabled audiences and on targeting long tails) may point out rather an evolution of the traditional film industry business model towards a new form, with a change in the value chain in the direction of an Internet networked model, where the orientation towards independent documentary seems guided from the opportunity of a market niche that has been little explored.

In principle, using crowd funding to support any creative accomplishments that would otherwise struggle to come to implementation can only enrich cultural expressions allowing independent movie features screening beyond the traditional gatekeepers. Nevertheless, it becomes necessary to ponder how this funding form impacts not only on existing industries and funding structures but also on the movie features themselves. As a funding model for documentary movie, crowd funding has the unintentional consequence that only certain types of documentaries are funded. Usually, the crowd funders are keener to favour issue-led movies and polemical documentaries at the expense of other kinds of documentaries. Likewise, the editorial standards and attributes traditionally associated with documentary may be potentially challenged in crowd funded projects.

Furthermore, although crowd funding provides some solution to funding and producing independent documentaries outside of the traditional patterns, the wider documentary industry is still dependent on the traditional gatekeepers and media institutions for the promotion, distribution and success of its movies. Documentary movie production and distribution are part of a value chain that is still dominated by established media institutions. At the moment, crowd funded movies still need the traditional distributors—festivals, cinemas and broadcasters—to reach their audiences. Also, in order to have the projects crowd funded online, producers and directors rely on crowd funding platforms and crowd funding consultants. It could be that these organizations and individuals will be benefit from innovation dynamics more than filmmakers and movie feature quality. Paradoxically, therefore, crowd funding could undermine the integrity and credibility of documentary movies as well as the plurality and diversity of screened content.

Conclusion

This study's exploration has uncovered evidence of two rising themes: audience engagement and innovation in the film industry value chain and business models. The case suggests that the film industry distribution might develop as a "social process" and the film industry value chain may advance innovative solutions through a user-centred design approach.

The case of *Movieday.it* has acted as a stimulus to identify the impact of emerging digital technologies on distribution and consumption processes, arguably revealing the beginning of a fundamental shift towards a demand-led independent market. In particular, the case study allows designing a provisional theory (represented through a conceptual model in Fig. 10.3) on *becoming platform* (which, as mentioned above, may be considered as being a *basic social psychological process*) in the substantive area of digital start-ups active in film industry and its being accomplished through the *marketizing of movies* (*basic social structural process*).

Moreover, through the identification of these two core categories, the case study provides a theoretical understanding of the implications of digitalization and related business models for new ventures in the cinema industry.

The case study also suggests that the cinema experience continues to be of great significance in the life of a movie, since audiences attach a special value to the collective experience, whereas a switch to user-driven distribution would allow cinemas to offer more varied programming, as well as giving screen space to more movies. Still, this would also expand the range of movies available to cinemagoers, in a market where only a very small fraction of the movies produced each year get a theatrical release.

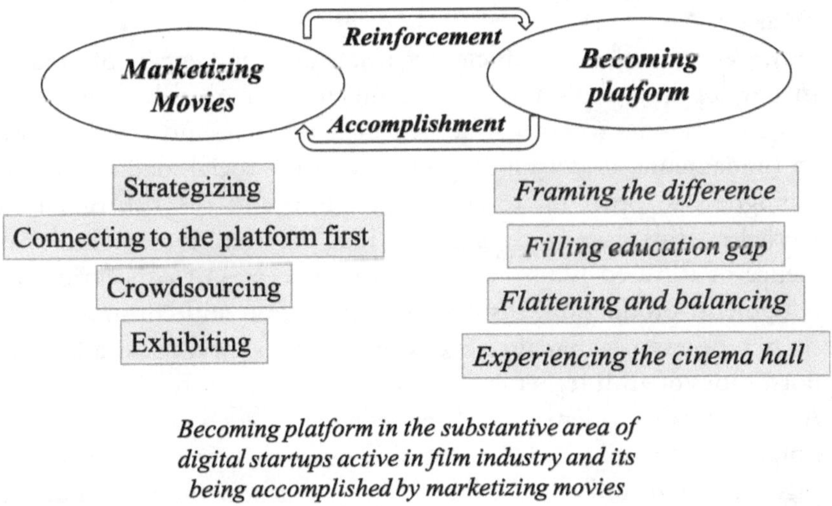

Fig. 10.3 Conceptual model of the theory on becoming platform in the substantive area of digital start-ups active in film industry and its being accomplished by marketizing movies

Nevertheless, for theatre operators, offering a great variety of movies remains a difficult task because of the complexity and several practical limitations and constraints. Platform (as those offered by Movieday.it) may help in this task since it offers to cinema theatres a wider range of movies available for programming, and determines beforehand the minimum average number of visitors per show, helping in better defining target audience.

In future, *these platforms* may potentially collaborate in an even closer way with cinema operators experimenting data analytics. Movie marketing and modelling are a new area for the application of marketing decision support systems in movie programming, as well as for achieving better performances in scheduling, practising both high-quality content diversity and promoting to individual customers via email, social media or text messages—possibly linked with a dynamic pricing approach.

Furthermore, *Movieday.it* case study shows how new ways of using the Internet and social media can offer opportunities not only for promoting and marketing feature movies (and doing so right from the beginning of the filmmaking process), but also for creating an accessible and highly effective point of entry to the film industry for aspiring new filmmakers.

However, in order to sufficiently reach core audiences, filmmakers must develop new skills and manage much of the distribution process themselves. Building personal audiences takes time and effort, requiring a fundamental understanding of how to use social media tools and a willingness to open up to strangers, critics and the risk of failure. Nonetheless, this case study suggests that the traditional value chain sequence of featured films—entailing the processes of conception and development, production, distribution, exhibition and consumption—need not necessarily remain strictly linear, in view of the additional opportunities of an Internet era.

A shift towards a demand-led independent market could help build a vibrant, sustainable and interesting European movie sector able to engage audiences and could collectively outperform the mass audience movies which currently fill the programming schedules of most local cinemas across Europe. The fact that there are some genuine success stories (the mentioned case of the documentary movie "Unlearning" but also others) indicates that the industry is moving towards solutions that could potentially generate sustainability for independent and documentary movies. As new business strategies and business models are adopted, the market may develop in two directions: one for independent filmmakers based on community engagement, crowd funding and crowd-ticketing and the other for big productions that will continue to use models centred on traditional mechanisms.

It is too early to confirm whether this is a true paradigm shift and, if so, define it concretely. Moreover, further empirical analysis of how becoming platform and marketizing movies is needed, especially regarding how new business models are developed by entrepreneurs with diverse skills, education and value propositions. Further analysis is also particularly important considering the emerging digital offering of cinema content questioning either the need for cinema halls or for a traditional distributor (i.e. Netflix, etc.).

In summary, some key questions remain unanswered, especially those in relation to the economic viability of new distribution models, such as to say if this demand-led approaches present a stronger financial return to distributors in comparison with the traditional model, and last but not least, if these new business models can also work for larger independent movies or are they best suited for niche markets.

Notes

1. An independent movie is a movie "that is not a studio picture, and whose development and/or production finance is provided by more than one source" (Davies & Wistreich, 2007: 8–9, 449). It has also been defined as a movie "that is developed without ties to a major studio, regardless of where subsequent production and/or distribution financing comes from", and/or where the producer shares some of the investment risk (Goodell, 1998: xvii; Vogel, 2007: 90–91).
2. Although there is not yet an agreement on the definition of **business model** (Massa, Viscusi, & Tucci, 2018; Massa, Tucci, & Afuah, 2017; Viscusi & Tucci, 2018; Afuah & Tucci, 2012), we adopt here the one provided by Zott and Amit (2010: 1), who consider it as "a system of

interdependent activities that transcends the focal firm and spans its boundaries. The activity system enables the firm, in concert with its partners, to create value and also to appropriate a share of that value". In particular, this perspective on what is a business model has been complemented by the two scholars with the identification of three key design elements characterizing the activity system of an organization that are its *content* (i.e. the selection of system activities), *structure* (i.e. the mode and sequence in which the activities are connected) and *governance* (Amit & Zott, 2001; Zott & Amit, 2010, 2017). Accordingly, this definition is useful for its fitting the idea of business model's innovation advanced by Foss and Saebi (2016: 216) as made up by "designed, novel, and nontrivial changes to the key elements of a firm's BM and/or the architecture linking these elements".

3. Crowdfunding is a "collective effort by consumers who network and pool their money together, usually via the Internet, in order to invest in and support efforts initiated by other people or organizations" (Ordanini, Miceli, Pizzetti, & Parasuraman, 2011: 443).

Appendix: Data collection

As for the case study, while the overall population includes 195 informants (the details are shown in Table 10.1), we are first considering for this paper a sample of 11 informants, comprising all the *Movieday.it* staff (5 interviewees), 2 providers, 1 director and 3 cinema halls owners.

Table 10.1 Informants for the case study

Organization	Informants	Total	Sample
Movieday.it	4 internal	9	4
	2 consultants (distribution and rights)		
	1 graphic designer		1
	2 developers (external software provider)		
Providers	130 cinemas	176	3
	40 digital archives		
	6 films campaigner		2
Network	10 directors and producers	10	1
		195	11

The field study and interviews have been started in March 2016 with one of the authors also organizing four screenings through *Movieday.it*, taking memos further discussed with the other author during monthly sessions of 1 hour through Skype or face-to-face meetings. Yet, the interview sessions started in December 2016 and have been closed in June 2017, further evaluating the degree of the theoretical saturation for the current codes and related concepts. The interviews are in Italian or English, depending on the language preference of each interviewee (the interview averaged one hour with a semi-structured protocol), and they are subsequently coded and analysed in parallel sessions by the two authors of this article on paper and with the support of MAXQDA 12.

References

Afuah, A., & Tucci, C. L. (2012). Crowdsourcing as a solution to distant search. *Academy of Management Review, 37*(3), 355–375.

Amit, R., & Zott, C. (2001). Value creation in e-business. *Strategic Management Journal, 22*(6–7), 493–520.

Christensen, C. M. (1997). *The innovator's dilemma: When new technologies cause great firms to fail.* Boston, MA: Harvard Business School Press.

Christensen, C. M., Raynor, M. E., & McDonald, R. (2015). What is disruptive innovation? *Harvard Business Review, 93*(12), 44–53.

Cinetel. (2017). *Annuario Cinetel.* https://www.cinetel.it/.

DaSilva, C. M., & Trkman, P. (2014). Business model: What it is and what it is not. *Long Range Planning, 47*(6), 379–389. https://doi.org/10.1016/j.lrp.2013.08.004.

Davies, A., & Wistreich, N. (2007). *The film finance handbook, new global edition.* London: Netribution.

Foss, N. J., & Saebi, T. (2016). Fifteen years of research on business model innovation. *Journal of Management, 43*(1), 200–227. https://doi.org/10.1177/0149206316675927.

Gioia, D. A., Corley, K. G., & Hamilton, A. L. (2013). Seeking qualitative rigor in inductive research: Notes on the Gioia methodology. *Organizational Research Methods, 16*(1), 15–31. https://doi.org/10.1177/1094428112452151.

Glaser, B. G. (1978). *Theoretical sensitivity: Advances in the methodology of grounded theory.* Mill Valley: The Sociology Press.

Goodell, G. (1998). *Independent feature film production.* New York, NY: St. Martins Griffin.

Gubbins, M. (2012). *Digital revolution: The active audience.* Retrieved August 14, 2017, from http://film-junction.co.uk/wp-content/uploads/DigitalRevolution2012_Final.pdf.

Gubbins, M. (2014). *Audience in the mind.* Cine-Regio. Retrieved from https://www.cineregio.org/dyn/files/pdf_download_items/16-file/CineRegio_AudienceInTheMind_Executive%20Summary%20160327.pdf. Accessed 10 May 2019.

Hewson, C. (2008). Internet-mediated research as an emergent method and its potential role in facilitating mixed methods research. In S. N. Hesse-Biber & P. Leavy (Eds.), *Handbook of emergent methods* (pp. 543–570). New York, NY: Guilford Press.

Jenkins H., Ito, M., & Boyd D. (2016). *Participatory culture in a networked era: A conversation on youth, learning, commerce, and politics.* Cambridge and Malden, MA: Polity Press.

Kallinikos, J. (2006). *The consequences of information—Institutional implications of technological change.* Cheltenham, UK; Northampton, MA: Edward Elgar.

Kallinikos, J. (2012). Form, function, and matter: Crossing the border of materiality. In P. M. Leonardi, B. A. Nardi, & J. Kallinikos (Eds.), *Materiality and organizing—Social interaction in a technological world* (pp. 67–87). Oxford: Oxford University Press.

Klein, H. K., & Myers, M. D. (1999). A set of principles for conducting and evaluating interpretive field studies in information systems. *MIS Quarterly, 23*(1), 67–93. https://doi.org/10.2307/249410.

Lawrence, T. B., Leca, B., & Zilber, T. B. (2013). Institutional work: Current research, new directions and overlooked issues. *Organization Studies, 34*(8), 1023–1033.

Lawrence, T. B., & Suddaby, R. (2006). Institutions and institutional work. In S. R. Clegg, C. Hardy, T. B. Lawrence, & W. R. Nord (Eds.), *The Sage handbook of organization studies* (2nd ed., pp. 215–254). London: Sage.

Markides, C. (2006). Disruptive innovation: In need of better theory. *Journal of Product Innovation Management.* https://doi.org/10.1111/j.1540-5885.2005.00177.x.

Massa, L., Tucci, C. L., & Afuah, A. (2017). A critical assessment of business model research. *Academy of Management Annals, 11*(1), 73–104. https://doi.org/10.5465/annals.2014.0072.

Massa, L., Viscusi, G., & Tucci, C. (2018). Business models and complexity. *Journal of Business Models, 6*(1), 59–71. https://doi.org/10.5278/ojs.jbm.v6i1.2579.

Matt, C., Hess, T., & Benlian, A. (2015). Digital transformation strategies. *Business and Information Systems Engineering (BISE), 57*(5), 339–343. https://doi.org/10.1007/s12599-015-0401-5.

Oliver, C. (1992). The antecedents of deinstitutionalization. *Organization Studies, 13*(4), 563–588. https://doi.org/10.1177/017084069201300403.

Ordanini, A., Miceli, L., Pizzetti, M., & Parasuraman, A. (2011). Crowdfunding: Transforming customers into investors through innovative service platforms. *Journal of Service Management, 4*(22), 443–470.

Rayport, J., & Sviokla, J. (1995, November/December). Exploiting the virtual value chain. *Harvard Business Review, 73*(6), 75–85.

Scholz, R. W., & Tietje, O. (2002). *Embedded case study methods: Integrating quantitative and qualitative knowledge*. London and Thousand Oaks, CA: Sage.

Star, S. L., & Ruhleder, K. (1996). Steps toward an ecology of infrastructure: Design and access for large information spaces. *Information Systems Research, 7*(1), 111–134.

Viscusi, G., & Tucci, C. (2018). Three's a crowd? In C. Tucci, A. Afuah, & G. Viscusi (Eds.), *Creating and capturing value through crowdsourcing*. Oxford: Oxford University Press.

Vogel, H. (2007). *Entertainment industry economics—A guide for financial analysis* (7th ed.). Cambridge, UK: Cambridge University Press.

Vorbach, S., Wipfler, H., & Schimpf, S. (2017). Business model innovation vs. business model inertia: The role of disruptive technologies. *BHM Berg- Und Hüttenmännische Monatshefte, 162*(9), 382–385. https://doi.org/10.1007/s00501-017-0671-y.

Walsham, G. (1993). *Interpreting information systems in organizations* (1st ed.). New York, NY: Wiley.

Yin, R. K. (2009). *Case study research: Design and methods* (4th ed.). Thousand Oaks, CA: Sage.

Zott, C., & Amit, R. (2010). Business model design: An activity system perspective. *Long Range Planning, 43*(2–3), 216–226. https://doi.org/10.1016/j.lrp.2009.07.004.

Zott, C., & Amit, R. (2017). Business model innovation: How to create value in a digital world. *GfK Marketing Intelligence Review, 9*(1), 18–23. https://doi.org/10.1515/gfkmir-2017-0003.

11

Afterword

Jesper Strandgaard Pedersen, Mukti Khaire and Barbara Slavich

In theory, we started the process of thinking specifically about putting together this volume on how technology interacts with the processes of creation, commerce, commentary about, and consumption of cultural goods, only after the papers in the Standing Workgroup sub-theme for the EGOS 2017 conference came together. In reality, however, the topics covered in this volume, and indeed in the 'Call for Papers' for that EGOS sub-theme, have been of relevance to scholars and citizens for some time now—how, if at all, does technology, associated with

J. Strandgaard Pedersen (✉)
Department for Organization, Copenhagen Business School, Københavns, Denmark
e-mail: Js.ioa@cbs.dk

M. Khaire
Cornell University, Ithaca, NY, USA
e-mail: mvk34@cornell.edu

B. Slavich
IÉSEG School of Management, Paris, France

J. Strandgaard Pedersen et al. (eds.), *Technology and Creativity*,
https://doi.org/10.1007/978-3-030-17566-5_11

machines and insentience, affect the very things, viz. expression and symbolism, that make us human? While this question has been relevant for several decades now, as Sgourev shows in this volume in his historical study of painting, the scale and speed at which digital technologies change and evolve is such that the topic gains special significance today as the digital medium has permeated every stage of the value chain in the creative and cultural industries. This was shown in the various chapters, like from pitches for crowd funding, in the chapter by Pershina and Soppe, over professional struggles in Cultural Journalism, in the chapter by Plesner, to new ways of reaching audiences, as shown in the chapters by Romanelli on museums, on visual art by Hartmann, and on film distribution and film exhibition by Solidoro and Viscusi. Our attempt in this volume was to shed light on some crucial aspects of this relationship between technology, creativity, and markets for cultural goods by drawing on a multitude—organizational, institutional, sociological, and cultural—of perspectives.

While the authors in this volume certainly have provided multifaceted insights into these questions, like all good research, these chapters, individually, and taken together, also raise questions that suggest directions for future scholarly investigations. For instance, the chapters by Sgourev and by Hartmann taken together suggest that scholars may need to expand the definitions of 'art' based on the possibility of the rise of new, technically advanced media, or even technologies that 'create' art (such as the artificial intelligence program that wrote a 'poem' or 'made a painting'), thus casting doubt on the very definition of artistic endeavors that has been widely accepted. Cattani et al., Collas, and Furnari, having raised the specter of a world of markets that are entirely mediated by digital technologies, thus question the very foundations of organizational and institutional literature, going beyond the limited scope of cultural and creative industries. How should scholars in the field think about traditionally, demarcated boundaries and constituents of institutional and organizational fields (even beyond the creative and cultural industries), when the digital medium provides the infrastructure for all parts of the supply chain in an industry?

In the context of creative and cultural industries in particular, if all steps, from creation, commerce, through commentary and consumption can be accomplished with the help of digital technologies, do we have to examine more critically the assumption that cultural goods have symbolic meaning and value, or that they embody (or intentionally challenge) beliefs and norms accepted by society? This further leads to the higher-level question of whether the seamless interpenetration of producer, commentator, and consumer roles that the digital medium has rendered possible (the so-called democratization movement) is a net positive or net negative impact. At this point in time, the jury is out on this question, as, anecdotally, the popular press provides articles that bolster both sides of the argument. It is, therefore, up to scholars to take a rigorous approach to addressing this question, which has serious and deep social as well as economic implications. The debate about digitalization and the Internet seems, however, to be changing. One example of research on the negative, social, and economic implications of the Internet is Shoshana Zuboff's book, '*The Age of Surveillance Capitalism*' (Zuboff, 2019). In a seven-year-long study, Zuboff has studied Google, Facebook, and other Internet-based social media and service providers, their modus operandi and associated business models. She identifies a new era of capitalism—Surveillance Capitalism—with Internet-based business models thriving on surveillance, gathering and sale of user data.[1] Information gathering, retrieval, storing, protection, and use are highly contested issues in particular in relation to the 'Four' (Amazon, Apple, Facebook, and Google) (Galloway, 2017), due to their monopolistic status (Iansiti and Lakhani, 2017).[2] These debates are conducted under headings of 'privacy rights,' and 'democracy' in the wake of numerous data leaks and associated scandals like, for example, Facebook's sale of data to Cambridge Analytica.[3] The use of big data and other forms of utilization of user-generated information and the resulting data protection regulations are all highly relevant for creative industry organizations as well. We find that more research is needed and would welcome further research into these issues in a context of creative industries.

Other issues of relevance for creative industries firms and organizations are related to intellectual property rights and how they are handled in the digital age. For example, previously when we as consumers bought music in the form of a record or CD or a movie on a DVD, we owned it and had the right to sell it again. However, in a digitalized world, when we buy and download a song or stream a film, we do not own it and cannot re-sell it. Another topic related to immaterial and intellectual property rights concerns how to make Internet services like Youtube, Facebook, and Instagram pay the artists for their music, film, images, and texts produced.[4] More research on digital business models and artists' intellectual property rights are also important topics for further research within the creative industries, we find.

Many industries and organizations claim that they are special and unique. We would call for the examination of structural variation in creative industries—both across the various creative industries and over time. This would allow us to consider the multiple ways in which similar practices and arrangements, like for example how the use of digital technologies and intellectual property rights is handled or how evaluative practices are organized or can change. Particularly in times of rapid change, comparisons of structural features of a given creative industry as it changes over time can provide valuable insights with regard to dynamics and mechanisms for transformation and change.

Finally, we hope that the chapters in this volume spark interest also in studying the opposite phenomenon—how, if at all, does humanism and human input change the perceived value of creative and cultural goods, in a world where human imperfections are all being eliminated by efficient and unerring technologies. This is a question that encompasses all the social, artistic/cultural, and economic dimensions that constitute the creative and cultural industries and is therefore one we, the editors are eager to see answered. We hope that readers of this volume will take up the challenge to address some of these questions and illuminate our understanding of the individual artists, firms, and markets that collectively make life worth living.

Notes

1. This book is not her first book on digitalization and its impact on society. In 1988, she published her influential and acclaimed book '*In the Age of the Smart Machine*' (Zuboff, 1988).
2. For more favorable accounts of Google and Apple see, for example, Schmidt and Rosenberg (2014) '*How Google Works*' and Lashinsky (2012) '*Inside Apple*'.
3. These leaks and scandals have called for various political initiatives for regulation like, for instance, the recent introduction of European General Data Protection Regulation (GDPR) that aptly demonstrates the many questions this data moment invokes.
4. The Internet-based services are regulated by the so-called Safe Harbor regulation from 2001, which was made with the ambition to enable and increase information exchange, connectivity, and business activities as much as possible. Since then 'the Four' and other Internet-based services have developed to large commercial platforms, some of which with almost monopolistic, global position. EU has since 2016 worked on a reform of the immaterial property rights.

References

Galloway, S. (2017). *The four: The hidden DNA of Amazon, Apple, Facebook and Google*. London, UK: Bantam Press.

Iansiti, M., & Lakhani, K. R. (2017, September–October). Managing our hub economy. *Harvard Business Review*, pp. 84–92.

Lashinsky, A. (2012). *Inside Apple: How America's most admired—And secreative—Company really works*. New York: Business Plus.

Schmidt, E., & Rosenberg, J. (2014). *How Google works*. New York: Grand Central Publishing, Hachette Book Group.

Zuboff, S. (1988). *In the age of the smart machine: The future of work and power*. New York: Basic Books.

Zuboff, S. (2019). *The age of surveillance capitalism: The fight for a human future at the New Frontier of power*. London, UK: Profile Books.

Correction to: Innovators' Acts of Framing and Audiences' Structural Characteristics in Novelty Recognition

Gino Cattani, Denise Falchetti and Simone Ferriani

Correction to:
Chapter 2 in: J. Strandgaard Pedersen et al. (eds.), *Technology and Creativity*, https://doi.org/10.1007/978-3-030-17566-5_2

The original version of the chapter was inadvertently published without the additional Acknowledgements content regarding the study in Chapter 2, which has now been included. The chapter has been updated with the necessary change.

The updated version of this chapter can be found at
https://doi.org/10.1007/978-3-030-17566-5_2

J. Strandgaard Pedersen et al. (eds.), *Technology and Creativity*,
https://doi.org/10.1007/978-3-030-17566-5_12

Index

J. Strandgaard Pedersen et al. (eds.), *Technology and Creativity*,
https://doi.org/10.1007/978-3-030-17566-5

M

Kolibri 360 GmbH
Ferdinand-Jühlke-Straße 7
99095 Erfurt, Deutschland
produktsicherheit@kolibri360.de